Arabic through the Qur'ān

Alan Jones

ARABIC THROUGH THE QUR'ĀN

Alan Jones

THE ISLAMIC TEXTS SOCIETY

This edition published 2005 by
THE ISLAMIC TEXTS SOCIETY
MILLER'S HOUSE
KINGS MILL LANE
GREAT SHELFORD
CAMBRIDGE CB22 5EN, U.K.

Reprint 2006, 2011, 2012, 2014, 2016, 2017, 2018, 2019

British Library Cataloguing-in-Publication Data.
A catalogue record for this book is
available from the British Library.

ISBN 978 0946621 67 5 cloth
ISBN 978 0946621 68 2 paper

Set with ArabTEX and teTEX
in Bembo and Naskh types.
The publishers wish to thank
Prof. Klaus Lagally (Stuttgart) for his generous help.

Printed by Mega Printing in Turkey

To
James Craig

لَا مُسْتَعْرِبَ أَعْلَمُ أَوْ أَفْصَحُ مِنْهُ

Contents

Acknowledgement xiii

Introductory Note xiv

The Arabic Alphabet 1

Lesson One
Nouns and Adjectives 7
Exercise One 14

Lesson Two
Plurals 16
Exercise Two 20

Lesson Three
The Declension of Nouns 22
Exercise Three 28

Lesson Four
Prepositions 30
Exercise Four 33

Lesson Five
The First Person Singular Genitive Suffix
and the Pronoun of Separation 35
Exercise Five 37

Lesson Six
Demonstratives 39
Exercise Six 42

Lesson Seven
Iḍāfa 44
Exercise Seven 48

Lesson Eight
The Perfect Tense 50
Exercise Eight 55

Lesson Nine
Pronominal suffixes 57
Exercise Nine 61

Lesson Ten
The particle *mā* 63
Exercise Ten 68

Lesson Eleven
Kull; baʿḍ; the accusative of time 70
Exercise Eleven 73

Lesson Twelve
Kāna; qāla; lammā 75
Exercise Twelve 80

Lesson Thirteen
The Dual 82
Exercise Thirteen 85

Lesson Fourteen
Cardinal Numbers 86
Exercise Fourteen 92

Lesson Fifteen
Derived Forms of the Verb 93
Exercise Fifteen 97

Lesson Sixteen
The Imperfect 99
Exercise Sixteen 103

Lesson Seventeen
Interrogatives 105
Exercise Seventeen 110

Lesson Eighteen
The Subjunctive 112
Exercise Eighteen 119

Lesson Nineteen
Inna 121
Exercise Nineteen 125

Lesson Twenty
The Jussive 127
Exercise Twenty 130

Lesson Twenty-One
Laysa; idh; idhā; man 132
Exercise Twenty-One 137

Lesson Twenty-Two
Verbs with a *hamza* as one of their Radicals 139
Exercise Twenty-Two 142

Lesson Twenty-Three
Relative Sentences 144
Exercise Twenty-Three 149

Lesson Twenty-Four
Assimilated Verbs 151
Exercise Twenty-Four 153

Lesson Twenty-Five
The Elative 155
Exercise Twenty-Five 160

Lesson Twenty-Six
Doubled Verbs 163
Exercise Twenty-Six 165

Lesson Twenty-Seven
Exceptive Sentences with *illā* 167
Exercise Twenty-Seven 170

Lesson Twenty-Eight
Hollow Verbs 172
Exercise Twenty-Eight 178

Lesson Twenty-Nine
The Vocative 180
Exercise Twenty-Nine 183

Lesson Thirty
Defective Verbs 185
Exercise Thirty 192

Lesson Thirty-One
Ordinal and Other Numbers 194
Exercise Thirty-One 197

Lesson Thirty-Two
The Imperative 199
Exercise Thirty-Two 202

Lesson Thirty-Three
The Passive 204
Exercise Thirty-Three 207

Lesson Thirty-Four
More about Nouns 210
Exercise Thirty-Four 216

Lesson Thirty-Five
More on the Accusative 218
Exercise Thirty-Five 225

Lesson Thirty-Six
Conditional Sentences 227
Exercise Thirty-Six 238

Lesson Thirty-Seven
More about *an*; *ᶜasa* and *laᶜalla* 240
Exercise Thirty-Seven 246

Lesson Thirty-Eight
Special verbs; *law-lā* 248
Exercise Thirty-Eight 253

Lesson Thirty-Nine
The Energetic; Oaths and Exclamations 255
Exercise Thirty-Nine 262

Lesson Forty
Special Uses of *mā kāna*;
Verbs of Wonder, Praise and Blame 264
Exercise Forty 268

Key to the Exercises 270

Technical Terms 290

General Vocabulary 296

Acknowledgement

Over the years I have received advice and comments from many friends, colleagues and students. I owe particular debts of gratitude to Kinga Dévényi, Philip Kennedy, Samir Haykal, Lucy Collard and Kahlan al-Kharusi.

I should also like to thank Fatima Azzam and Juan Acevedo of the Islamic Texts Society for all their efforts and skill in turning a difficult manuscript into a published book.

Finally, my thanks go, as ever, to my wife Margaret, who copes with my presence at home 'in retirement' with care and equanimity.

AJ

Introductory Note

Over the years it has often been suggested to me that there is a need for an Arabic grammar that will enable readers of English to learn enough Arabic to be able to read the Qur'ān in its original language. This book attempts to fill that gap.

In its 40 lessons the book covers all the important points of the grammar of Quranic Arabic—though not every point, as there are some problems of Qur'ānic grammar that the grammarians, Arab and non-Arab alike, have never solved. Like grammarians in the past, I have occasionally taken a sentence somewhat out of context or changed a case-ending so that a phrase can stand alone. Without these minor and traditional pedagogic liberties, examples of some grammatical points would be very scarce. This is hardly surprising, given the relatively small size of the text of the Qur'ān. Nevertheless, Quranic examples are used in most places in the explanatory material, and all the exercises consist of Quranic quotations. The three topics in which I had to use most non-Quranic examples were the numerals, relative sentences and exceptive sentences. Here I have used a number of non-Quranic examples to help me to provide a full explanation. Elsewhere such examples are rare.

I have tried, wherever possible, to show the grammar of the Qur'ān within the broader framework of Arabic as defined by the classical grammarians and also that of later Arabic. For most of the book this is a relatively straightforward task, even though the language of the Qur'ān predates that of classical Arabic and though it contains a range of expressions and constructions that are not normally found in later texts (unless, of course, they crop up in a Qur'ānic quotation). For the greater part of the book the reader may be assured that there is relatively little difference between Qur'ānic and later Arabic, except in vocabulary. However, the topics covered in the last five lessons show greater or lesser variation from later developments. In particular, conditional sentences became, for a time at least, more uniform than those we find in the Qur'ān—and more recently they have become less so.

Though some of those who use this book will be familiar with Arabic script, many others will not be. For the latter the exercises of the first five lessons have transliterations to help them to master Arabic script thoroughly. A certain amount of transliteration is used throughout the rest of the book, particularly when it helps the grammatical explanations to run smoothly.

The text of the Qur'ān referred to throughout this book is that of the Egyptian standard edition, first issued in 1342/1923 and revised in 1381/1960 and subsequently. There are, however, certain problems. First, the style of writing used in the standard edition is somewhat ornate, and it also looks decidedly archaic in comparison with the printing norms of the period when it first appeared. Secondly, in more recent times the move to computer type-setting of Arabic has somewhat reduced the options that used to be available with hot metal type-setting. The result is that the Arabic printed in this book lacks the ornate and calligraphic touches of the standard edition, though there is the consolation that it is slightly easier to read. However, two attempts have been made to provide something of the feel of the standard edition. The first is the intermittent use of short *alif* (see p. 3), and the second is the use of the archaic spellings of a handful of common words (see p. 4).

Grammatical terms, largely English but sometimes Arabic, are used throughout the book. For those not familiar with grammatical terminology there is a glossary of technical terms (pp.290–295), which may be of some help, even though explanations of grammatical terms are always turgid.

It is assumed that most readers will be studying alone, and it is to them that the following remarks are addressed. (Those fortunate enough to have teachers will find that the teachers will have plenty of their own guidance to offer.) Each lesson consists of three parts: (a) exposition of a number of grammatical topics. Each piece of grammar should be mastered before moving on to the next. Particular attention should be paid to understanding the examples given in a section. The grammatical sections are followed by (b) the Vocabulary for that lesson. The vocabularies are intended to be read from right to left. In the first 7 lessons the first column contains the singular form of nouns, together with pronouns, adverbs, prepositions, etc.; the second column contains such plurals as are needed; and the third column has the English translation. From Lesson 8 onwards there is a further column of Arabic to allow the Perfect, Imperfect and Verbal Noun (*maṣdar*) forms to be printed together. In Vocabularies 15–40 the Perfects of derived forms are preceded by a number (e.g. 2) to show which derived form is involved. There is also a General Vocabulary, which puts together all the words in Vocabularies 1–40 in Arabic alphabetical order. This is to enable a reader who has forgotten a word to look it up without having to remember which lesson it was first used in.

Every attempt should be made to become familiar with the words in a lesson's vocabulary before the reader moves on to (c) the exercise for that lesson. One can then test one's absorption of the lesson by tackling the exercise. Some of the sentences will turn out to be less straightforward than they might at first appear. This is often because they are without a wider context. Each exercise should be attempted in the first place without reference to the Key. If readers find that they still have problems, they should turn to the Key, and look at the sentence and its translation together. Once the sentences in an exercise are understood, the vocabulary should be revised and fully mastered.

At various points there are exhortations to the reader to learn the vocabulary and to learn it in a certain way. These are based on experience with students over a nearly half a century and are a reminder of how readers might help themselves. The same applies to exhortations to learn declensions and conjugations. Effort put in at an early stage has real rewards.

Let me stress again that this book's basic aim is to help the reader to learn to read the Qur'ān. To go beyond the texts referred to in this work, the reader will need a text, a translation, such as my own, and a dictionary. Dictionaries are a problem. Hava's Arabic Dictionary is quite helpful, but it has long been out of print and it is difficult to find. Penrice's Dictionary and Glossary of the Qur'ān was hardly at the cutting edge of scholarship when it was first printed in 1873. However, it was reprinted by the Curzon Press in 1971 and is sometimes available. It should be noted that Wehr's Arabic Dictionary, whether in the original German or in Milton Cowan's English translation, is a dictionary of modern Arabic. For the Qur'ān it is largely useless. However, it is an excellent work, and those readers of this book who go on to modern Arabic (and I hope that most of them will do) will find it indispensable. The great reference grammar for early and classical Arabic is Wright's Arabic Grammar, still being issued by the Cambridge University Press. However, the first edition was published in 1859/1862, and thus it does not cover modern Arabic.

This book is largely concerned with reading the Qur'ān. However, it is essential to remember that *al-Qur'ān* means 'the Recitation', that the Prophet delivered the Qur'ān orally, and that its oral dimension is crucial. With the knowledge that the reader has acquired, I hope that he or she will learn to understand the text both in written and recited form.

Letters	Independent	Initial	Medial	Final	Transliteration
alif	ا			ـا	
bā'	ب	بـ	ـبـ	ـب	*b*
tā'	ت	تـ	ـتـ	ـت	*t*
thā'	ث	ثـ	ـثـ	ـث	*th*
jīm	ج	جـ	ـجـ	ـج	*j*
ḥā'	ح	حـ	ـحـ	ـح	*ḥ*
khā'	خ	خـ	ـخـ	ـخ	*kh*
dāl	د			ـد	*d*
dhāl	ذ			ـذ	*dh*
rā'	ر			ـر	*r*
zāy	ز			ـز	*z*
sīn	س	سـ	ـسـ	ـس	*s*
shīn	ش	شـ	ـشـ	ـش	*sh*
ṣād	ص	صـ	ـصـ	ـص	*ṣ*
ḍād	ض	ضـ	ـضـ	ـض	*ḍ*
ṭā'	ط	طـ	ـطـ	ـط	*ṭ*
ẓā'	ظ	ظـ	ـظـ	ـظ	*ẓ*
ʿayn	ع	عـ	ـعـ	ـع	ʿ
ghayn	غ	غـ	ـغـ	ـغ	*gh*
fā'	ف	فـ	ـفـ	ـف	*f*
qāf	ق	قـ	ـقـ	ـق	*q*
kāf	ك	كـ	ـكـ	ـك	*k*
lām	ل	لـ	ـلـ	ـل	*l*
mīm	م	مـ	ـمـ	ـم	*m*
nūn	ن	نـ	ـنـ	ـن	*n*
hā'	ه	هـ	ـهـ	ـه	*h*
wāw	و			ـو	*w*
yā'	ي	يـ	ـيـ	ـي	*y*

The Arabic Alphabet

Introduction to the Arabic Alphabet

Arabic is written from right to left in a script that has an alphabet of 29 letters. (Perhaps 28 would be more accurate—see the notes on *hamza* below). Various forms of the script developed over the centuries, one of them, Kūfic, being particularly associated with the writing of the Qur'ān in the early centuries of Islam. The user of this book will need to be familiar with only one form. This is known as *naskh*, the primary printed form. The standard Egyptian text of the Qur'ān is written in a more elegant way than one finds in ordinary printing and has certain modifications that are explained below. (It should be noted that copies of the Qur'ān from North Africa are written in a different script, Maghribī, with different forms for the letters *fā'* and *qāf*.)

The alphabet set out on the opposite page has developed in a number of ways since the time of the Prophet Muḥammad. At that period dots were used relatively rarely to differentiate the letters, and for a time, as the early Kūfic script evolved, they appear not to have been used in the writing of the Qur'ān. However, by the end of the first Islamic century, determined efforts were being made to differentiate the letters fully by the use of dots, though it was some considerable time before all scribes used them. During the same period, the writing of *hamza* was introduced, and signs to indicate the short vowels were also added. A hybrid letter, *tā' marbūṭa*, was introduced to indicate the final letter of words that take the main feminine grammatical ending. This is a *hā'* to which the dots of the letter *tā'* have been added. From time to time the standard text uses an ordinary *tā'* where a *tā' marbūṭa* might have been expected. Printed *naskh*, and handwriting akin to it, have fewer combinations of letters, usually known as ligatures, than other styles of writing. The letters concerned are normally clear enough. One ligature has almost attained the status of a letter. This is the combination of *lām* and *alif* (لا).

Hamza (ء)

With the passage of time Arabic developed various spellings to indicate the presence of a glottal stop, *hamza* (full name *hamzat al-qaṭʿ*). The rules for these spellings are complicated, and are something of a nuisance for beginners. They owe their existence to historical circumstances. In seventh-century Arabic, the *hamza* had more or less dropped out of use in some dialects, including that of Quraysh, Muḥammad's tribe; but in other dialects it survived, as it did in the higher registers of language, including most poetry. Classical Arabic owed more to those dialects that preserved the *hamza* than to those that did not. The resulting orthography of *hamza*, where a 'seat', or *kursiyy*, indicated an absent *hamza*, was a compromise, allowing for texts to be comprehensible whether the *hamza* was actually written in or not. As time went on, forms with *hamza* prevailed over those without, and the need for complex spellings disappeared. However, by that time the writing system was largely fixed, and it preserved what is in effect various forms of double spelling, with the majority of forms having both a *hamza* and a 'seat' (*kursiyy*). The latter gives an indication of the pronunciation without *hamza*. There is a further complication. The writing system also developed a way of indicating a vowel placed before a word or a cluster that would otherwise begin with a vowelless consonant. This secondary form of *hamza* (full name *hamzat al-waṣl*) was born from theories about pronunciation held by the Arab grammarians, who took the view that such words and clusters could not begin without a vowel. To avoid the problem, an *alif* and a vowel without the *hamza* sign are placed at the beginning of the word or cluster. If that were all, the process would be relatively simple; but if the word preceding the word or cluster that begins without a vowel ends with (or can be given) a final vowel to which the vowelless letter can be linked (and thus pronounced without an extra vowel being added to the vowelless word or cluster), an *alif* and a joining sign, *waṣla*, are written instead. If you cannot immediately understand the last sentence, do not be surprised. It takes time to absorb the complicated logic of these rules, but they are not such a problem for those whose initial aim is to read texts. Those wanting to write vocalised Arabic need a lot of practice to enable them to co-ordinate their use of these rules.

Vowels

The Qur'ān has long been written with full vocalisation. This is a feature found in few texts. Most Arabic, from the earliest times to the present day, carries no indication of short vowels. The signs for the short vowels were developed in Umayyad times. This is in contrast to the long vowels, which often occur in the earliest surviving documents from the Islamic period. The system of vocalisation that evolved is able to indicate three short vowels, three long vowels and two diphthongs. The short vowels are:

> *a* (Arabic name *fatḥa*), written َ, e.g. أَ
>
> *i* (Arabic name *kasra*), written ِ, e.g. إِ
>
> *u* (Arabic name *ḍamma*), written ُ, e.g. أُ

The basic ways of writing the long vowels are:
ā, indicated by writing an *alif* after a *fatḥa*,
ī, indicated by writing a *yā'* after a *kasra*,
ū, indicated by writing a *wāw* after a *ḍamma*,

However, there are alternative ways of writing the long vowels, and some of these are to be found in the standard text of the Qur'ān. Those for *ī* and *ū* are simple. A small independent form of *yā'*, now obsolete, is used to indicate *ī*; and a small independent form of *wāw* is used to indicate *ū*. The writing of the alternative forms of *ā* is more complex. There are two principal forms:

1. SHORT ALIF. In this form a *fatḥa* is written perpendicularly, so that it resembles a short *alif* written independently. Thus one finds both كِتَاب and كِتٰب for *kitāb*. With many words, and *kitāb* is one of these, the short *alif* predominates. It should be noted that this use of short *alif* has become less frequent as time has passed. It is

relatively uncommon in modern Arabic for the *alif* indicating long *ā* not to be written as a full letter, except in the demonstratives, where the written forms have become fossilised. (See Lesson 6.)

2. ALIF IN THE FORM of a *yā'* [*alif maqṣūra*]. Under rules that need not be set out in this book, the letter that indicates *ā* at the end of a word may be written as a *yā'* instead of an *alif*. This is known, perhaps not surprisingly, as *alif* in the form of a *yā'*. In the Qur'ān it frequently has a short *alif* written above it. The Arab grammarians had various theories about its origin, and the argument that it indicated some variation in pronunciation appears to have some validity. It must be noted that *alif* in the form of a *yā'* can occur only at the end of a word. If a word is extended by the addition of a suffix, *yā'* reverts to *alif*. Thus *ramā* 'he threw' is written with *alif* in the form of a *yā'*: رَمَى. When the suffix for 'it' is added, this becomes *ramā-hu*, written رَمَاهُ. It should also be noted that in a small number of words *ā* is indicated by a *wāw* and a short *alif*. The most common of these words are زَكَوٰة *zakāt* 'alms-giving', صَلَوٰة *ṣalāt* 'ritual prayer', حَيَوٰة *ḥayāt* 'life', and اَلرِّبَوا *al-ribā* 'usury'. This special spelling may originally have indicated an *o* sound.

The diphthongs are *aw* and *ay* represented by *fatḥa* + *wāw* (أَوْ) and *fatḥa* + *yā'* (أَيْ) respectively.

Madda

It has become standard for a *hamza* followed by a long *ā* to be written as two *alif*s, one vertical and one horizontal (آ). This piece of orthography is not used in the standard text of the Qur'ān, a convention that is not always easy to follow. In this book آ is used for purposes of clarity.

Sukūn

This is the sign to indicate the absence of a vowel. The usual form is a little circle placed above the consonant concerned (ْ), but the standard Egyptian text more frequently uses the sign ۡ.

Tanwīn

The final vowel of a noun or adjective may have an *n* sound to indicate that it is indefinite. This is shown by writing the vowel twice, to give ٌ *un*, ً *an* or ٍ *in*.

Tashdīd

The sign ّ (*shadda*) indicates the doubling (*tashdīd*) of a letter. *Kasra* with a *shadda* is printed immediately under the *shadda* in this book.

PRONUNCIATION

It is impossible to give a proper explanation of pronunciation by written description alone, and the notes that follow give only brief indications. Much can be learned from listening to recorded recitations of the Qur'ān, particularly if these are not too highly stylised.

alif	nil	bearer for *hamza* or sign of long *ā*.
bā'	*b*	
tā'	*t*	
thā'	*th*	as in '*th*ink'.
jīm	*j*	as in '*j*am'.
ḥā'		a hoarse, much stronger aspiration than *hā'*.
khā'		like the *ch* in the Scottish 'lo*ch*' or the German 'a*ch*'.
dāl	*d*	
dhāl		transcribed as *dh*, but sounds like the *th* in '*th*e'.
rā'	*r*	a rolled *r*, always fully sounded.
zāy	*z*	
sīn	*s*	
shīn	*sh*	as in 'shingle'.
ṣād		an emphatic form of *s*.
ḍād		an emphatic form of *d*.
ṭā'		an emphatic form of *t*.

ẓā'		an emphatic form of *dh* (not of *z*).
ʿayn		a guttural produced by compression of the throat, found in very few languages and best learned from a native speaker.
ghayn		a gargling sound, much like the *gr* in the French '*gr*and'.
fā'	*f*	
qāf		a *k* sound produced from the back of the throat.
kāf	*k*	
lām	*l*	
mīm	*m*	
nūn	*n*	
hā'	*h*	always pronounced.
wāw	*w*	also part of *ū* and *aw*.
yā'	*y*	also part of *ī* and *ay*.

Lesson One
Nouns and Adjectives

Grammatically Arabic nouns and adjectives may be either definite or indefinite.

Indefinite

There is no indefinite article equivalent to the English 'a', 'an'. However, the large majority of nouns and adjectives have *tanwīn* (the addition of the sound *n* to the final vowel of a word) to indicate that the word is indefinite:

أَجْرٌ	*ajrun*	a reward
عَذَابٌ	*ʿadhābun*	a punishment
كِتَابٌ كِتَٰبٌ	*kitābun*	a scripture, document
آيَةٌ	*āyatun*	a sign, verse
رَحْمَةٌ	*raḥmatun*	a mercy
قُرْآنٌ	*qur'ānun*	a recitation

However, you will come across a considerable number of words that do **not** take *tanwīn* when they are indefinite. At this stage you can only learn what these words are by experience. Two examples are:

آخَرُ	*ākharu*	other
أَوَّلُ	*awwalu*	first

You must remember that it is impossible to add *tanwīn* to words that are shown as not taking it (either in the text or in the vocabularies), and **any attempt to do so is incorrect**.

DEFINITE

A noun may be made definite in one of two ways:

1. by being preceded by the definite article, equivalent to the English 'the'.
2. by being followed by the genitive of possession.

We shall deal here only with the definite article; on (2) see Lesson 7.

THE DEFINITE ARTICLE

Traditional wisdom tells us that the definite article is أَلْ (*al*) prefixed inseparably to a word, and that is the way that it has always been written:

أَلْبَلَدُ	*al-baladu*	the town
أَلْعَذَابُ	*al-ʿadhābu*	the punishment

In fact, the definite article is in essence simply a *lām* (*l*) but as Arabic phonetic theory holds that words cannot begin with an unvowelled consonant, the vowel *a* (*fatḥa*) is added to the *lām* to give *al*. Theory also holds that this *a* vowel is not an integral part of the definite article and is required only when no other vowel precedes the *l*. In effect this means that the added vowel is used only at the beginning of a sentence. In other places the vowel *a* (*fatḥa*) is replaced by a 'joining sign' ٱ (*waṣla*), which tells you to link the *l* of the definite article to the final vowel of the preceding word.

In short, you will find أَلْ at the beginning, and ٱلْ elsewhere in the sentence/verse. The use of the two can be seen in:

أَلْكِتَابُ ٱلْمُبِينُ *al-kitābu l-mubīnu*

This is the first of two pieces of manipulation required by the definite article. The second initially appears more complicated, but you will soon get used to it. The sooner you do so the better, because until you have mastered it, you will not be able to read or pronounce correctly.

1. When it precedes half of the letters of the alphabet, the *l* of the definite article is pronounced as *l*.
   These letters are: ء ي و ه م ك ق ف غ ع خ ح ج ب.
   In Arabic terminology this group of letters is known as 'the moon letters' (because the word for 'moon' begins with one of them).
   With such letters a *sukūn* is written over the *l* of the definite article:

اَلْيَوْمُ	*al-yawmu*	the day
اَلْكِتَابُ	*al-kitābu*	the document

2. For words beginning with all the other letters of the alphabet the pronunciation of the *l* is assimilated to the sound of the following consonant. These letters are:
   ن ل ظ ط ض ص ش س ز ر ذ د ث ت.
   They are known as 'the sun letters' (the word for 'sun' beginning with one of them). With such letters a *shadda* is written over the letter after the ال (i.e. the letter to which the *lām* is assimilated). This is a clear indication of the doubling of the sound of the following letter.

اَلرَّحْمَةُ	*al-raḥmatu* (*ar-raḥmatu*)	the mercy
اَلرَّسُولُ	*al-rasūlu* (*ar-rasūlu*)	the messenger

   The correct form of pronunciation is the one given in brackets. However, most systems of transliteration retain the spelling of the article with *l* and expect the reader to make the correct assimilation. Thus one normally sees *al-Raḥīmu* 'the Compassionate', which has to be read and pronounced as *ar-Raḥīmu*. This convention is followed in this book.

Note that in the Qur'ān when the definite article is prefixed to a word beginning with *lam*, only one *lam* is written. Thus *al-laylu* 'the night' is written اَلَّيْل. This is not normally the case in modern Arabic.

With reading practice you should soon become accustomed to these rules for reading and pronouncing the definite article.

Whatever you do, you must not forget that **if a word has the definite article, it cannot also have *tanwīn***. (Words cannot be definite and indefinite at the same time.)

The word اَللّٰهُ Allāhu

Allāhu 'God' is a combination of the definite article and the word إِلٰهٌ *ilāhun* 'a god', with the dropping of the initial *hamza* of the noun. Literally, it means 'the God', though that is not a natural English expression and will not be used in this book. Note that in some versions of the Qur'ān *Allāhu* is written without any indication of the long vowel.

GENDER

There are two genders in Arabic: masculine and feminine.

The simplest working rule is to treat words as masculine unless you have a reason for treating them as feminine. As you proceed, you will find that words may be feminine because of form, meaning, category or convention.

From the outset you will encounter a small number of words that are feminine through meaning, such as أُمٌّ *umm(un)* 'mother', or through convention, such as أَرْضٌ *arḍ(un)* 'earth'.

However, the first important group of feminine words that you have to deal with are those that take the ending ـَةٌ *-atun* when indefinite [also occasionally *atu*]. A couple of these have already been mentioned. Here are examples of the definite and indefinite feminine forms together:

اَلْآيَةُ	*al-āyatu*	آيَةٌ	*āyatun*
اَلرَّحْمَةُ	*al-raḥmatu*	رَحْمَةٌ	*raḥmatun*

There are a few masculine words with this ending, but the only common one is خَلِيفَةٌ *khalīfatun*. In the Qur'ān this word has the strict sense of 'successor' or 'viceroy'. In later times this was generalized to 'caliph'.

This ending in *-atun* is the one most commonly used to form a feminine adjective from a masculine one:

اَلْكَبِيرُ	كَبِيرٌ	m.	*kabīrun / al-kabīru*
اَلْكَبِيرَةُ	كَبِيرَةٌ	f.	*kabīratun / al-kabīratu*
اَلشَّدِيدُ	شَدِيدٌ	m.	*shadīdun / al-shadīdu*
اَلشَّدِيدَةُ	شَدِيدَةٌ	f.	*shadīdatun / al-shadīdatu*

USE OF ADJECTIVES

An adjective used attributively follows the noun and must agree with the noun in **four** things:

1. Definiteness
2. Gender
3. Number
4. Case

You should now be able to deal with the first two:

اَلْفَوْزُ ٱلْعَظِيمُ	*al-fawzu l-ʿaẓīmu*	the great victory
اَلْيَوْمُ ٱلْآخِرُ	*al-yawmu l-ākhiru*	the last day
قُرْآنٌ مُبِينٌ	*qur'ānun mubīnun*	a clear recitation
رَحْمَةٌ وٰسِعَةٌ	*raḥmatun wāsiʿatun*	a widespread mercy

Number and case will be dealt with shortly.

SIMPLE NON-VERBAL SENTENCES

The rule about agreement in definiteness is crucial, because a definite noun followed by an indefinite adjective is a complete sentence—a subject and a predicate—not requiring a verb. Arabic is thus able to manage without a verb for 'to be' in the present tense. Hence many sentences are complete though they have no verb.

اَللّٰهُ عَزِيزٌ	*Allāhu ʿazīzun*	God is mighty
اَللّٰهُ قَوِيٌّ	*Allāhu qawiyyun*	God is strong
اَللّٰهُ قَوِيٌّ عَزِيزٌ	*Allāhu qawiyyun ʿazīzun*	God is powerful and mighty

Note that in this last example it is necessary to link the adjectives in English by using 'and'. This is not necessary in Arabic, though the particle وَ (*wa-*) 'and' could be used. Single letter words in Arabic cannot be written separately, so *wa-* is linked to the following word, as will be seen in later lessons.

LEARNING VOCABULARY

The vocabulary that accompanies each lesson is intended to include all the words you need to understand the examples in the text of the lesson and to do the translation exercise that follows it. To make progress you will have to learn the vocabulary of each lesson as you come to it, and you should learn all the forms that are given: with nouns (and adjectives) you should learn the singular and the plural together; with verbs you should learn three forms—the perfect, imperfect and *maṣdar*—together (see Lesson 8).

Because of the limits of Qur'ānic vocabulary, one often finds only a singular form or a plural form of a word in the Qur'ān, though the corresponding plural and singular may be common elsewhere. Two good examples of this are the plural *manāfiʿu*, 'benefits', commonly used in the Qur'ān, whilst the singular *manfaʿatun* is not found; and *arḍun*, 'earth', even more common, though its plurals *arāḍin* and *araḍūna* do not occur. There are similar gaps in the incidence of verb forms. These missing forms are listed in the General Vocabulary and occasionally used as examples.

Vocabulary One

Singular		Plural		
اَللّٰهُ	*Allāhu*			God
إِلٰهٌ	*ilāhun*	آلِهَةٌ	*ālihatun*	a god
أَجْرٌ	*ajrun*	أُجُورٌ	*ujūrun*	reward
آيَةٌ	*āyatun*	آيَاتٌ	*āyātun*	sign, verse
بَلَدٌ	*baladun*	بِلَادٌ	*bilādun*	town
رَسُولٌ	*rasūlun*	رُسُلٌ	*rusulun*	messenger
رَحْمَةٌ	*raḥmatun*			mercy
عَذَابٌ	*ʿadhābun*			punishment
فَوْزٌ	*fawzun*			victory
قُرْآنٌ	*qur'ānun*			Qur'ān, recitation
كِتَابٌ	*kitābun*	كُتُبٌ	*kutubun*	scripture, document, book
خَلِيفَةٌ	*khalīfatun*	خُلَفَاءُ	*khulafā'u*	successor, viceroy, caliph
أَرْضٌ	*arḍun* (f.)			earth
أُمٌّ	*ummun*	أُمَّهَاتٌ	*ummahātun*	mother
يَوْمٌ	*yawmun*	أَيَّامٌ	*ayyāmun*	day
أَمِينٌ	*amīnun*			faithful, secure
آخِرٌ	*ākhirun*			last, [next]
شَدِيدٌ	*shadīdun*	شِدَادٌ	*shidādun*	strong, severe
عَزِيزٌ	*ʿazīzun*			mighty

Singular		Plural		
عَظِيمٌ	*ʿaẓīmun*			great, mighty
قَوِيٌّ	*qawiyyun*			strong
كَبِيرٌ	*kabīrun*			big, great
كَرِيمٌ	*karīmun*	كِرَامٌ	*kirāmun*	noble, generous
مَجِيدٌ	*majīdun*			glorious
وَاسِعٌ	*wāsiʿun*			wide, ample
مُبِينٌ	*mubīnun*			clear
أَوَّلُ	*ʾawwalu*	أَوَّلُونَ	*awwalūna*	first
أُولَى	*ūlā* (f.)			
آخَرُ	*ākharu*	آخَرُونَ	*ākharūna*	other
أُخْرَى	*ukhrā* (f.)	أُخَرُ	*ukharu*	

Exercise One

1.	اَلْكِتَابُ ٱلْمُبِينُ	*al-kitābu l-mubīnu*	[12:1]
2.	كِتَابٌ مُبِينٌ	*kitābun mubīnun*	[5:15]
3.	كِتَابٌ كَرِيمٌ	*kitābun karīmun*	[27:29]
4.	قُرْآنٌ مُبِينٌ	*qur'ānun mubīnun*	[15:1]
5.	اَلْقُرْآنُ ٱلْمَجِيدُ	*al-qur'ānu l-majīdu*	[50:1]
6.	قُرْآنٌ كَرِيمٌ	*qur'ānun karīmun*	[56:77]
7.	قُرْآنٌ مَجِيدٌ	*qur'ānun majīdun*	[85:21]
8.	اَلْقُرْآنُ ٱلْعَظِيمُ	*al-qur'ānu l-ʿaẓīmu*	[15:87]

9.	رَحْمَةٌ وٰسِعَةٌ	*raḥmatun wāsiʿatun*	[6:147]
10.	آيَـةٌ أُخْرَى	*āyatun ukhrā*	[20:22]
11.	اَلْيَوْمُ الْآخِرُ	*al-yawmu l-ākhiru*	[2:126]
12.	يَوْمٌ كَبِيرٌ	*yawmun kabīrun*	[11:3]
13.	اَلْعَذَابُ الشَّدِيدُ	*al-ʿadhābu l-shadīdu*	[10:70]
14.	يَوْمٌ عَظِيمٌ	*yawmun ʿaẓīmun*	[6:15]
15.	عَذَابٌ شَدِيدٌ	*ʿadhābun shadīdun*	[3:4]
16.	أَجْرٌ عَظِيمٌ	*ajrun ʿaẓīmun*	[3:172]
17.	أَجْرٌ كَرِيمٌ	*ajrun karīmun*	[57:11]
18.	عَذَابٌ عَظِيمٌ	*ʿadhābun ʿaẓīmun*	[2:7]
19.	أَجْرٌ كَبِيرٌ	*ajrun kabīrun*	[11:11]
20.	رَسُولٌ أَمِينٌ	*rasūlun amīnun*	[26:107]
21.	رَسُولٌ كَرِيمٌ	*rasūlun karīmun*	[44:17]
22.	اَلْبَلَدُ الْأَمِينُ	*al-baladu l-amīnu*	[95:3]
23.	إِلٰهٌ آخَرُ	*ilāhun ākharu*	[15:96]
24.	رَسُولٌ مُبِينٌ	*rasūlun mubīnun*	[43:29]
25.	اَلْأَوَّلُ وَالْآخِرُ	*al-awwalu wa-l-ākhiru*	[57:3]
26.	اَلْأُولٰى وَالْآخِرَةُ	*al-ūlā wa-l-ākhiratu*	[28:70]
27.	اَللّٰهُ عَزِيزٌ	*Allāhu ʿazīzun*	[2:209]
28.	اَللّٰهُ قَوِيٌّ	*Allāhu qawiyyun*	[8:52]
29.	اَللّٰهُ قَوِيٌّ عَزِيزٌ	*Allāhu qawiyyun ʿazīzun*	[58:21]
30.	اَلْقَوِيُّ الْأَمِينُ	*al-qawiyyu l-amīnu*	[28:26]

Lesson Two
Plurals

Arabic has two types of plural, known as sound plurals and broken plurals. In general, broken plurals are much more common than sound plurals. However, in the Qur'ān, the proportion of sound plurals is considerably higher than it is in later Arabic.

Sound plurals

There are masculine and feminine sound plurals. These are indicated by word endings. Words with sound plurals are analogous to *house/houses* and *ox/oxen* in English.

Masculine sound plural

	Singular		Plural
ظَالِمٌ	*ẓālimun*	ظَالِمُونَ	*ẓālimūna*
تَوَّابٌ	*tawwābun*	تَوَّابُونَ	*tawwābūna*
أَعْجَمِيٌّ	*aʿjamiyyun*	أَعْجَمِيُّونَ	*aʿjamiyyūna*

The masculine sound plural is very restricted in use. The only three common categories of words that take it are: participles, or nouns that were originally participles, like ظَالِمٌ *ẓālimun* 'wrongdoer'; words of the same form as تَوَّابٌ *tawwābun* 'relenting', most of which now refer to professions and occupations, though in the Qur'ān they normally have an intensive meaning; and relative adjectives like أَعْجَمِيٌّ *aʿjamiyyun.*

There are a few words in the Qur'ān that are feminine singulars, ending in *-atun* but nevertheless have a sound masculine plural. The only common word is سَنَةٌ *sanatun* 'a year', with the plural سِنُونَ *sinūna*—though in modern Arabic سِنُونَ has been superseded by the sound feminine plural سَنَوَاتٌ *sanawātun*.

Feminine sound plural

This is particularly, though not entirely, associated with the feminine singular ending in *-atun*.

Singular		Plural	
مُؤْمِنَةٌ	*mu'minatun*	مُؤْمِنَاتٌ	*mu'minātun*
آيَةٌ	*āyatun*	آيَاتٌ	*āyātun*

However, you cannot assume that all words ending in ـَةٌ take a sound feminine plural. Many do not. Conversely, there are some words that have a sound feminine plural form though the singular gives no indication that this might be so, e.g. سَمَاءٌ *samā'un*, plural سَمَاوَاتٌ *samāwātun*.

Broken Plurals

Broken plurals are formed by a change of vowel pattern from the singular to plural. Words with broken plurals are analogous to *mouse/mice* and *foot/feet* in English. The vast majority of Arabic nouns and a fair number of adjectives have broken plurals; and there are many forms of broken plural. Eventually you will find that, within certain limits, experience allows you to predict from the singular of the noun what the broken plural form is likely to be. At the outset it is impossible to make such predictions.

Singular		Plural	
عَبْدٌ	*ʿabdun*	عِبَادٌ	*ʿibādun*
قَرْنٌ	*qarnun*	قُرُونٌ	*qurūnun*
فَٰكِهَةٌ	*fākihatun*	فَوَٰكِهُ	*fawākihu*
كِتَابٌ	*kitābun*	كُتُبٌ	*kutubun*

رَجُلٌ	*rajulun*	رِجَالٌ	*rijālun*
قَرْيَةٌ	*qaryatun*	قُرًى	*quran*[A]

There is a crucial grammatical rule that you must remember:

> Broken plurals are treated grammatically as **feminine singulars**, unless they refer to male persons, when they are treated as masculine plurals (or to female persons, when they are treated as feminine plurals).

Thus قُرُونٌ *qurūnun*, فَوٰكِهُ *fawākihu*, قُرًى *quran* and كُتُبٌ *kutubun* are all feminine singulars; and adjectives agreeing with them and similar nouns must, in all normal circumstances, be in the feminine singular.

كُتُبٌ قَيِّمَةٌ	*kutubun qayyimatun*	valuable documents
مَنٰفِعُ كَثِيرَةٌ	*manāfiʿu kathīratun*	many benefits
اَلْقُرُونُ ٱلأُولَى	*al-qurūnu l-ūlā*	the first generations

However, because رِجَالٌ *rijālun* and عِبَادٌ *ʿibādun* refer to male persons, they take either a broken plural adjective form or a sound masculine plural form:

رِجَالٌ مُؤْمِنُونَ	*rijālun mu'minūna*	believing men
عِبَادٌ مُكْرَمُونَ	*ʿibādun mukramūna*	honoured servants

There are some nouns in the Qur'ān that are singular in form but plural in meaning. These normally take plural adjectives. Prominent amongst them is قَوْمٌ *qawm*, 'people':

اَلْقَوْمُ ٱلْكٰفِرُونَ	*al-qawmu l-kāfirūna*	the unbelieving people

[A] On this form see Lesson 3

Some broken plural nouns not referring to persons also take broken plural adjectives, e.g. أَيَّامٌ أُخَرُ *ayyāmun ukharu* 'other days'.

Occasionally such nouns are also found in the Qur'ān with feminine plural adjectives, but with the passing of time this has become increasingly rare, and it is surprising when one sees this usage in modern Arabic. A common mistake for beginners is to expect that a broken plural form of an adjective may have a feminine ending added to it. This is totally impossible.

VOCABULARY TWO

SINGULAR		PLURAL		
رَجُلٌ	*rajulun*	رِجَالٌ	*rijālun*	man
سَمَاءٌ	*samā'un*	سَمَاوَاتٌ	*samāwātun*	heaven, sky
عَبْدٌ	*ᶜabdun*	عِبَادٌ	*ᶜibādun*	servant, slave
قَرْنٌ	*qarnun*	قُرُونٌ	*qurūnun*	generation [horn]
قَرْيَةٌ	*qaryatun*	قُرًى	*quran*	settlement, village
قَوْمٌ	*qawmun*	أَقْوَامٌ	*aqwāmun*	people
مَنْفَعَةٌ	*manfaᶜatun*	مَنَافِعُ	*manāfiᶜu*	benefit
كَافِرٌ	*kāfirun*	كَافِرُونَ	*kāfirūna*	unbeliever, ungrateful
مُؤْمِنٌ	*mu'minun*	مُؤْمِنُونَ	*mu'minūna*	believer
ظَالِمٌ	*ẓālimun*	ظَالِمُونَ	*ẓālimūna*	wrongdoer
أَعْجَمِيٌّ	*aᶜjamiyyun*	أَعْجَمِيُّونَ	*aᶜjamiyyūna*	foreign
عَرَبِيٌّ	*ᶜarabiyyun*	عَرَبٌ	*ᶜarabun*	Arab, Arabic
مُسْلِمٌ	*muslimun*	مُسْلِمُونَ	*muslimūna*	Muslim
نَصْرَانِيٌّ	*naṣrāniyyun*	نَصَارَى	*naṣārā*	Christian
يَهُودِيٌّ	*yahūdiyyun*	يَهُودٌ	*yahūdun*	Jew, Jewish

Singular		Plural		
سَنَةٌ	*sanatun*	سِنُونَ	*sinūna*	year
فَاكِهَةٌ	*fākihatun*	فَوَاكِهُ	*fawākihu*	fruit
كَثِيرٌ	*kathīrun*	كَثِيرُونَ	*kathīrūna*	many
		كِثَارٌ	*kithārun*	
تَوَّابٌ	*tawwābun*	تَوَّابُونَ	*tawwābūna*	relenting (s.)
				repenting (pl.)
مُكْرَمٌ	*mukramun*	مُكْرَمُونَ	*mukramūna*	honoured

Exercise Two

1.	آلِهَةٌ أُخْرَىٰ	*ālihatun ukhrā*	[6:19]
2.	مَنَافِعُ كَثِيرَةٌ	*manāfiʿu kathīratun*	[23:21]
3.	فَوَاكِهُ كَثِيرَةٌ	*fawākihu kathīratun*	[23:19]
4.	اَلْقُرُونُ ٱلْأُولَىٰ	*al-qurūnu l-ūlā*	[20:51]
5.	اَلْقُرَىٰ ظَالِمَةٌ	*al-qurā ẓālimatun*	[11:102]
6.	قَرْيَةٌ ظَالِمَةٌ	*qaryatun ẓālimatun*	[21:11]
7.	اَلْيَهُودُ وَٱلنَّصَارَىٰ	*al-yahūdu wa-l-naṣārā*	[5:18]
8.	اَلسَّمٰوَاتُ وَٱلْأَرْضُ	*al-samawātu wa-l-arḍu*	[15:85]
9.	أَعْجَمِيٌّ وَعَرَبِيٌّ	*aʿjamiyyun wa-ʿarabiyyun*	[41:44]
10.	اَلْقَوْمُ ٱلظَّالِمُونَ	*al-qawmu l-ẓālimūna*	[6:47]
11.	اَلْقَوْمُ ٱلْكَافِرُونَ	*al-qawmu l-kāfirūna*	[12:87]
12.	كَافِرٌ وَمُؤْمِنٌ	*kāfirun wa-mu'minun*	[64:2]
13.	رِجَالٌ مُؤْمِنُونَ	*rijālun mu'minūna*	[48:25]

14.	اَلْمُؤْمِنُونَ وَٱلْمُؤْمِنَاتُ	*al-mu'minūna wa-l-mu'minātu*	[24:12]
15.	مُؤْمِنُونَ وَمُؤْمِنَاتٌ	*mu'minūna wa-mu'minātun*	[48:25]
16.	اَلْأَوَّلُونَ وَٱلْآخِرُونَ	*al-awwalūna wa-l-ākhirūna*	[56:49]
17.	اَللّٰهُ تَوَّابٌ	*Allāhu tawwābun*	[49:12]
18.	عِبَادٌ مُكْرَمُونَ	*ʿibādun mukramūna*	[21:26]
19.	رَجُلٌ مُؤْمِنٌ	*rajulun mu'minun*	[40:28]
20.	أَيَّامٌ أُخَرُ	*ayyāmun ukharu*	[2:184]
21.	اَلسَّمَاءُ وَٱلْأَرْضُ	*al-samā'u wa-l-arḍu*	[44:29]
22.	اَلْمُسْلِمُونَ وَٱلْمُسْلِمَاتُ	*al-muslimūna wa-l-muslimātu*	[33:35]

Lesson Three
The Declension of Nouns

Arabic has three cases: nominative, accusative and genitive. A slightly simplistic explanation of their functions covers all main points:

1. The nominative is used for the subject (in most places) and for some predicates in non-verbal sentences.
2. The genitive is used after prepositions and to denote possession.
3. The accusative is used if you cannot use the nominative or genitive.

In Lessons 1 and 2 the nominative has been used. In Lesson 4 the use of the genitive will be introduced; and in Lesson 8 the use of the accusative will be introduced.

Forms of Declension

There are five basic types of declension, the first three of which have sub-divisions. There are also special declension forms for the sound feminine plural and the sound masculine plural. The types are set out below in tables, and it is useful to learn them as they are set out. Learning the types in this way is not the theoretical exercise it might seem to be. It helps to give structure to one's knowledge, and, as with the verb tables that come later, it is akin to learning multiplication tables for arithmetic.

Type One

Type One consists of words that have the feminine ending ةٌ. These are the simplest forms to decline. There are two sub-divisions: a) those words which are fully inflected and have three case endings; and b) those that are not and have only two case endings. In Type One this latter sub-division is confined to proper names. Therefore although the words in the sub-division may appear indefinite in form, they are definite in meaning. This means that any adjective attached to them has to have the definite article.

Fully inflected (3 case endings)

	Indefinite			Definite
قَرْيَةٌ	*qaryatun*	nom.	اَلْقَرْيَةُ	*al-qaryatu*
قَرْيَةً	*qaryatan*	acc.	اَلْقَرْيَةَ	*al-qaryata*
قَرْيَةٍ	*qaryatin*	gen.	اَلْقَرْيَةِ	*al-qaryati*

Partially inflected

nom.	مَكَّةُ	*makkatu*
acc.	مَكَّةَ	*makkata*
gen.	مَكَّةَ	*makkata*

The crucial difference between the fully and partially inflected form here (and in Type Two) is in the genitive. This can be clearly seen when an adjective is added, *al-mukarramatu*, commonly used to describe Mecca in later times. The adjective has to have the definite article because *makkatu*, as a proper noun, is definite.

nom.	مَكَّةُ اَلْمُكَرَّمَةُ	*makkatu l-mukarramatu*
acc.	مَكَّةَ اَلْمُكَرَّمَةَ	*makkata l-mukarramata*
gen.	مَكَّةَ اَلْمُكَرَّمَةِ	*makkata l-mukarramati*

Type Two

Type Two embraces most nouns and adjectives. There are two points of special note with this type:

1. An *alif* is added to the indefinite accusative form of fully inflected words:

   رَجُلًا *rajulan* a man

2. Partially inflected words have the same form for the accusative and genitive when they are indefinite; but when they are definite, they act like fully inflected words and have all three case endings. You can see this by looking at the declension of:

Fully inflected

	Indefinite		Definite	
nom.	يَوْمٌ	*yawmun*	اَلْيَوْمُ	*al-yawmu*
acc.	يَوْمًا	*yawman*	اَلْيَوْمَ	*al-yawma*
gen.	يَوْمٍ	*yawmin*	اَلْيَوْمِ	*al-yawmi*

Partially inflected

	Indefinite		Definite	
nom.	أَسْوَدُ	*aswadu*	اَلْأَسْوَدُ	*al-aswadu*
acc.	أَسْوَدَ	*aswada*	اَلْأَسْوَدَ	*al-aswada*
gen.	أَسْوَدَ	*aswada*	اَلْأَسْوَدِ	*al-aswadi*

Type Three

Type Three consists of words whose indefinite nominative ends with *-in*. Most, though not all, come from roots with *wāw* or *yā'* as the last radical. Beginners usually find this type the most difficult to learn. Pay special attention to the endings and in particular to the sole difference between the singular and plural forms, which is in the indefinite accusative:

Singulars

	Indefinite		Definite	
nom.	وَادٍ	*wādin*	اَلْوَادِي	*al-wādī*
acc.	وَادِيًا	*wādiyan*	اَلْوَادِيَ	*al-wādiya*
gen.	وَادٍ	*wādin*	اَلْوَادِي	*al-wādī*

Plurals

	Indefinite		Definite	
nom.	جَوَارٍ	*jawārin*	اَلْجَوَارِي	*al-jawārī*
acc.	جَوَارِيَ	*jawāriya*	اَلْجَوَارِيَ	*al-jawāriya*
gen.	جَوَارٍ	*jawārin*	اَلْجَوَارِي	*al-jawārī*

Type Four

This consists of words ending in اً or ىً. Such words do not change for case, but they lose *tanwīn* when they are definite.

Indefinite			Definite	
عَصًا	*ʿaṣan*	nom., acc., gen.	اَلْعَصَا	*al-ʿaṣa*
قُرًى	*quran*	nom., acc., gen.	اَلْقُرَى	*al-qurā*

Type Five

This consists of words ending in اَ or ىَ. Words of this type are the same whether they are definite or indefinite, and they do not change for case.

Indefinite			Definite	
بُشْرَى	*bushrā*	nom., acc., gen.	اَلْبُشْرَى	*al-bushrā*
دُنْيَا	*dunyā*	nom., acc., gen.	اَلدُّنْيَا	*al-dunyā*

SOUND FEMININE PLURALS

Indefinite			Definite	
سَمٰوٰتٌ	*samāwātun*	nom.	اَلسَّمٰوٰتُ	*al-samāwātu*
سَمٰوٰتٍ	*samāwātin*	acc.	اَلسَّمٰوٰتِ	*al-samāwāti*
سَمٰوٰتٍ	*samāwātin*	gen.	اَلسَّمٰوٰتِ	*al-samāwāti*

SOUND MASCULINE PLURALS

Indefinite			Definite	
ظٰلِمُونَ	*ẓālimūna*	nom.	اَلظّٰلِمُونَ	*al-ẓālimūna*
ظٰلِمِينَ	*ẓālimīna*	acc.	اَلظّٰلِمِينَ	*al-ẓālimīna*
ظٰلِمِينَ	*ẓālimīna*	gen.	اَلظّٰلِمِينَ	*al-ẓālimīna*

PRONOUNS: NOMINATIVE FORMS

The nominative forms of the pronouns are:

أَنَا	*ana*	I	نَحْنُ	*naḥnu*	We
أَنْتَ	*anta*	You (m.s.)	أَنْتُمْ	*antum*	You (m.p.)
أَنْتِ	*anti*	You (f.s.)	أَنْتُنَّ	*antunna*	You (f.p.)
هُوَ	*huwa*	He, it	هُمْ	*hum*	They (m.p.)
هِيَ	*hiya*	She, it, they	هُنَّ	*hunna*	They (f.p.)

Notes on pronouns:

a) In all normal circumstances the plural forms can refer only to persons.

b) In general terms *ana* is either masculine or feminine and *naḥnu* is either masculine or feminine or both. *ana* and *naḥnu* are much more commonly used of males than of females but *ana* refers to a woman in 11:72 and 12:51.

c) The third feminine singular form *hiya* will commonly mean 'they', as it is the pronoun that refers to broken plurals of nouns that do not denote male persons.
d) Despite the spelling, the second vowel of *ana* is short. The *alif* is a spelling convention only.

Vocabulary Three

Singular		Plural		
جَنَّةٌ	*jannatun*	جَنَّاتٌ	*jannātun*	garden
جَارِيَةٌ	*jāriyatun*	جَوَارٍ	*jawārin*	ship, young woman
حَقٌّ	*ḥaqqun*	حُقُوقٌ	*ḥuqūqun*	truth; true
فِتْنَةٌ	*fitnatun*	فِتَنٌ	*fitanun*	affliction, temptation
بُشْرَى	*bushrā*			good tidings
اَلدُّنْيَا	*dunyā*			world
وَادٍ	*wādin*			valley
عَصًا	*ʿaṣan*			stick, staff
نَذِيرٌ	*nadhīrun*	نُذُرٌ	*nudhurun*	warner
هُدًى	*hudan*			guidance
مَكَّةُ	*makkatu*			Mecca
فَقِيرٌ	*faqīrun*	فُقَرَاءُ	*fuqarā'u*	poor
أَسْوَدُ	*aswadu*	سُودٌ	*sūdun*	black
سَوْدَاءُ	*sawdā'u* (f.)			
أَبْيَضُ	*abyaḍu*	بِيضٌ	*bīḍ*	white
بَيْضَاءُ	*bayḍā'u* (f.)			
عَالٍ	*ʿālin*			high, lofty

Singular		Plural		
عَالِيَةٌ	*ʿāliyatun* (f.)			
لَطِيفٌ	*laṭīfun*			gentle
جَاهِلٌ	*jāhilun*	جَاهِلُونَ	*jāhilūna*	ignorant

Exercise Three

A. 1.	أَنْتُمْ مُسْلِمُونَ	*antum muslimūna*	[2:132]
2.	هُمْ مُسْلِمُونَ	*hum muslimūna*	[27:81]
3.	نَحْنُ فِتْنَةٌ	*naḥnu fitnatun*	[2:102]
4.	أَنَا نَذِيرٌ	*ana nadhīrun*	[29:50]
5.	جَنَّةٌ عَالِيَةٌ	*jannatun ʿāliyatun*	[69:22]
6.	أَنْتَ ٱلتَّوَّابُ	*anta l-tawwābu*	[2:128]
7.	أَنْتُمْ ظَالِمُونَ	*antum ẓālimūna*	[2:92]
8.	أَنْتُمُ ٱلْفُقَرَاءُ	*antumu l-fuqarāʾu*	[35:15]
9.	هِيَ ظَالِمَةٌ	*hiya ẓālimatun*	[11:102]
10.	هُوَ مُؤْمِنٌ	*huwa muʾminun*	[16:97]
11.	هُوَ ٱللَّطِيفُ	*huwa l-laṭīfu*	[67:14]
12.	أَنْتُمْ مُؤْمِنُونَ	*antum muʾminūna*	[60:11]
13.	أَنَا ٱللّٰهُ ٱلْعَزِيزُ	*ana llāhu l-ʿazīzu*	[27:9]
14.	هِيَ بَيْضَاءُ	*hiya bayḍāʾu*	[7:108]
15.	هُوَ شَدِيدٌ	*huwa shadīdun*	[13:13]
16.	أَنْتَ ٱلْعَزِيزُ	*anta l-ʿazīzu*	[5:118]

17.	هِيَ فِتْنَةٌ	*hiya fitnatun*	[39:49]
18.	أَنْتَ نَذِيرٌ	*anta nadhīrun*	[11:12]
19.	أَنْتُمْ جَاهِلُونَ	*antum jāhilūna*	[12:89]
20.	أَنَا ٱلتَّوَّابُ	*ana l-tawwābu*	[2:160]

B. Write out in Arabic the nominative, accusative and genitive of the following:

fitnatun, rijālun, jannātun, ẓālimūna, wādin, al-arḍu, jāhilun, manāfiᶜu, al-mu'minūna, aswadu.

Lesson Four
Prepositions

All prepositions in Arabic take the genitive case:

فِي ٱلسَّمَآءِ	*fī l-samā'i*	in the sky/heaven
إِلَى ٱلنَّارِ	*ilā l-nāri*	to the fire
عَلَى سَفَرٍ	*'alā safarin*	on a journey
مِنْ قُرْآنٍ	*min qur'ānin*	from a recitation

Note that when *min* is followed by the article or a word beginning with *hamzat al-waṣl* it becomes *mina*:

مِنَ ٱلْجَنَّةِ	*mina l-jannati*	from the garden

The majority of prepositions are written separately from the word they govern, as in the above example. However, those that consist of a single letter are prefixed to the word they govern, the most important being *li-* and *bi-*:

لِأَهْلٍ	*li-ahlin*	to/for a people
بِرَحْمَةٍ	*bi-raḥmatin*	by a mercy

If *li-* is prefixed to a word that also has the definite article, the preposition and the article are written together as لِلْ:

لِلْعِبَادِ	*li-l-'ibādi*	to/for the servants

Note also لِلّٰهِ *li-llāhi*, 'to/for God'. The article after *bi-* is written in full:

بِٱلْوَادِي	*bi-l-wādī*	in the valley

Note the use of *wa-* with the genitive to start an oath (see also Lesson 38):

وَٱللّٰهِ	*wa llāhi*	by God!
وَٱلشَّمْسِ	*wa l-shamsi*	by the sun!

On the spelling of the *basmala* see Lesson 7.

A PREPOSITIONAL PHRASE AS THE PREDICATE OF A NON-VERBAL SENTENCE

a) If the subject is definite, the subject comes first, followed by the prepositional phrase as predicate:

اَللّٰهُ مَعَ ٱلصّٰبِرِينَ	*Allāhu maʿa al-ṣābirīna* God is with the patient ones
اَلظّٰلِمُونَ فِي ضَلٰلٍ مُبِينٍ	*al-ẓālimūna fī ḍalālin mubīnin* the wrongdoers are in manifest error
اَلصَّدَقٰتُ لِلْفُقَرَاءِ	*al-ṣadaqātu li-l-fuqarāʾi* alms are for the poor

b) If the subject is indefinite, the prepositional phrase must come first, followed by the subject:

فِي ٱلْأَرْضِ فَسَادٌ كَبِيرٌ	*fī l-arḍi fasādun kabīrun* there is much corruption on earth
عَلَى ٱلْأَعْرَافِ رِجَالٌ	*ʿalā l-aʿrāfi rijālun* there are men on the heights

'TO HAVE'

One of the most common uses of *li-* is to express the verb 'to have' or its equivalent in non-verbal sentences:

لِلْكٰفِرِينَ عَذَابٌ	*li-l-kāfirīna ʿadhābun*	
	(to the unbelievers a punishment)	
	the unbelievers have a punishment	
اَلْحَمْدُ لِلّٰهِ	*al-ḥamdu li-llāhi*	
	(the praise to God)	
	praise belongs to God	

Vocabulary Four

Singular		Plural		
نَارٌ	*nārun* (f.)	نِيرَانٌ	*nīrānun*	fire, Hell
صَدَقَةٌ	*ṣadaqatun*	صَدَقَاتٌ	*ṣadaqātun*	alms
عُرْفٌ	*ʿurfun*	أَعْرَافٌ	*aʿrāfun*	crest, ridge, height
سَبِيلٌ	*sabīlun* (f.)	سُبُلٌ	*subulun*	way, road, path
سَفَرٌ	*safarun*	أَسْفَارٌ	*asfārun*	journey
ضَلَالٌ	*ḍalālun*			error
فَسَادٌ	*fasādun*			corruption
حَمْدٌ	*ḥamdun*			praise
أَهْلٌ	*ahlun*	أَهْلُونَ	*ahlūna*	people, family, folk
شَمْسٌ	*shāmsun*			sun
رَحِيمٌ	*raḥīmun*			compassionate
صَابِرٌ	*ṣābirun*			patient, steadfast

مِنْ	*min*	from, of
فِي	*fī*	in, concerning
لِ	*li-*	to, for
بِ	*bi-*	in, at, by
عَلَىٰ	*ʿalā*	on, against
إِلَىٰ	*ilā*	to (motion)
مَعَ	*maʿa*	with
بَيْنَ	*bayna*	between, among

Exercise Four

1.	فِي ٱلصَّدَقَٰتِ	*fī l-ṣadaqāti*	[9:58]
2.	فِي ضَلَٰلٍ مُّبِينٍ	*fī ḍalālin mubīnin*	[6:74]
3.	عَلَى ٱلنَّارِ	*ʿalā l-nāri*	[51:13]
4.	بَيْنَ ٱلسَّمَآءِ وَٱلْأَرْضِ	*bayna l-samāʾi wa-l-arḍi*	[2:164]
5.	بَيْنَ ٱلْمُؤْمِنِينَ	*bayna l-muʾminīna*	[9:107]
6.	بَيْنَ ٱلْقَوْمِ	*bayna l-qawmi*	[5:25]
7.	مَعَ ٱلْقَوْمِ ٱلظَّٰلِمِينَ	*maʿa l-qawmi l-ẓālimīna*	[6:68]
8.	مَعَ ٱلْمُؤْمِنِينَ	*maʿa l-muʾminīna*	[4:146]
9.	مَعَ ٱلرَّسُولِ	*maʿa l-rasūli*	[25:27]
10.	عَلَىٰ هُدًى	*ʿalā hudan*	[22:67]
11.	عَلَى ٱلرَّسُولِ	*ʿalā l-rasūli*	[29:18]
12.	عَلَى ٱلْكَٰفِرِينَ	*ʿalā l-kāfirīna*	[16:27]
13.	مِنْ سَبِيلٍ	*min sabīlin*	[42:46]
14.	إِلَىٰ بَلَدٍ	*ilā baladin*	[35:9]

15.	إِلَىٰ عَذَابٍ عَظِيمٍ	*ilā ʿadhābin ʿaẓīmin*	[9:101]
16.	مِنَ ٱلرُّسُلِ	*mina l-rusuli*	[5:19]
17.	مِنْ أَيَّامٍ أُخَرَ	*min ayyāmin ukhara*	[2:185]
18.	مِنْ إِلَـٰهٍ	*min ilāhin*	[28:72]
19.	بِٱللَّهِ	*bi-llāhi*	[2:67]
20.	بِٱلْآخِرَةِ	*bi-l-ākhirati*	[2:4]
21.	بِوَادٍ	*bi-wādin*	[14:37]
22.	بُشْرَىٰ لِلْمُسْلِمِينَ	*bushrā li-l-muslimīna*	[16:89]
23.	لِلْقَوْمِ ٱلظَّـٰلِمِينَ	*li-l-qawmi l-ẓālimīna*	[11:44]
24.	لِلْمُؤْمِنَـٰتِ	*li-l-mu'mināti*	[24:31]
25.	لِلَّهِ ٱلْآخِرَةُ وَٱلْأُولَىٰ	*li-llāhi l-ākhiratu wa-l-ūlā*	[53:25]

Lesson Five
The First Person Singular Genitive Suffix and the Pronoun of Separation

FIRST PERSON SINGULAR GENITIVE SUFFIX

To express 'of me', or, as it will normally be translated, 'my', the suffix *-ī* is added to the noun. Any short final vowel (and of course *tanwīn*, if applicable) that the noun may originally have had is suppressed:

رَبِّي *rabb-ī* my Lord

عِبَادِي *ʿibād-ī* my servants

Once the *-ī* suffix has been added, there can be no variation for case. With wording ending with *ta' marbūṭa*, this is replaced by *ta' maftūḥa*:

حَيَاتِي *ḥayāt-ī* my life

نِعْمَتِي *niʿmat-ī* my blessing, bounty

If the dropping of *tanwīn* before the addition of a suffix produces a long vowel or a diphthong at the end of the word, the suffix becomes *-ya*:

هُدَايَ *hudā-ya* my guidance

The genitive suffix makes the noun definite, and so any adjective attached to this noun must have the definite article:

عِبَادِي ٱلصَّٰلِحُونَ *ʿibād-ī l-ṣāliḥūna* my righteous servants

If the adjective is without the definite article, it is a predicate:

عِبَادِي صَٰلِحُونَ *ʿibād-ī ṣāliḥūna* my servants are righteous

رَبِّي قَرِيبٌ *rabb-ī qarībun* my Lord is near

أَرْضِي وٰسِعَةٌ *arḍ-ī wāsiʿatun* my land is wide

One will of course find similar sentences where the predicate is a prepositional phrase:

اِبْنِي مِنْ أَهْلِي *ibn-ī min ahl-ī* my son is from my people

According to the use of *li-* set out in Lesson 4, *lī* 'to me', will mean 'I have . . . ' or '. . . is mine' or '. . . to my credit':

لِي عَمَلِي *lī ʿamal-ī* my work is to my credit

لِي آيَةٌ *lī āyatun* I [shall] have a sign

THE PRONOUN OF SEPARATION

You have now seen how an indefinite predicate and a prepositional phrase predicate are expressed. However, one can also have definite predicates in sentences such as 'my book is the new one' or 'God is the truth'.

To separate a definite predicate from a definite subject, a third person pronoun (known as *ḍamīr al-faṣl*, the pronoun of separation) is inserted between subject and predicate:

اَلْكٰفِرُونَ هُمُ ٱلظّٰلِمُونَ *al-kāfirūna humu l-ẓālimūna*

(the unbelievers they the wrongdoers)
the unbelievers are the wrongdoers

اَللّٰهُ هُوَ ٱلتَّوَّابُ *Allāhu huwa l-tawwābu*

(God He the relenting)
God is the Relenting one

عَذَابِي هُوَ ٱلْعَذَابُ ٱلْأَلِيمُ *ʿadhāb-ī huwa l-ʿadhābu l-'alīmu*

(my punishment it the painful punishment)
my punishment is the painful one

Vocabulary Five

Singular		Plural		
اِبْنٌ	*ibnun*	أَبْنَاءٌ/بَنُونَ	*banūna/abnā'un*	son
وَلِيٌّ	*waliyyun*	أَوْلِيَاءُ	*awliyā'u*	friend, protector
خَالِدٌ	*khālidun*	خَالِدُونَ	*khālidūna*	remaining in, everlasting
صَالِحٌ	*ṣāliḥun*			righteous
نِعْمَةٌ	*niʿmatun*			blessing, bounty
أَخٌ	*akhun*	إِخْوَانٌ	*ikhwānun*	brother
		إِخْوَةٌ	*ikhwatun*	
رَبٌّ	*rabbun*	أَرْبَابٌ	*arbābun*	lord
عَمَلٌ	*ʿamalun*	أَعْمَالٌ	*aʿmālun*	work
حَسْبٌ	*ḥasbun*			sufficiency, reckoning
قَرِيبٌ	*qarībun*			near
سَمِيعٌ	*samīʿun*			hearing (adjective)
حَيَاةٌ (also حَيَوٰةٌ)	*ḥayātun*			life

Exercise Five

1. عَذَابِي شَدِيدٌ *ʿadhāb-ī shadīdun* [14:7]
2. رَبِّي رَحِيمٌ *rabb-ī raḥīmun* [11:90]
3. رَبِّي قَرِيبٌ *rabb-ī qarībun* [11:61]
4. وَلِيِّيَ ٱللَّهُ *waliyy-ī Allāhu* [7:196]

5.	اَللّٰهُ رَبِّي	*Allāhu Rabb-ī*	[3:51]
6.	اِبْنِي مِنْ أَهْلِي	*ibn-ī min ahl-ī*	[11:45]
7.	عَذَابِي هُوَ ٱلْعَذَابُ ٱلْأَلِيمُ	*ʿadhāb-ī huwa l-ʿadhābu l-alīmu*	[15:50]
8.	مَعِي رَبِّي	*maʿ-ī Rabb-ī*	[26:62]
9.	بَيْنِي وَبَيْنَ إِخْوَتِي	*bayn-ī wa-bayna ikhwat-ī*	[12:100]
10.	حَسْبِي ٱللّٰهُ	*ḥasb-ī llāhu*	[39:38]
11.	اَللّٰهُ هُوَ ٱلْهُدَىٰ	*Allāhu huwa l-hudā*	[2:120]
12.	اَللّٰهُ هُوَ ٱلْحَقُّ	*Allāhu huwa l-ḥaqqu*	[22:6]
13.	رَبِّي لَطِيفٌ	*Rabb-ī laṭīfun*	[12:100]
14.	هُوَ ٱللّٰهُ رَبِّي	*huwa llāhu Rabb-ī*	[18:38]
15.	هِيَ عَصَايَ	*hiya ʿaṣā-ya*	[20:18]
16.	اَللّٰهُ هُوَ ٱلسَّمِيعُ	*Allāhu huwa l-samīʿu*	[40:20]
17.	اَللّٰهُ هُوَ رَبِّي	*Allāhu huwa Rabb-ī*	[43:64]
18.	أَنَا وَرُسُلِي	*ana wa-rusul-ī*	[58:21]
19.	هُوَ مِنَ ٱلْكِتَابِ	*huwa mina l-kitābi*	[3:78]
20.	هُوَ فِي ضَلَالٍ مُبِينٍ	*huwa fī ḍalālin mubīnin*	[67:29]
21.	عَذَابِي شَدِيدٌ	*ʿadhāb-ī shadīdun*	[14:7]
22.	هُوَ خَالِدٌ فِي ٱلنَّارِ	*huwa khālidun fī l-nāri*	[47:15]
23.	هُوَ ٱلْأَوَّلُ وَٱلْآخِرُ	*huwa l-awwalu wa-l-ākhiru*	[57:3]
24.	أَنَا مِنَ ٱلْمُسْلِمِينَ	*ana mina l-muslimīna*	[10:90]
25.	أَجْرِي عَلَى ٱللّٰهِ	*ajr-ī ʿalā llāhi*	[11:29]

Lesson Six
Demonstratives

هٰذَا[A]	This	m.s.	ذٰلِكَ	That
هٰذِهِ	This, these	f.s.	تِلْكَ	That, those
هٰؤُلَآءِ	These	pl.	أُولَٰئِكَ	Those

Demonstratives are used **either** as pronouns **or** adjectivally.

In the Qur'ān the only forms that are used at all frequently as adjectives are *hādhā* and *hādhihi*. *dhālika, tilka, hā'ulā'i* and *ulā'ika* are usually used as pronouns, and only occasionally are they used adjectivally.

Some alternative forms of *dhālika* are found: ذٰلِكُمْ *dhālikum* etc. The apparent change of the 'final pronoun' is due to the context.

Occasionally instead of *hā'ulā'i* the simple أُولَآءِ is found. Despite the spelling, the first vowel is short, as it is in *ulā'ika*.

ADJECTIVAL USE

The demonstrative **precedes the noun and is linked to it by the definite article**:

هٰذَا ٱلْقُرْآنُ	this recitation
هٰذِهِ ٱلنَّارُ	this fire
هٰذِهِ ٱلْأَنْهَارُ	these rivers
هٰؤُلَآءِ ٱلْقَوْمُ	these people
ذٰلِكَ ٱلْكِتَابُ	that book

[A] From here onwards, Arabic text will normally be given without transliteration.

هٰذِهِ ٱلْقَرْيَةُ	this settlement
تِلْكَ ٱلْقُرَى	those settlements
أُولَائِكَ ٱلْأَحْزَابُ	those parties

The three elements of demonstrative, definite article and noun form an indivisible unit. The article is the essential link between the demonstrative and the noun. If the article cannot be used, for example when the noun carries a pronoun suffix (as in 'this shirt of mine'), the demonstrative cannot precede the noun. Instead, it must follow the phrase, in apposition to it.

كِتَابِي هٰذَا	this book of mine
قَمِيصِي هٰذَا	this shirt of mine
يَوْمُهُمْ هٰذَا	this day of theirs

The other usages of the demonstrative are pronominal:

هٰذِهِ نَاقَةٌ	this is a she-camel
هٰذَا أَخِي	this is my brother
هٰذَا هُوَ ٱلْحَقُّ	this is the truth
قَبْلَ هٰذَا	before this
هٰؤُلَاءِ بَنَاتِي	these are my daughters
أُولَاءِ عَلَى أَثَرِي	these men are on my track
تِلْكَ أُمَّةٌ	that is a community
ذٰلِكَ هُوَ ٱلضَّلَالُ	that is the error
أُولَائِكَ هُمُ ٱلظَّالِمُونَ	those are the wrongdoers
بَعْدَ ذٰلِكَ	after that

VOCABULARY SIX

SINGULAR	PLURAL	
أُمَّةٌ	أُمَمٌ	community
اِبْنَةٌ	بَنَاتٌ	daughter
شَيْءٌ	أَشْيَاءُ	thing
دَارٌ (f.)	دُورٌ / دِيَارٌ	abode
حِزْبٌ	أَحْزَابٌ	party
أَثَرٌ	آثَارٌ	track; effect
لِسَانٌ	أَلْسِنَةٌ	tongue
نَاقَةٌ	إِبِلٌ	she-camel
نَهْرٌ	أَنْهَارٌ	river
فَضْلٌ		bounty
سِحْرٌ		magic
صِرَاطٌ		way, path
قَمِيصٌ		shirt
مُجْرِمٌ		sinner
قَلِيلٌ		few
مُسْتَقِيمٌ		straight
عَجِيبٌ		amazing, strange, wonderful
حَلَالٌ		permissible
حَرَامٌ		forbidden, sacred
بَعِيدٌ		far reaching, distant

SINGULAR

يَسِيرٌ	easy
عَسِيرٌ	difficult
قَبْلَ	before
بَعْدَ	after

The prepositions *baʿda* and *qabla* are commonly used after *min*, becoming *min baʿdi* and *min qabli*. There is no change in meaning.

EXERCISE SIX

1. ذَٰلِكَ هُوَ ٱلْفَضْلُ ٱلْكَبِيرُ [42:22]
2. هَٰذَا حَلَالٌ وَهَٰذَا حَرَامٌ [16:116]
3. هَٰذَا نَذِيرٌ مِنَ ٱلنُّذُرِ ٱلْأُولَىٰ [53:56]
4. هَٰذَا لِسَانٌ عَرَبِيٌّ [16:103]
5. هَٰذَا رَحْمَةٌ مِنْ رَبِّي [18:98]
6. ذَٰلِكَ ٱلْفَضْلُ مِنَ ٱللَّهِ [4:70]
7. هَٰذَا صِرَاطٌ مُسْتَقِيمٌ [3:51]
8. هَٰذِهِ ٱلْحَيَوٰةُ [29:64]
9. تِلْكَ ٱلدَّارُ ٱلْآخِرَةُ [28:83]
10. هَٰذَا شَيْءٌ عَجِيبٌ [50:2]
11. أُولَٰئِكَ عَلَىٰ هُدًى [2:5]
12. ذَٰلِكَ هُوَ ٱلضَّلَالُ ٱلْبَعِيدُ [14:18]
13. هَٰذِهِ سَبِيلِي [12:108]
14. ذَٰلِكَ يَوْمٌ عَسِيرٌ [74:9]

15. أُولَائِكَ هُمُ ٱلْمُؤْمِنُونَ [8:74]
16. هٰذَا رَبِّي [6:76]
17. هٰذَا سِحْرٌ مُبِينٌ [61:6]
18. ذٰلِكَ عَلَى ٱللّٰهِ يَسِيرٌ [22:70]
19. أُولَائِكَ مِنَ ٱلصَّالِحِينَ [3:114]
20. هٰؤُلَاءِ قَوْمٌ مُجْرِمُونَ [44:22]
21. أُولَائِكَ فِي جَنَّاتٍ مُكْرَمُونَ [70:35]
22. هٰؤُلَاءِ قَلِيلُونَ [26:54]
23. ذٰلِكَ فِي كِتَابٍ [22:70]
24. هٰذَا صِرَاطِي [6:153]
25. تِلْكَ آيَاتُ ٱللّٰهِ [3:108]
26. رَبِّي عَلَى صِرَاطٍ مُسْتَقِيمٍ [11:56]
27. لِلْكَافِرِينَ عَذَابٌ مُهِينٌ [2:90]

Lesson Seven
Iḍāfa

Iḍāfa, 'annexation', commonly called in European grammars 'the Construct', is used primarily to represent the association of one noun with another. It very frequently shows the possession of one thing by another, hence the looser, though more easily comprehensible, description of it as the 'genitive of possession'. However, the 'genitive' need not be a noun. You have already been introduced to the use of the suffix for 'my'. This pronominal suffix is fully equivalent to a noun in the genitive case. It is also possible for the 'genitive' to be a clause. This is a common feature in the Qur'ān and will be dealt with in Lesson 34.

The crucial points to remember are:

1. A noun that is followed by this genitive **cannot** take **either** the definite article **or** *tanwīn*. In other words, a noun can **either** take *tanwīn* **or** have the definite article **or** have a following genitive, but only one of these three.
2. In normal circumstances, a noun followed by a genitive is definite in meaning. If an indefinite meaning is required another construction must be used. (There are some exceptions to this rule, but these are rare and need not be dealt with here).
3. The following genitive itself may be definite or indefinite in meaning.
4. Nothing must intervene between the noun and the following genitive. The only apparent exception is when the genitive also has a demonstrative, but this is not a real exception because the demonstrative + article + genitive noun is an indivisible unit.
5. The strict rule about the order of adjectives, that adjectives describing the genitive come before adjectives describing any preceding noun, is not really relevant to Qur'ānic

phraseology, in which complex phrases are broken up, normally by the use of *min* or *li-* or *fī*.

Here are some examples to show how the *iḍāfa* works:

شَفَا حُفْرَةٍ	the edge of a pit
أَهْلُ ٱلْكِتَابِ	the people of the book
رَبُّ ٱلْعَالَمِينَ	the Lord of [all] created beings
رَحْمَةُ ٱللّٰهِ	God's mercy
أَهْلُ هٰذِهِ ٱلْقَرْيَةِ	the people of this settlement
عَذَابُ يَوْمٍ عَظِيمٍ	the punishment of a mighty day

These are all the examples you need in the first instance. There is no point in spending time at this stage on the tightly knit *iḍāfa* phrases that one finds in later Arabic.

To express possession of a noun with an indefinite meaning, prepositional constructions with *min* and *li-* are used:

حُفْرَةٌ مِنَ ٱلنَّارِ	a pit of the Fire
طَائِفَةٌ مِنَ ٱلْمُؤْمِنِينَ	a group of the faithful
نِسْوَةٌ مِنَ ٱلْمَدِينَةِ	some women of the city
عَدُوٌّ لِي	an enemy of mine
وَلِيٌّ لِلشَّيْطَانِ	a friend of the devil

IDIOMATIC USES OF *iḍāfa*

Idiomatic uses of *iḍāfa* are common in the Qur'ān, as indeed they are in all Arabic. Among the uses that you will come across frequently are:

1. The use of two nouns in *iḍāfa* to represent an idea that has to be translated as a noun and a qualifying adjective:

   قَوْمُ سَوْءٍ people of evil = an evil people

2. The use of certain words, such as *umm, ab, ibn, ahl, ṣāḥib and dhū* (accusative *dhā*, genitive *dhī* found only with a following genitive, see also Lesson 34) to represent a single idea:

اِبْنُ ٱلسَّبِيلِ son of the road = traveller

أَهْلُ بَيْتٍ family of a house = a household

ذُو ٱلْفَضْلِ possessed of bounty = bountiful

All these words, apart from *dhū*, can have their full meaning:

أَصْحَابُ ٱلنَّارِ the inhabitants of Hell

[This is not a full list of such words, but it is enough to introduce the idiomatic phrases in which they are used.]

Iḍāfa AND THE SOUND MASCULINE PLURAL

Sound masculine plurals with a following genitive lose the final *nūn + fatḥa* of the sound masculine plural. This is best shown with the word *ulū*, which is a plural equivalent of *dhū* and is found only with a following genitive:

أُولُو ٱلْأَلْبَابِ	nom.	men of understanding (lit. possessors of hearts)
أُولِي ٱلْأَبْصَارِ	acc., gen.	men of insight (lit. possessors of sight)

Note also *banū isrā'īla* (nom.), *banī isrā'īla* (acc., gen.), the 'Children of Israel'. Other examples, apart from some with pronominal suffixes, are rare and need not be mentioned here.

THE *basmala*

All the *sūras* in the Qur'ān, apart from Sūra 9, are prefaced by the formula 'In the name of the Merciful and Compassionate God'.

In this formula alone the *alif* of the word 'name' اِسْمٌ is dropped giving:

بِسْمِ ٱللّٰهِ ٱلرَّحْمٰنِ ٱلرَّحِيمِ

Vocabulary Seven

Singular	Plural	
اَلرَّحْمٰنُ		the Merciful
	اَلْعَالَمِينَ (gen. pl. only)	created beings
شَفًا		lip, rim, edge
حُفْرَةٌ		pit
أَبٌ	آبَاءٌ	father
صَاحِبٌ	أَصْحَابٌ	companion, inhabitant
طَائِفَةٌ		group, number, party
اِمْرَأَةٌ	نِسَاءٌ/نِسْوَةٌ	woman
أَمْرٌ	أُمُورٌ	affair, matter,command
إِنْسَانٌ	اَلنَّاسُ	man; people (pl.)
ذُو	أُولُو	possessor of
اِسْمٌ	أَسْمَاءٌ	name
	أَلْبَابٌ	hearts, intellects
بَصَرٌ	أَبْصَارٌ	sight; eye
يَدٌ (f.)	أَيْدٍ	hand

Singular	Plural	
عَدُوٌّ	أَعْدَاءٌ	enemy
شَيْطَانٌ	شَيَاطِينُ	devil
سَوْءٌ		evil
عَاقِبَةٌ		end, consequence
مَدِينَةٌ	مُدُنٌ	city
بَيْتٌ	بُيُوتٌ	house

Exercise Seven

1. فِي سَبِيلِ ٱللّٰهِ [2:154]
2. بَنَاتُ ٱلْأَخِ [4:23]
3. قَلِيلٌ مِنَ ٱلْآخِرِينَ [56:14]
4. سَبِيلُ ٱلْمُجْرِمِينَ [6:55]
5. ٱلْفَضْلُ بِيَدِ ٱللّٰهِ [3:73]
6. أَيْدِي ٱلنَّاسِ [30:41]
7. آيَاتُ ٱلرَّحْمٰنِ [19:58]
8. أَرْضُ ٱللّٰهِ وَاسِعَةٌ [4:97]
9. هٰذِهِ نَاقَةُ ٱللّٰهِ [7:73]
10. قَبْلَ يَوْمِ ٱلْحِسَابِ [38:16]
11. أُولَائِكَ حِزْبُ ٱلشَّيْطَانِ [58:19]
12. ٱللّٰهُ ذُو ٱلْفَضْلِ ٱلْعَظِيمِ [57:29]
13. كَثِيرٌ مِنَ ٱلنَّاسِ [22:18]

14. [2:81] أُولَائِكَ أَصْحَابُ ٱلنَّارِ
15. [2:98] اَللَّهُ عَدُوٌّ لِلْكَافِرِينَ
16. [30:50] آثَارُ رَحْمَةِ ٱللَّهِ
17. [7:143] أَنَا أَوَّلُ ٱلْمُؤْمِنِينَ
18. [44:7] رَبُّ ٱلسَّمَوَاتِ وَٱلْأَرْضِ
19. [3:69] طَائِفَةٌ مِنْ أَهْلِ ٱلْكِتَابِ
20. [61:14] طَائِفَةٌ مِنْ بَنِي إِسْرَائِيلَ
21. [3:68] اَللَّهُ وَلِيُّ ٱلْمُؤْمِنِينَ
22. [31:22] إِلَى ٱللَّهِ عَاقِبَةُ ٱلْأُمُورِ
23. [8:73] فِتْنَةٌ فِي ٱلْأَرْضِ وَفَسَادٌ كَبِيرٌ
24. [3:103] عَلَى شَفَا حُفْرَةٍ مِنَ ٱلنَّارِ
25. [1:2] اَلْحَمْدُ لِلَّهِ رَبِّ ٱلْعَالَمِينَ

Lesson Eight
The Perfect Tense

Now that you are aware of the basic uses of the nominative and genitive, it is time to turn to the accusative. The best way to introduce the accusative is through the verb, since most verbs have their direct object in the accusative.

The vast majority of verbs in Arabic are **triliteral verbs**, which means that they have a root made of three radicals. Some verbs have four radicals, and are called **quadriliteral verbs**. These are not common in the Qur'ān and are dealt with very briefly in Lesson 15.

The verb has two main tenses, the *māḍī* and the *muḍāriʿ*. The *māḍī* is usually known in English as the 'perfect' tense. It normally indicates a completed action or state, and is translated into English as a past tense.

The first class of verbs to be dealt with is that of 'the sound verbs'. These are verbs that do not have a *wāw*, or a *yā'* or a *hamza* as one of their radicals, and do not have the same letter as both second and third radical. Although sound verbs need to be understood first, you should be aware that a fair number of verbs have different forms and conjugations because they have one or more weak radicals or doubled radicals. In fact, the two most common verbs in the Qur'ān, قَالَ *qāla*, 'to say' and كَانَ *kāna* 'to be', are verbs that have a *wāw* as their middle radical. These two verbs will be introduced gradually in Lessons 12, 15, 18 and 20.

SOUND VERBS

Let us take the example of the verb 'to write', whose three radical consonants are *k-t-b*. In a dictionary, the verb is listed under its radical in its simplest form, *kataba*, meaning 'he wrote'. The *māḍī* of *kataba* conjugates as follows:

	SINGULAR	PLURAL
3 m.	كَتَبَ	كَتَبُوا
3 f.	كَتَبَتْ	كَتَبْنَ
2 m.	كَتَبْتَ	كَتَبْتُمْ
2 f.	كَتَبْتِ	كَتَبْتُنَّ
1	كَتَبْتُ	كَتَبْنَا

Learn these forms by heart, and learn them well. Only four forms of the *māḍī* of *kataba* occur in the Qur'ān, but the verb is a standard example in grammars. Knowing the singular and plural of *kataba* will enable you to handle countless verb forms.

NOTES

a) Note that before the definite article or any other word beginning with *hamzat al-waṣl* the 3 f.s. form كَتَبَتْ *katabat* becomes كَتَبَتِ *katabati.*

b) Note also the otiose *alif* added to the end of the 3 m.p. كَتَبُوا *katabū*. The *alif* acts as a word separator and is not pronounced. There are a number of places in the Qur'ān where this *alif* is not written.

c) The vowel of the middle radical of the *māḍī* is a variable. Most verbs have a *fatḥa*, as *kataba* does. However, there are a fair number of verbs that have *kaṣra*, including some of the most common ones in the Qur'ān, such as *ʿalima, samiʿa, ʿamila, shahida* and *shariba*. Verbs with *ḍamma* on the second radical, such as *kabura*, are rare.

d) As explained in Lesson 1, the vocabularies will give the 3 m.s. of the perfect, the 3 m.s. of the imperfect and the verbal noun (*maṣdar*) of every verb. The best practice is to learn the three forms together, even at this stage, when the imperfect and the *maṣdar* have yet to be explained. Wherever possible, all three forms are given in this book, whether the imperfect or the *maṣdar* occurs in the Qur'ān or not.

USE OF THE VERB

At this stage the verb may be divided into three kinds: those that are linked to an object by the accusative (transitive verbs); those that are linked to an object by a preposition (*e.g.* the verb *naẓara* 'to look'—*naẓara ilā* 'to look at' and *naẓara fī* 'to look into'); and those that do not have an object (intransitive verbs). As in English some verbs that are basically transitive (*e.g.* 'to enter', as in 'he entered the house') may also be used intransitively ('he entered', with no object specified). A transitive verb may take more than one accusative in Arabic.

1. The direct object is placed in the accusative:

بَلَغَ مَغْرِبَ ٱلشَّمْسِ	he reached the place where the sun set
سَمِعْتُمْ آيَاتِ ٱللّٰهِ	you heard God's signs
عَمِلُوا ٱلصَّالِحَاتِ	they did righteous deeds
كَتَبْنَاهَا	we wrote it (f.)

2. The most common word order in a sentence with a verb is:
   1. Verb 2. Subject 3. Object 4. Adverbial phrase

   However, the Qur'ān contains so many sentences in which this order is varied that you should note it only as a general point. The basic rule for the Qur'ān is that the verb will come first unless there is a reason for it not to do so. (What these reasons are will be set out later.)
3. a. If the verb precedes the subject, the verb normally agrees with the subject in gender, **but the verb must be in the singular no matter what the number of the subject is**.

كَرِهَ ٱلْمُجْرِمُونَ	the sinners were reluctant
قَالَ ٱلظَّالِمُونَ	the wrongdoers said

b. There are some examples where a feminine subject is preceded by a masculine verb. This is a standard feature of early Arabic, which has never entirely disappeared:

كَانَ صَلَاتُهُمْ	[8:35]	their prayer was...
قَالَ نِسْوَةٌ	[12:30]	some women said...
ذَهَبَ ٱلسَّيِّئَاتُ	[11:10]	the ills have gone

4. If the verb follows the subject, it agrees both in number and gender.

أُولَائِكَ يَئِسُوا مِنْ رَحْمَتِي [29:23][A]

these have despaired of my mercy

وَٱللّٰهُ أَمَرَنَا بِهَا [7:28]

and God has ordered us [to do it]

5. The verb has an active participle and a passive participle. The active participle of *kataba* is كَاتِبٌ *kātibun* and the passive participle is مَكْتُوبٌ *maktūbun*. Up to and including Lesson 12 any participles used are treated as separate items of vocabulary.

Uses of the perfect which are not to be translated by a past tense will be dealt with later.

Vocabulary Eight

Perfect	Imperfect	Verbal noun	
بَعَثَ	يَبْعَثُ	بَعْثٌ	to send, raise
بَلَغَ	يَبْلُغُ	بُلُوغٌ	to reach
جَعَلَ	يَجْعَلُ	جَعْلٌ	to make, assign, appoint

[A] For verbs with *hamza* as a radical see Lesson 22.

Perfect	Imperfect	Verbal noun	
حَمَلَ	يَحْمِلُ	حَمْلٌ	to carry
خَلَقَ	يَخْلُقُ	خَلْقٌ	to create
دَخَلَ	يَدْخُلُ	دُخُولٌ	to enter
ذَكَرَ	يَذْكُرُ	ذِكْرٌ	to mention
ذَهَبَ	يَذْهَبُ	ذَهَابٌ	to go away
سَمِعَ	يَسْمَعُ	سَمْعٌ	to hear
شَرِبَ	يَشْرَبُ	شُرْبٌ	to drink
شَهِدَ	يَشْهَدُ	شَهَادَةٌ	to witness
ضَرَبَ	يَضْرِبُ	ضَرْبٌ	to strike, coin, journey
عَمِلَ	يَعْمَلُ	عَمَلٌ	to do, work
كَتَبَ	يَكْتُبُ	كِتَابَةٌ	to write
وَجَدَ	يَجِدُ	وُجُودٌ	to find
وَعَدَ	يَعِدُ	وَعْدٌ	to promise
رَجَعَ	يَرْجِعُ	رُجُوعٌ	to return
ظَهَرَ	يَظْهَرُ	ظُهُورٌ	to appear
كَرِهَ	يَكْرَهُ	كَرْهٌ	to be reluctant, hate
لَبِثَ	يَلْبَثُ	لَبْثٌ	to tarry, linger

Singular	Plural	
سَيِّئَةٌ	سَيِّئَاتٌ	evil, ill
قَمَرٌ		moon
ضِيَاءٌ		light, illumination

Singular	Plural	
نُورٌ	أَنْوَارٌ	light
مَثَلٌ	أَمْثَالٌ	likeness, parallel
مَطْلِعٌ		rising-place
مَغْرِبٌ	مَغَارِبُ	setting-place
بَرٌّ		land
بَحْرٌ	بِحَارٌ	sea
حَمْلٌ		load
يَوْمُ ٱلْبَعْثِ		Day of Resurrection
اَلزَّبُورُ		the Psalms
خَفِيفٌ		light (adj.)

Exercise Eight

1. دَخَلَ ٱلْمَدِينَةَ [28:15]
2. دَخَلُوا قَرْيَةً [27:34]
3. جَعَلَ ٱلشَّمْسَ ضِيَاءً وَٱلْقَمَرَ نُورًا [10:5]
4. بَعَثَ ٱللّٰهُ رَسُولًا [25:41]
5. حَمَلَتْ حَمْلًا خَفِيفًا [7:189]
6. خَلَقَ ٱلسَّمٰوَاتِ وَٱلْأَرْضَ [7:54]
7. خَلَقَ ٱللّٰهُ ذٰلِكَ [10:5]
8. خَلَقْنَا ٱلْإِنْسَانَ [90:4]
9. ذَكَرُوا ٱللّٰهَ [3:135]
10. رَجَعْنَا إِلَى ٱلْمَدِينَةِ [63:8]

11. رَجَعْتُمْ [9:94]
12. ضَرَبَ ٱللَّهُ مَثَلًا [39:29]
13. ضَرَبْتُمْ فِي سَبِيلِ ٱللَّهِ [4:94]
14. لَبِثُوا فِي ٱلْعَذَابِ ٱلْمُهِينِ [34:14]
15. لَبِثْتُمْ فِي كِتَابِ ٱللَّهِ إِلَى يَوْمِ ٱلْبَعْثِ [30:56]
16. كَتَبْنَا فِي ٱلزَّبُورِ مِنْ بَعْدِ ٱلذِّكْرِ [21:105]
17. وَجَدَ قَوْمًا [18:93]
18. وَجَدْتُ ٱمْرَأَةً [27:23]
19. وَجَدُوا ٱللَّهَ تَوَّابًا [4:64]
20. وَعَدَ ٱللَّهُ ٱلْمُؤْمِنِينَ وَٱلْمُؤْمِنَاتِ جَنَّاتٍ [9:72]
21. بَلَغَ مَطْلِعَ ٱلشَّمْسِ [18:90]
22. ظَهَرَ أَمْرُ ٱللَّهِ [9:48]
23. ظَهَرَ ٱلْفَسَادُ فِي ٱلْبَرِّ وَٱلْبَحْرِ [30:41]
24. بَعَثْنَا فِي كُلِّ أُمَّةٍ رَسُولًا [16:36]

Lesson Nine
Pronominal suffixes

FIRST PERSON SINGULAR

In the first person singular, the accusative and genitive suffixes are distinct and are not interchangeable. We have already dealt with the first person singular genitive suffix *-ī* in Lesson 5. The accusative suffix is *-nī*.

بَلَغَنِي	it reached me
أَمَرْتَنِي	you ordered me

With other persons, the suffix is the same for both accusative and genitive.

SECOND PERSON SINGULAR

m + noun	كِتَابُكَ	your book
m + verb	وَجَدَكَ	he found you
f + noun	ذَنْبُكِ	your sin
f + verb	طَهَّرَكِ	he has purified you

THIRD PERSON SINGULAR

m + noun	يَدُهُ	his hand
m + verb	رَفَعْنَاهُ	We raised it
f + noun	وَلَدُهَا	her child
f+ verb	وَعَدَهَا	he promised it (f.)

Note that if the 3 m.s. suffix is preceded immediately by *i, ī*, or *ay*, the form changes to *-hi*:

فِيهِ	in it
لِأَهْلِهِ	to its folk
بِرَحْمَتِهِ	through His mercy

If any letter comes between these vowels and the suffix, the rule does not apply, *e.g.* مِنْهُ *min-hu*.

PLURAL FORMS

First person + noun	نَصْرُنَا	our help
First person + verb	بَعَثَنَا	he sent us
Second person m + noun	قَرْيَتُكُمْ	your village
Second person m + verb	نَصَرَكُمْ	he helped you
Second person f + noun	بُيُوتُكُنَّ	your houses
Second person f + verb[A]	طَلَّقَكُنَّ	he divorced you
Third person m + noun	رَبُّهُمْ	their Lord
Third person m + verb	أَخَذَهُمْ	he seized them
Third person f + noun	أَوْلَادُهُنَّ	their children
Third person f + verb	خَلَقَهُنَّ	he created them

Note that the vowel change from *u* to *i* that occurs with the 3 m.s. suffix also applies to the two plural suffixes:

إِلَى قَوْمِهِمْ	to their people
بَيْنَ أَيْدِهِنَّ وَأَرْجُلِهِنَّ	between their hands and feet

[A] For these verbs see Lesson 15. There are few examples of this sufix with verbs.

Before *hamzat al-waṣl*, *hum* and *kum* become *humu* and *kumu*.

ALTERATIONS TO VERB FORMS WHEN SUFFIXES ARE ATTACHED

1. The otiose *alif* of the 3 m.p. is dropped:

   نَصَرُوهُ they helped him

2. The end of the 2 m.p. becomes *-tumū:*

   سَمِعْتُمُوهُ you heard it
   عَلِمْتُمُوهُنَّ you recognised them (f.)

ALTERATIONS TO PREPOSITIONS WHEN SUFFIXES ARE ATTACHED

1. إِلَى *ilā* and عَلَى *ʿalā* become *ilay-* and *ʿalay-*:

إِلَيَّ	*ilay-ya*	إِلَيْنَا	*ilay-nā*
إِلَيْكَ	*ilay-ka*	عَلَيْكُمْ	*ʿalay-kum*
عَلَيْكِ	*ʿalay-ki*	إِلَيْكُنَّ	*ilay-kunna*
إِلَيْهِ	*ilay-hi*	عَلَيْهِمْ	*ʿalay-him*
عَلَيْهَا	*ʿalay-hā*	إِلَيْهِنَّ	*ilay-hinna*

2. لِ *li-* with the suffix *-ī* becomes لِي *lī*. Before all other suffixes *li-* becomes *la-*: لَهُ *lahu*, لَهُمْ *lahum*, لَنَا *lanā*, etc.
3. With the first person singular suffix the prepositions مِنْ *min* and عَنْ *ʿan*become مِنِّي *minnī*and عَنِّي *ʿannī*, respectively.

VOCABULARY NINE

PERFECT	IMPERFECT	VERBAL NOUN	
أَخَذَ	يَأْخُذُ	أَخْذٌ	to take, seize
أَمَرَ	يَأْمُرُ	أَمْرٌ	to order
تَبِعَ	يَتْبَعُ	تَبَعٌ	to follow
خَرَجَ	يَخْرُجُ	خُرُوجٌ	to go out
رَفَعَ	يَرْفَعُ	رَفْعٌ	to raise
سَأَلَ	يَسْأَلُ	سُؤَالٌ	to ask
فَعَلَ	يَفْعَلُ	فَعْلَةٌ	to do
كَذَبَ	يَكْذِبُ	كِذْبٌ	to tell lies
نَصَرَ	يَنْصُرُ	نَصْرٌ	to help
عَلِمَ	يَعْلَمُ	عِلْمٌ	to know

SINGULAR	PLURAL	
إِذْنٌ		permission
نَهْرٌ	أَنْهَارٌ	river
ذَنْبٌ	ذُنُوبٌ	sin
لَعْنَةٌ		curse
سَلَامٌ		peace
رِجْلٌ (f.)	أَرْجُلٌ	foot
نَفْسٌ (f.)	أَنْفُسٌ	soul, self
وَلَدٌ	أَوْلَادٌ	child

خِلَالَ	through
عَنْ	away from; concerning

Exercise Nine

1. مِنَ آللّٰهِ وَرَسُولِهِ [2:279]
2. هُنَّ أُمَّهَاتُهُمْ [58:2]
3. فَعَلْتَ فَعْلَتَكَ [26:19]
4. جَعَلَ خِلَالَهَا أَنْهَارًا [27:61]
5. خَرَجُوا مِنْ دِيَارِهِمْ [2:243]
6. خَرَجْنَا مَعَكُمْ [9:42]
7. اَلْأَمْرُ بَيْنِي وَبَيْنَكُمْ [6:58]
8. عَلَيْكَ لَعْنَتِي [38:78]
9. جَعَلْنَا آبْنَ مَرْيَمَ وَأُمَّهُ آيَةً [23:50]
10. نَصَرَكُمُ آللّٰهُ بِبَدْرٍ [3:123]
11. رَجَعُوا إِلَيْهِمْ [9:122]
12. اَلْأَمْرُ إِلَيْكِ [27:33]
13. كَذَبُوا عَلَى أَنْفُسِهِمْ [6:24]
14. تَبِعَ هُدَايَ [2:38]
15. سَأَلْتُمُوهُنَّ [33:53]
16. بِإِذْنِ رَبِّهِ [7:58]
17. نِعْمَتِي عَلَيْكُمْ [2:150]

18. دَخَلْتُمُوهُ [5:23]

19. بِإِذْنِ أَهْلِهِنَّ [4:25]

20. سَأَلَهَا قَوْمٌ مِنْ قَبْلِكُمْ [5:102]

21. سَأَلَكَ عِبَادِي عَنِّي [2:186]

22. تَبِعَكَ [7:18]

23. تَبِعَنِي [14:36]

24. رَفَعَهُ ٱللّٰهُ إِلَيْهِ [4:158]

25. سَلَامٌ عَلَيْكُمْ كَتَبَ رَبُّكُمْ عَلَى نَفْسِهِ ٱلرَّحْمَةَ [6:54]

26. دَخَلَ جَنَّتَهُ [18:35]

27. أَخَذَهُمُ ٱللّٰهُ بِذُنُوبِهِمْ [3:11]

Lesson Ten
The particle *mā*

There is very little of the Qur'ān that you can read without coming across *mā*, as it occurs over 2,000 times in the text. It is traditional to talk about the particle *mā* as a particle having various uses. In reality it is a series of words that have evolved into the same form. Most of these occur in the Qur'ān. Here are notes on the two most frequent, and most important, ones.

NEGATION WITH *mā*

1. مَا *mā* is put in front of the perfect verb to negate the *māḍī*. This is the standard usage throughout the ages:

مَا لَبِثَ	he did not tarry
مَا ظَلَمُونَا	they did not wrong us
مَا مَنَعَنَا	he did not prevent us

2. *mā* is also used to negate nominal sentences. This occurs much more frequently in the Qur'ān than it does in later Arabic. In the negation of nominal sentences *mā* is frequently followed by the subject in the nominative, as one would expect, but the predicate is then introduced by *bi-* with the genitive. This is an archaic usage, known to the Arab grammarians as the 'Ḥijāzī *mā*', as it was a feature of the Arabic of western Arabia. Here are two examples:

مَا هُوَ بِمَيِّتٍ	he is not dead
مَا صَاحِبُكُمْ بِمَجْنُونٍ	your companion is not possessed

Much less frequently the Ḥijāzī *mā* has its predicate in the accusative:

مَا هٰذَا بَشَرًا this is not a human being

If *mā* is followed at a relatively short distance by إِلَّا *illā* 'except', it will be negative, the combined sense of the *mā* and the *illā* being 'only'.

مَا أَنْتُمْ إِلَّا بَشَرٌ you are only men

مَا مِنَّا إِلَّا لَهُ مَقَامٌ مَعْلُومٌ everyone of us [will] have a known station

مَا مِنْ إِلَاهٍ إِلَّا ٱللّٰهُ there is no god but God

From time to time the negative *mā* is followed by a phrase that begins with *min*, the *min* being partitive and giving the sense 'any'.

مَا لِلظَّالِمِينَ مِنْ نَصِيرٍ wrongdoers have no helper

مَا لَكَ مِنَ ٱللّٰهِ مِنْ وَلِيٍّ you have no protector against God

The phrase introduced by *min* is usually the real subject, but sometimes it is the object:

مَا عَلِمْنَا عَلَيْهِ مِنْ سُوءٍ we know no wrong against/of him

However, if you see *mā* followed shortly by *min*, do not assume that it is the negative *mā*. It *may* be, but, as you will shortly see, it could be the relative *mā*. Only the context will make this clear.

THE PRONOMINAL USE OF *mā*

Mā is also a relative pronoun meaning 'that which', 'what', 'whatsoever'. This is easily spotted when *mā* follows a verb or a noun.

عَلِمْتُمْ مَا فَعَلْتُمْ you knew what you did

نِصْفُ مَا تَرَكَ half of what he left

If *mā* is immediately followed by a prepositional phrase, it is likely to be the relative:

مَا فِي ٱلسَّمٰوَاتِ وَٱلْأَرْضِ what is in the heavens and the earth

If *mā* follows a demonstrative, it is likely to be the relative at the start of the predicate:

هٰذَا مَا وَعَدَ ٱلرَّحْمٰنُ this is what the Merciful promised

If *mā* introduces a clause after a preposition it will be the relative:

بِمَا عَمِلْتُمْ because of what you did

If a verb has its construction completed by a preposition as is the case of *amara* [أَمَرَ ٱلرَّجُلَ بِشَيْءٍ *amara l-rajula bi-shay'in* 'he ordered the man (accusative) to do (*bi-*) something'], that preposition will take the 3 m.s. pronominal suffix to complete the construction and refer back to the *mā*:

مَا أَمَرْتَنِي بِهِ that which you have ordered me to do

Usually with the accusative there is no pronoun referring back to the *mā*, but occasionally the pronoun *-hu* will be found with this function.

It is quite common for the relative *mā* to be followed, with or without an intervening phrase, by *min* and a noun in the genitive. The meaning imparted by *min* is quite different from that given by *min* after the negative *mā*:

مَا ... مِنْ خَيْرٍ whatever good, such good as...

مَا ... مِنْ سُوءٍ whatever evil, such evil as ...

مَا ... مِنْ عَمَلٍ whatever deed, such deeds as ... (all) the deeds

Two sentences will show how the construction works in context:

فَرِحُوا بِمَا عِنْدَهُمْ مِنَ ٱلْعِلْمِ [40:83]

they rejoiced in the knowledge they had

[25:23] قَدِمْنَا إِلَى مَا عَمِلُوا مِنْ عَمَلٍ

we have advanced on whatever work they have done

The notes given above should enable the reader to differentiate between the negative *mā* and the relative *mā* in most cases. In cases of doubt, context is crucial. Without it, for example, *mā ʿalima* could mean either 'he did not know' or 'what he knew'. On the other hand, when the phrase *mā khalaqa llāhu* occurs in two consecutive verses [10:5 and 6], the context makes it clear that in verse 5 it is negative—it is followed by *illā*—and that in verse 6 it is relative—shown both by the preceding and following phrases.

Vocabulary Ten

Perfect	Imperfect	Verbal noun	
تَرَكَ	يَتْرُكُ	تَرْكٌ	to leave
ظَلَمَ	يَظْلِمُ	ظُلْمٌ	to do wrong
كَسَبَ	يَكْسِبُ	كَسْبٌ	to acquire, earn, gain
عَمِلَ	يَعْمَلُ	عَمَلٌ	to do, work
فَرِحَ	يَفْرَحُ	فَرَحٌ	to rejoice in
فَرَضَ	يَفْرِضُ	فَرْضٌ	to assign, prescribe
قَدِمَ	يَقْدَمُ	قُدُومٌ	to come, advance on
كَنَزَ	يَكْنُزُ	كَنْزٌ	to store
مَنَعَ	يَمْنَعُ	مَنْعٌ	to prevent
وَقَعَ	يَقَعُ	وُقُوعٌ	to fall, come to pass

Singular	Plural	
بَشَرٌ		human being (s.); men, human beings (pl.)
سُوءٌ		evil, wrong
شَهِيدٌ	شُهَدَاءُ	witness
قَوْلٌ	أَقْوَالٌ [أَقَاوِيلُ]	saying, words
مَقَامٌ		station
مُلْكٌ		sovereignty, kingdom
عِلْمٌ	عُلُومٌ	knowledge
نَاصِرٌ/نَصِيرٌ	أَنْصَارٌ	helper
نِصْفٌ		half
خَيْرٌ		good
مَجْنُونٌ		possessed (by *Jinn*)
مَعْرُوفٌ		kindness; proper
مَعْلُومٌ		known
مَيِّتٌ	مَيِّتُونَ	dead
خَلْفَ		behind
عِنْدَ		with, in the possession of
إِلَّا		except

EXERCISE TEN

1. [3:117] مَا ظَلَمَهُمُ ٱللّٰهُ
2. [4:90] مَا جَعَلَ ٱللّٰهُ لَكُمْ عَلَيْهِمْ سَبِيلًا
3. [14:20] مَا ذٰلِكَ عَلَى ٱللّٰهِ بِعَزِيزٍ
4. [41:47] مَا مِنَّا مِنْ شَهِيدٍ
5. [3:56] وَمَا لَهُمْ مِنْ نَاصِرِينَ
6. [4:66] مَا فَعَلُوهُ
7. [34:14] مَا لَبِثُوا فِي ٱلْعَذَابِ ٱلْمُهِينِ
8. [34:47] مَا سَأَلْتُكُمْ مِنْ أَجْرٍ
9. [42:41] مَا عَلَيْهِمْ مِنْ سَبِيلٍ
10. [46:9] مَا أَنَا إِلَّا نَذِيرٌ مُبِينٌ
11. [53:28] مَا لَهُمْ بِهِ مِنْ عِلْمٍ
12. [57:27] مَا كَتَبْنَاهَا عَلَيْهِمْ
13. [37:58] مَا نَحْنُ بِمَيِّتِينَ
14. [7:44] وَجَدْنَا مَا وَعَدَنَا
15. [2:240] مَا فَعَلْنَ فِي أَنْفُسِهِنَّ مِنْ مَعْرُوفٍ
16. [8:68] فِي مَا أَخَذْتُمْ
17. [9:35] هٰذَا مَا كَنَزْتُمْ لِأَنْفُسِكُمْ
18. [13:21] مَا أَمَرَ ٱللّٰهُ بِهِ
19. [19:64] مَا بَيْنَ أَيْدِينَا وَمَا خَلْفَنَا
20. [33:50] عَلِمْنَا مَا فَرَضْنَا عَلَيْهِمْ

21. مَا عَمِلَتْهُ أَيْدِيهِمْ [36:35]

22. لِلّٰهِ مُلْكُ ٱلسَّمٰوَاتِ وَٱلْأَرْضِ وَمَا فِيهِنَّ [5:120]

23. وَقَعَ ٱلْقَوْلُ عَلَيْهِمْ بِمَا ظَلَمُوا [27:85]

24. وَجَدُوا مَا عَمِلُوا [18:49]

25. مَا فِي ٱلْبَرِّ وَٱلْبَحْرِ [6:59]

26. نِصْفُ مَا فَرَضْتُمْ [2:237]

27. ظَهَرَ ٱلْفَسَادُ فِي ٱلْبَرِّ وَٱلْبَحْرِ بِمَا كَسَبَتْ أَيْدِي ٱلنَّاسِ [30:41]

Lesson Eleven
Kull; baʿḍ; the accusative of time

كُلٌّ *kull*

The masculine noun *kullun*, meaning 'each' or 'every', most commonly takes the indefinite genitive singular, but is also followed by an indefinite genitive plural when the plural is being used as a collective or is divisible into parts:

كُلُّ شَيْءٍ each, every thing

كُلُّ نَفْسٍ each, every soul

كُلُّ أُنَاسٍ each, every people

With the meaning 'all', it takes the definite genitive plural or is followed by the genitive of a singular noun that is being used as a collective or is divisible into parts.

كُلُّ ٱلثَّمَرَاتِ all the fruits

كُلُّ ٱلطَّعَامِ all the food

Note also كُلُّ ذٰلِكَ *kullu dhālika* 'all that'.

بَعْضٌ *baʿḍ*

The basic construction of the masculine noun *baʿḍ*, meaning 'some', is that it takes the definite genitive plural or is followed by the genitive of a noun that is being used as a collective or is divisible into parts:

بَعْضُ ٱلْكِتَابِ some of the book

بَعْضُ ٱلنَّبِيِّينَ some of the prophets

بَعْضُ ٱلْأَقَاوِيلِ some of the stories

Sometimes بَعْضٌ means 'one of':

بَعْضُ ٱلسَّيَّارَةِ one of the caravans

No other construction is normally allowed. However, the Qur'ān does have one phrase in which *baᶜḍ* is followed by an indefinite genitive:

بَعْضُ يَوْمٍ part of a day

Very rarely *baᶜḍ* is used without any following genitive (see 4:150), but this tends to be confined to phrases in which it occurs twice, first with a following genitive/pronominal suffix, then as an indefinite:

[A] فَضَّلْنَا بَعْضَ ٱلنَّبِيِّينَ عَلَى بَعْضٍ

We have preferred some prophets over others

Often the construction is best translated as 'one another':

بَعْضُهُمْ أَوْلِيَاءُ بَعْضٍ they are friends of one another

The rule of agreement with phrases containing كُلّ and بَعْض is that verbs or adjectives can agree either with كُلّ / بَعْض themselves or with the logical subject (the following genitive). In the Qur'ān there is a strong tendency for the verb or adjective to agree with the logical subject.

كُلُّ نَفْسٍ رَهِينَةٌ every soul is pledged

[A] On this form of the verb see Lesson 15.

In this example [74:38] the adjective رَهِينَةٌ agrees with the logical subject, the genitive نَفْسٍ, rather than the formal grammatical subject كُلُّ.

ACCUSATIVE OF TIME

Arabic can express an adverbial phrase by putting a noun (or a phrase equivalent to a noun) into the accusative:

يَوْمًا أَوْ بَعْضَ يَوْمٍ	for a day or part of a day
لَيْلًا وَنَهَارًا	by night and day
أَوَّلَ مَرَّةٍ	on / for the first time

This use of the accusative is common in the Qur'ān.

Vocabulary Eleven

Perfect	Imperfect	Verbal noun	
حَفِظَ	يَحْفَظُ	حِفْظٌ	to guard, preserve, keep
فَتَحَ	يَفْتَحُ	فَتْحٌ	to open
نَظَرَ	يَنْظُرُ	نَظَرٌ	to look at (إِلَى), into (فِي)

Singular	Plural	
إِثْمٌ		sin
أَجَلٌ		term
ثَمَرَةٌ	ثَمَرَاتٌ	fruit
حَفِيظٌ	حَفَظَةٌ	guardian
رَهِينٌ		hostage, pledged
سَيَّارَةٌ	سَيَّارَاتٌ	caravan

SINGULAR	PLURAL	
ظَنٌّ	ظُنُونٌ	thought, supposition, suspicion, conjecture
مَغْفِرَةٌ		forgiveness
مَكَانٌ	أَمْكِنَةٌ	place, side
لَيْلٌ	لَيَالٍ	night, night time
مَرَّةٌ	مَرَّاتٌ /مِرَارٌ	time, occasion
مَوْتٌ		death
نَهَارٌ		day, daytime
طَعَامٌ		food
نَبِيٌّ	أَنْبِيَاءُ	prophet
بَابٌ	أَبْوَابٌ	gate, door
رَجِيمٌ		accursed
مُسْتَطَرٌ		inscribed
صَغِيرٌ		small
قَدِيرٌ		having power over
فَوْقَ		above, over (sometimes used as a synonym for *alā*, 'on'.)

EXERCISE ELEVEN

1. جَعَلْنَا بَعْضَكُمْ لِبَعْضٍ فِتْنَةً [25:20]
2. بَعْضُكُمْ لِبَعْضٍ عَدُوٌّ [20:123]
3. رَفَعْنَا بَعْضَهُمْ فَوْقَ بَعْضٍ [43:32]

4. بَعْضَ ٱلظَّنِّ إِثْمٌ [49:12]

5. أُولَٰئِكَ بَعْضُهُمْ أَوْلِيَاءُ بَعْضٍ [8:72]

6. تَرَكْنَا بَعْضَهُمْ [18:99]

7. نَظَرَ بَعْضُهُمْ إِلَىٰ بَعْضٍ [9:127]

8. ٱلْمُؤْمِنُونَ وَٱلْمُؤْمِنَاتُ بَعْضُهُمْ أَوْلِيَآءُ بَعْضٍ [9:71]

9. ٱللَّهُ عَلَىٰ كُلِّ شَيْءٍ قَدِيرٌ [5:40]

10. أَنْتَ عَلَىٰ كُلِّ شَيْءٍ شَهِيدٌ [5:117]

11. فَتَحْنَا عَلَيْهِمْ أَبْوَابَ كُلِّ شَيْءٍ [6:44]

12. جَعَلْنَا لِكُلِّ نَبِيٍّ عَدُوًّا مِنَ ٱلْمُجْرِمِينَ [25:31]

13. لِكُلِّ أُمَّةٍ أَجَلٌ [7:34]

14. ٱلْمَوْتُ مِنْ كُلِّ مَكَانٍ [14:17]

15. ذَهَبَ كُلُّ إِلَٰهٍ بِمَا خَلَقَ [23:91]

16. بَعَثْنَا فِي كُلِّ أُمَّةٍ رَسُولًا [16:36]

17. رَبُّكَ عَلَىٰ كُلِّ شَيْءٍ حَفِيظٌ [34:21]

18. كُلُّ نَفْسٍ بِمَا كَسَبَتْ رَهِينَةٌ [74:38]

19. وَكُلُّ صَغِيرٍ وَكَبِيرٍ مُسْتَطَرٌ [54:53]

20. لَهُمْ فِيهَا مِنْ كُلِّ ٱلثَّمَرَاتِ وَمَغْفِرَةٌ [47:15]

21. كُلُّ مَا سَأَلْتُمُوهُ [14:34]

22. لَبِثْنَا يَوْمًا أَوْ بَعْضَ يَوْمٍ [18:19]

23. دَخَلُوهُ أَوَّلَ مَرَّةٍ [17:7]

Lesson Twelve
Kāna; qāla; lammā

The two most common verbs in the Qur'ān are *kāna* and *qāla*. They belong to a type of verb known as the 'hollow verb' because it has a weak letter, in the case of these two verbs a *wāw*, as the middle of three radicals (with *kāna* the radicals are *kāf, wāw, nūn;* with *qāla* they are *qāf, wāw, lām*). The weak letters *wāw* and *yā'* are in general liable to suppression or modification in such verbs and thus they have different patterns of conjugation from sound verbs like *kataba*. There are rules to govern such modifications, but it is easier and more effective to learn the verb forms thoroughly, without bothering about such rules.

كَانَ *kāna*

The verb *kāna* is used for those parts of the English verb 'to be' that can be expressed verbally in Arabic.

Learn the singular and plural of the *māḍī* of *kāna* from the table below and learn them well.

	Singular	Plural
3 m.	كَانَ	كَانُوا
3 f.	كَانَتْ	كُنَّ
2 m.	كُنْتَ	كُنْتُمْ
2 f.	كُنْتِ	كُنْتُنَّ
1	كُنْتُ	كُنَّا

Kāna has one other feature that must be mastered from the outset. Its predicate goes into the **accusative, as though *kāna* were a transitive verb**.

كَانَ مَرِيضًا	he was ill
كُنَّا مُؤْمِنِينَ	we were believers
مَا كَانَ إِبْرَاهِيمُ يَهُودِيًّا	Abraham was not a Jew
كَانُوا ظَالِمِينَ	they were wrongdoers

Note:

a) *Kāna* is not used impersonally in the way that the verb 'to be' is used in English.

b) When *kāna/kānat* begins a sentence that is otherwise composed of a prepositional phrase followed by its indefinite subject, the verb simply signifies the past:

كَانَ لَهُ إِخْوَةٌ	he had brothers
كَانَ فِي قَصَصِهِمْ عِبْرَةٌ لِأُولِي ٱلْأَلْبَابِ	in their story there was a warning for men of understanding
كَانَ لَكُمْ أُسْوَةٌ حَسَنَةٌ فِي إِبْرَاهِيمَ	you have had a fine example in Abraham

The accusative will be found, but the meaning is then quite different:

كَانَ لِلنَّاسِ عَجَبًا	it has been a wonder for mankind
كَانَ فَاحِشَةً	it was an abomination

The Pluperfect

Kāna is also used with another perfect verb to represent the pluperfect. Over time, it has become ever more common for this second verb to be preceded by the particle *qad*. The construction of *kāna* with the Perfect of the second verb is to be found in the Qur'ān, but it is rare, in contrast to the common use of *kāna* with the Imperfect of the second verb (see Lesson 16). It should also be noted that, unlike the situation in later Arabic, none of the examples of *kāna* with the Perfect has the particle *qad*, though the particle occurs over 220 times in the Qur'ān.

Although the basic meaning of *kāna* is 'he was', it is very frequently used in the Qur'ān with the sense of the present: 'he is'. This is shown most clearly by phrases referring to God: كَانَ اَللّٰهُ غَفُورًا رَحِيمًا means 'God is Forgiving and Compassionate'.

The use of the Perfect with a present meaning was a standard feature of early Arabic, but became less common as time went on. *Kāna* is only one of numerous verbs that exemplify this usage, but it stands out because the Imperfect of *kāna* cannot be used to express 'is'.

The Qur'ān also contains one or two idiomatic uses of *kāna*, which will be dealt with later.

قَالَ *qāla*

The verb *qāla* means 'to say' or 'to speak'. It is the main way of introducing direct speech. Its Perfect is formed in the same way as that of *kāna*:

	SINGULAR	PLURAL
3 m.	قَالَ	قَالُوا
3 f.	قَالَتْ	قُلْنَ
2 m.	قُلْتَ	قُلْتُمْ
2 f.	قُلْتِ	قُلْتُنَّ
1	قُلْتُ	قُلْنَا

لَمَّا *lammā*

The conjunction *lammā* means 'when', 'after'. It is used with the *māḍī* only, and indicates that the verb of the subordinate clause is prior in time to that of the main verb.

لَمَّا رَجَعَ مُوسَى إِلَى قَوْمِهِ قَالَ	when Moses returned to his people, he said...

لَمَّا دَخَلُوا عَلَيْهِ قَالُوا	when they went in to see him, they said...

Note that when the verb *dakhala* is followed by the preposition ʿ*alā*, it means 'to go in to see'.

WORD ORDER

The word order at the end of a sentence is often inverted if it coincides with the end of the verse, with the inversion producing the end-of-verse assonance. It is particularly common for a prepositional phrase that depends on a verb or a participle to precede the verb or participle. For example, غَافِلٌ *ghāfil* 'heedless' takes the preposition عَنْ ʿ*an* to indicate 'of'. The simplest way of saying 'you are heedless of it' is أَنْتُمْ غَافِلُونَ عَنْهُ *antum ghāfilūna* ʿ*an-hu*. However, what one expects to find in the Qur'ān is أَنْتُمْ عَنْهُ غَافِلُونَ *antum* ʿ*an-hu ghāfilūna*. Similarly, مُؤْمِنٌ *mu'min* 'believer' takes بِ *bi-* to indicate 'in'. 'You are believers in it' in its simplest form is أَنْتُمْ مُؤْمِنُونَ بِهِ *antum mu'minūna bi-hi*. In the Qur'ān this is likely to be أَنْتُمْ بِهِ مُؤْمِنُونَ *antum bi-hi mu'minūna*.

VOCABULARY TWELVE

PERFECT	IMPERFECT	VERBAL NOUN	
كَانَ	يَكُونُ	كَوْنٌ	to be
قَالَ	يَقُولُ	قَوْلٌ	to say
سَكَتَ	يَسْكُتُ	سُكُوتٌ	to abate; (+ʿ*an*) to leave

SINGULAR	PLURAL	
مَلَكٌ	مَلَائِكَةٌ	angel

Singular	Plural	
حَرَجٌ		trouble, difficulty
أُسْوَةٌ		example
بِضَاعَةٌ	بَضَائِعُ	merchandise
رَقِيبٌ		watcher
سَارِقٌ	سَارِقُونَ	thief
عِبْرَةٌ		lesson, warning
عَجَبٌ		wonder
غَضَبٌ		anger
غَفْلَةٌ		heedlessness
قَصَصٌ		story
لَوْحٌ	أَلْوَاحٌ	tablet
مَتَاعٌ	أَمْتِعَةٌ	goods, baggage
فَاحِشَةٌ	فَوَاحِشُ	abomination
هَشِيمٌ		dry twigs, stubble
بَصِيرٌ		observant, seeing
حَسَنٌ		fine, good
غَافِلٌ		heedless
خَبِيرٌ		aware
غَفُورٌ		forgiving
مَفْعُولٌ		done
مَرِيضٌ	مَرْضَى	ill, sick
مُوسَى		Moses

SINGULAR	PLURAL	
إِبْرَاهِيمُ		Abraham

EXERCISE TWELVE

1. كَانَ لَهُنَّ وَلَدٌ [4:12]
2. كَانُوا قَوْمًا مُجْرِمِينَ [7:133]
3. كَانُوا كَهَشِيمِ [54:31]
4. كُنَّا مُسْلِمِينَ [27:42]
5. كُنْتَ فِي غَفْلَةٍ مِنْ هٰذَا [50:22]
6. كَانَ أَمْرُ ٱللهِ مَفْعُولًا [4:47]
7. كَانَ عَدُوًّا لِلّٰهِ وَمَلَائِكَتِهِ وَرُسُلِهِ [2:98]
8. كَانَ مَعَهُ [23:91]
9. كَانَ بِعِبَادِهِ خَبِيرًا بَصِيرًا [17:96]
10. كَانَ رَبُّكَ بَصِيرًا [25:20]
11. كَانُوا عَلَيْهِ شُهَدَآءَ [5:44]
12. كَانَ ٱلنَّاسُ أُمَّةً [2:213]
13. كُنْتَ أَنْتَ ٱلرَّقِيبَ عَلَيْهِمْ [5:117]
14. مَا كُنَّا سَارِقِينَ [12:73]
15. كُنْتُمْ مُجْرِمِينَ [34:32]
16. كُنْتُمْ عَلَىٰ شَفَا حُفْرَةٍ مِنَ ٱلنَّارِ [3:103]
17. كَانَ مِنَ ٱلْقُرُونِ مِنْ قَبْلِكُمْ [11:116]
18. كَانُوا قَوْمَ سَوْءٍ [21:74]
19. كَانَ ذٰلِكَ عَلَى ٱللهِ يَسِيرًا [4:169]

20. كَانَتْ مِنْ قَوْمٍ كَافِرِينَ [27:43]

21. مَا كَانَ عَلَى ٱلنَّبِيِّ مِنْ حَرَجٍ [33:38]

22. كَانَ لَكُمْ فِي رَسُولِ ٱللّٰهِ أُسْوَةٌ حَسَنَةٌ [33:21]

23. كَانَ فِي ضَلَالٍ مُبِينٍ [43:40]

24. لَمَّا سَكَتَ عَنْ مُوسَى ٱلْغَضَبُ أَخَذَ ٱلْأَلْوَاحَ [7:154]

25. لَمَّا فَتَحُوا مَتَاعَهُمْ وَجَدُوا بِضَاعَتَهُمْ [12:65]

26. كُنَّا عَنْ هٰذَا غَافِلِينَ [7:172]

Lesson Thirteen
The Dual

In addition to the singular and plural, Arabic has a dual.

NOUNS

	MASCULINE		FEMININE	
	indef.	def.	indef.	def.
nom.	رَجُلَانِ	اَلْوَالِدَانِ	مَرَّتَانِ	اَلْفِئَتَانِ
acc., gen.	رَجُلَيْنِ	اَلْوَالِدَيْنِ	مَرَّتَيْنِ	اَلْفِئَتَيْنِ

Notice that in the feminine dual the *tā' marbūṭa* of the singular changes to *tā' maftūḥa*.

The above examples show that the dual is the same whether it is indefinite or has the definite article. However, if the dual has a following genitive, the final *nūn* of the dual ending is dropped:

nom.	يَدَاهُ	his hands
acc., gen.	يَدَيْهِ	

If the accusative/genitive ending is followed by *hamzat al-waṣl*, the *sukūn* of the dual ending becomes a *kasra*:

[49:1] بَيْنَ يَدَيِ ٱللَّهِ

All the occurrences of the dual of يَدٌ *yad* 'hand' in the Qur'ān are as the first element of an *iḍāfa*. So too are all the examples of the singular and the plural, apart from *ulī l-aydī* [38:45].

Note that *bayna yaday-*, originally 'between the hands of' means 'before', not only of space but also of time.

With the dual, the first person suffix becomes *-ya*, according to the rule given in Lesson 5.

Pronouns

There is a third person pronoun هُمَا *humā* and a second person pronoun كُمَا *kumā*. In the nominative these are independent forms, in the accusative and genitive they are suffixes. The suffix *-humā* may become *-himā* according to the rule already given about third person pronouns in Lesson 10.

Demonstratives

Unlike the singular and plural these decline:

	These two		Those two	
	m.	f.	m.	f.
nom.	هٰذَانِ	هٰتَانِ	ذَانِكَ	تَانِكَ
acc., gen.	هٰذَيْنِ	هٰتَيْنِ	ذَيْنِكَ	تَيْنِكَ

Verbs

There are three perfect forms. Again, the example is *kataba*:

3 m.d.	كَتَبَا
3 f.d.	كَتَبَتَا
2 d.	كَتَبْتُمَا

None of these perfect dual forms is common in the Qur'ān, but they do occur from time to time:

أَكَلَا مِنْهَا the two of them ate some of it

Remember that if a dual subject is preceded by a verb, **that verb will be in the singular**.

قَالَ رَجُلَانِ two men said

قَدَّمَتْ[A] يَدَاهُ his hands have sent forward

[A] On this form of the verb see Lesson 15.

Dūna AND ITS DERIVATIVES

The preposition دُونَ *dūna*, originally 'on this side of', frequently means 'without', and this is almost always the case with the compound *bi-dūni*. However, the compound *min dūni* is not so easily translated. It most frequently means 'to the exclusion of' or 'apart from', but it can simply mean 'without'.

VOCABULARY THIRTEEN

PERFECT	IMPERFECT	VERBAL NOUN	
أَكَلَ	يَأْكُلُ	أَكْلٌ	to eat

SINGULAR	PLURAL	
سِجْنٌ		prison
وَالِدٌ		father; (dual) parents
فَتًى	فِتْيَةٌ	youth
سَاحِرٌ		magician, sorcerer
بُرْهَانٌ		proof
مَجْمَعٌ		meeting, meeting-place, confluence
عَيْنٌ[A] (f.)	عُيُونٌ	spring
حِجَابٌ		obstacle, partition, veil
شَرِيكٌ	شُرَكَاءُ	partner, associate
زَرْعٌ		cultivation; green crops
نَخْلٌ		date-palms
رُمَّانٌ		pomegranates
مَبْسُوطٌ		spread, extended
فِئَةٌ		party, group

[A] When عَيْنٌ has the sense of 'eye', its Qur'ānic plural is أَعْيُنٌ

Exercise Thirteen

1. مِمَّا تَرَكَ ٱلْوَالِدَانِ [4:33]
2. قَالَ رَجُلَانِ [5:23]
3. يَدَاهُ مَبْسُوطَتَانِ [5:64]
4. آخَرَانِ [5:106]
5. دَخَلَ مَعَهُ ٱلسِّجْنَ فَتَيَانِ [12:36]
6. هٰذَانِ سَاحِرَانِ [20:63]
7. وَجَدَ فِيهَا رَجُلَيْنِ [28:15]
8. ذَانِكَ بُرْهَانَانِ مِنْ رَبِّكَ [28:32]
9. طَائِفَتَانِ مِنَ ٱلْمُؤْمِنِينَ [49:9]
10. فِيهِمَا عَيْنَانِ [55:50]
11. اِبْنَتَيَّ هٰتَيْنِ (genitive) [28:27]
12. وَجَدَ مِنْ دُونِهِمُ ٱمْرَأَتَيْنِ [28:23]
13. بَلَغَا مَجْمَعَ بَيْنِهِمَا [18:61]
14. فِيهِمَا إِثْمٌ كَبِيرٌ [2:219]
15. بَيْنَهُمَا حِجَابٌ [7:46]
16. جَعَلَا لَهُ شُرَكَآءَ [7:190]
17. وَمَا نَحْنُ لَكُمَا بِمُؤْمِنِينَ [10:78]
18. خَلَقْنَا ٱلسَّمٰوَاتِ وَٱلْأَرْضَ وَمَا بَيْنَهُمَا [15:85]
19. جَعَلْنَا بَيْنَهُمَا زَرْعًا [18:32]
20. مَا خَلَقْنَاهُمَا إِلَّا بِٱلْحَقِّ [44:39]
21. فِيهِمَا فَاكِهَةٌ وَنَخْلٌ وَرُمَّانٌ [55:68]
22. جَعَلْنَا ٱللَّيْلَ وَٱلنَّهَارَ آيَتَيْنِ [17:12]

Lesson Fourteen
Cardinal Numbers

It takes a good deal of practice and no little mental agility to learn to handle the Arabic cardinal numbers correctly. However, if you learn each rule and how to apply it correctly and then learn how to apply the rules in combination, you will find the numbers much less difficult than they might appear at the outset.

Here are the basic forms:

	with masculine noun	*with feminine noun*
one	أَحَدٌ	إِحْدَى
two	إِثْنَانِ	إِثْنَتَانِ
three	ثَلَاثَةٌ	ثَلَاثٌ
four	أَرْبَعَةٌ	أَرْبَعٌ
five	خَمْسَةٌ	خَمْسٌ
six	سِتَّةٌ	سِتٌّ
seven	سَبْعَةٌ	سَبْعٌ
eight	ثَمَانِيَةٌ	ثَمَانٍ
nine	تِسْعَةٌ	تِسْعٌ
ten	عَشَرَةٌ	عَشْرٌ
eleven	أَحَدَ عَشَرَ	إِحْدَى عَشْرَةَ
twelve	إِثْنَا عَشَرَ	إِثْنَتَا عَشْرَةَ
thirteen	ثَلَاثَةَ عَشَرَ	ثَلَاثَ عَشْرَةَ

	with masculine noun	*with feminine noun*
fourteen	أَرْبَعَةَ عَشَرَ	أَرْبَعَ عَشْرَةَ
fifteen	خَمْسَةَ عَشَرَ	خَمْسَ عَشْرَةَ
sixteen	سِتَّةَ عَشَرَ	سِتَّ عَشْرَةَ
seventeen	سَبْعَةَ عَشَرَ	سَبْعَ عَشْرَةَ
eighteen	ثَمَانِيَةَ عَشَرَ	ثَمَانِيَ عَشْرَةَ
nineteen	تِسْعَةَ عَشَرَ	تِسْعَ عَشْرَةَ

	with both genders
twenty	عِشْرُونَ
thirty	ثَلَاثُونَ
forty	أَرْبَعُونَ
fifty	خَمْسُونَ
sixty	سِتُّونَ
seventy	سَبْعُونَ
eighty	ثَمَانُونَ
ninety	تِسْعُونَ
one hundred	مِائَةٌ
one thousand	أَلْفٌ

The Qur'ān has a reasonably full range of numerals, but it would be surprising if in a work of its size all the numerals were to be covered. Basically we can find all the cardinal numbers up to twelve, though not necessarily with both masculine and feminine nouns. Above that, the only figures involving units are nineteen and ninety-nine (though 309 is dealt with by periphrasis). The tens (twenty, thirty, etc.) are all there, as are some larger numbers (100, 200, 300, 1,000, 5,000, 50,000 and 100,000 etc.). The outline given below uses Qur'ānic examples where possible, but it would be wrong not to try to explain the whole system fully. The Qur'ān contains two or three apparently anomalous examples, of some interest to specialists in grammar. At this stage they can be ignored.

BASIC RULE

The gender of a numeral is decided by the singular of the noun associated with it, even if the construction of the numeral requires the plural of that noun.

DETAILED RULES

The cardinal numbers as fall into three basic groupings: a) 3–10; b) 11–99; c) 100 etc.

A. Apart from compound numerals, 1 and 2 can be left out of major consideration.

However remember:

1. a) *aḥadun* is a noun, used (i) in compound numbers, and (ii) in some idiomatic phrases. Of the latter only one deserves attention at this stage: *aḥadun* frequently means 'any one' or 'some one' or, after a negative, 'no one'. There are examples of the partitive phrase *min aḥadin* 'any one' in the Qur'ān, sometimes as subject, sometimes as object.
   b) In addition to *aḥadun/iḥdā*, basically a noun, there is a form *wāḥidun/wāḥidatun*, which is basically an adjective. Note, however, *kullu wāḥidin* 'each one'.
2. **Requires the use of the dual**. No other construction is possible.

B. 3–10 take the *genitive plural*, but it is essential here to remember that the number goes into the opposite gender to that of the singular of the noun:

ثَلَاثَةُ أَيَّامٍ three days

أَرْبَعَةُ شُهَدَاءَ	four witnesses
سَبْعُ سَمٰوَاتٍ	seven heavens
تِسْعُ آيَاتٍ	nine verses

Note

a) The form of eight used with feminine nouns declines like the definite forms of *wādin*:

ثَمَانِي حِجَجٍ eight years

b) The form of ten used with feminine nouns is vocalised with a *sukūn* on the *shīn*: عَشْرُ سُوَرٍ *ʿashru suwarin* . However, the form used with masculine nouns has a *fatḥa* on the *shīn*: عَشَرَةُ مَسَاكِينَ *ʿasharatu masākīna* 'ten poor people'. This is the opposite to the forms of ten used in the numerals eleven to nineteen.

C. 11–99 take the accusative singular.

11. Both numerals agree in gender with the noun and are undeclinable:

إِحْدَى عَشْرَةَ مَدِينَةً	eleven cities
أَحَدَ عَشَرَ كَوْكَبًا	eleven stars

12. Both numerals agree in gender with the noun. The ten does not decline, but the unit declines:

m. nom.	اِثْنَا عَشَرَ شَهْرًا	twelve months
f. nom.	اِثْنَتَا عَشْرَةَ عَيْنًا	twelve springs
m. acc., gen.	اِثْنَيْ عَشَرَ نَقِيبًا	twelve chiefs
f. acc., gen.	اِثْنَتَيْ عَشْرَةَ مَدِينَةً	twelve cities

13–19. The unit goes into the gender opposite to that of the noun, the ten is in the same gender as the noun. Both ten and the unit are undeclinable.

The only form found in the Qur'ān [*tisʿata ʿashara*] is not followed by a noun. If it were, it would be a masculine one, as the context implies.
20–90. These are sound masculine plurals and are declined as such. Questions of gender do not arise:

ثَلَٰثُونَ شَهْرًا	thirty months
(acc.) أَرْبَعِينَ سَنَةً	forty years
(gen.) سِتِّينَ مِسْكِينًا	sixty poor people
(acc.) ثَمَانِينَ جَلْدَةً	eighty lashes

With 21, 22, 23 etc. the patterns of agreement and disagreement recur. Note that if the unit can normally have *tanwīn*, **it cannot be dropped**.

إِحْدَى وَعِشْرُونَ مَدِينَةً	twenty-one cities
اِثْنَانِ وَثَلَاثُونَ رَسُولًا	thirty-two messenger
ثَلَاثَةٌ وَأَرْبَعُونَ كِتَابًا	forty-three books
أَرْبَعٌ وَخَمْسُونَ قَرْيَةً	fifty-four villages

D. 100, 200/1,000, 2,000 etc. take the genitive singular. Again questions of gender do not arise.

100	مِائَةُ عَامٍ	one hundred years
200	مِائَتَا رَجُلٍ	two hundred men (note the dual *mi'atā* without *nūn*)
300	ثَلَاثُ مِائَةِ يَوْمٍ	three hundred days

[In 300–900 *mi'a* irregularly stays in the singular]

1,000	أَلْفُ سَنَةٍ	one thousand years
2,000	أَلْفَا رَجُلٍ	two thousand men (again no *nūn*)

3,000	ثَلَاثَةُ آلَافِ مَلَكٍ	three thousand angels (the Qur'ān deals with this example by periphrasis: ثَلَاثَةُ آلَافٍ مِنَ ٱلْمَلَائِكَةِ)

The genitive singular construction applies only on the hundred or thousand. For an additional one or two the noun is repeated—in the singular or dual, as is appropriate—in the same case as the hundred or thousand, *e.g.* أَلْفُ لَيْلَةٍ وَلَيْلَةٌ, 'a thousand and one nights'. Once there is an additional three etc. (right up to ninety-nine), the rules for the additional numeral apply:

208	مِائَتَانِ وَثَمَانِي مَنَافِعَ	208 benefits
456	أَرْبَعُ مِائَةٍ وَسِتٌّ وَخَمْسُونَ آيَةً	456 verses

Ordinal numbers and fractions are dealt with in Lesson 31.

Note that the numerals *sabᶜun ᶜijāfun* 'seven lean ones' [12:46], *sabᶜun shidādun* 'seven hard ones' [12:48] and *ᶜishrūna ṣābirūna* 'twenty men of patience' [8:65] are examples of the relatively rare construction where the numeral is qualified by an adjective.

At this point you should try and learn the numerals as set out in the tables above and as many of the examples as possible.

Vocabulary Fourteen

Singular	Plural	
حِجَّةٌ	حِجَجٌ	year
عَامٌ	أَعْوَامٌ	year
شَهْرٌ	شُهُورٌ/أَشْهُرٌ	month
كَوْكَبٌ	كَوَاكِبُ	star
نَقِيبٌ	نُقَبَاءُ	chief

Singular	Plural	
مِسْكِينٌ	مَسَاكِينُ	poor, destitute
جَلْدَةٌ		lash, stripe
عَجِيفٌ	عِجَافٌ	thin

Exercise Fourteen

Revise the numerals given in the lesson.

Lesson Fifteen
Derived Forms of the Verb

Virtually all languages have some way of modifying verbs to produce other verbs. In some cases there will be a close link in meaning, in others virtually none. One common way with Indo-European languages is to put prepositions and other prefixes before verbs, *e.g.* 'stand' $\rightarrow$ 'withstand' 'understand'; 'see' $\rightarrow$ 'oversee'. The Latin verb '*mitto*' has not come into English; but from its forms modified by a prepositional prefix we get 'admit', 'demit', 'emit', 'omit', 'permit, 'remit', 'submit', 'transmit'. The role played by the root structure in Arabic precludes such developments. Instead, modifications to vowel patterns, including the use of prefixes and infixes, take place. These modified forms of the verb are known as the derived forms of the verb, the form we have dealt with so far being the first, or base, form. There are fourteen derived forms, of which eight (2–8 and 10) are important. Grammars tend to discuss at length the various shades of sense imparted by each form. This is unhelpful initially, as the so-called norms are often misleading or inapplicable. The crucial step at this stage is to learn and recognise the base within each derived form and how the bases are manipulated. As all the patterns are predetermined, this is not difficult.

Remember to learn the derived form of the verb in its correct derived form. You should learn *arsala* not *rasala* [4] or anything like that.

The basic forms of the triliteral verb are to be found in the following tables. At this stage you should try to commit the 3 m.s. perfect forms to memory. For the verb *qabila* these are:

Form	Perfect	Imperfect	Verbal noun	Active participle	Passive participle
2	قَبَّلَ	يُقَبِّلُ	تَقْبِيلٌ	مُقَبِّلٌ	مُقَبَّلٌ
3	قَابَلَ	يُقَابِلُ	مُقَابَلَةٌ or قِبَالٌ	مُقَابِلٌ	مُقَابَلٌ
4	أَقْبَلَ	يُقْبِلُ	إِقْبَالٌ	مُقْبِلٌ	مُقْبَلٌ
5	تَقَبَّلَ	يَتَقَبَّلُ	تَقَبُّلٌ	مُتَقَبِّلٌ	مُتَقَبَّلٌ
6	تَقَابَلَ	يَتَقَابَلُ	تَقَابُلٌ	مُتَقَابِلٌ	مُتَقَابَلٌ
7	اِنْقَبَلَ	يَنْقَبِلُ	اِنْقِبَالٌ	مُنْقَبِلٌ	مُنْقَبَلٌ
8	اِقْتَبَلَ	يَقْتَبِلُ	اِقْتِبَالٌ	مُقْتَبِلٌ	مُقْتَبَلٌ
10	اِسْتَقْبَلَ	يَسْتَقْبِلُ	اِسْتِقْبَالٌ	مُسْتَقْبِلٌ	مُسْتَقْبَلٌ

NOTES ON THE FIFTH AND SIXTH FORMS

1. In the Qur'ān and some other early texts the initial prefix *ta-* is dropped from the imperfect tenses:

   Indicative: تَكَلَّمُ *takallamu* (for *tatakallamu*); تَنَزَّلُ *tanazzalu* (for *tatanazzalu*); تَذَكَّرُونَ *tadhakkarūna* (for *tatadhakkarūna*); تَسَاءَلُونَ *tasā'alūna* (for *tatasā'alūna*); تَنَاصَرُونَ *tanāṣarūna* (for *tatanāṣarūna*).

   Other tenses: تَصَدَّقُوا *taṣaddaqū* (for *tataṣaddaqū*); تَعَاوَنُوا *taʿā-wanū* (for *tataʿāwanū*); تَفَرَّقُوا *tafarraqū* (for *tatafarraqū*)

2. For the 5th and 6th forms the Qur'ān contains a range of examples of Ḥijāzī dialect forms which, instead of the *ta-* prefix use the prefix *it-*. The *tā'* of this prefix then assimilates to a following *thā', dāl, dhāl, zāy, sīn, ṣād,* or *ṭā'*. Most instances are 5th forms, and most are in the imperfect tenses, but there are some perfect forms and a few participles. Here are some of the verbs involved (the finite verbs are given in

the perfect, regardless of their Qur'ānic tense—and the list is not complete):

اِدَّبَّرَ اِذَّكَّرَ اِزَّيَّنَ اِسَّمَّعَ اِصَّدَّقَ اِصَّعَّدَ اِطَّوَّفَ
اطَّيَّرَ اِثَّاقَلَ اِدَّارَكَ مُدَّثِّرٌ مُزَّمِّلٌ

NOTE ON THE EIGHTH FORM

The infixed *t* of this form may change to *d* or to *ṭ* under the influence of the preceding first radical:

اِدَّعَى *iddaʿā* (see Lesson 30); اِدَّخَرَ (from *dhakhara*); اِزْدَجَرَ *izdajara*; اِزْدَادَ *izdāda* (Lesson 28); اِصْطَبَرَ *iṣṭabara*; اِصْطَادَ *iṣṭāda* (Lesson 28); اِضْطَرَّ *iḍṭarra* (Lesson 26); اِطَّلَعَ *iṭṭalaʿa*, etc.

[For the full extent of the rule see Wright 1, 66–67.]

NOTES ON OTHER FORMS

The 9th form of the verb, which works in the same way as the doubled verb (see Lesson 26), is in general very rare and does not merit special attention. In the Qur'ān it is found only a dozen times, always connected with colours. There are two 3 f.s. perfect: اِبْيَضَّتْ *ibyaḍḍat* 'to be white' and اِسْوَدَّتْ *iswaddat* 'to be black'; the same verbs in the 3 f.s. imperfect: تَبْيَضُّ *tabyaḍḍu*, تَسْوَدُّ *taswaddu*; and three participles: مُسْوَدٌّ *muswaddun*, and also مُخْضَرٌّ *mukhḍarrun* 'green' and مُصْفَرٌّ *musfarrun* 'yellow'. There is also one 11th form participle: مُدْهَامٌّ *mudhāmmun* 'dark green'.

QUADRILITERAL VERBS

Quadriliteral verbs have four radicals instead of three. They are quite rare in the Qur'ān, and most of those that do occur are onomatopoeic, like دَمْدَمَ *damdama* and وَسْوَسَ *waswasa* . Genuine quadriliterals are بَعْثَرَ *ba*ᶜ*thara* and the two derived forms اِشْمَأَزَّ *ishma'azza* and اِقْشَعَرَّ *iqsha*ᶜ*arra* . In all cases the radicals are obvious, and no special attention needs to be paid to these verbs in the Qur'ān. Their role in other Arabic is more important.

VOCABULARY FIFTEEN

PERFECT	IMPERFECT	VERBAL NOUN	
أَخَّرَ 2	يُؤَخِّرُ	تَأْخِيرٌ	to defer
عَلَّمَ 2	يُعَلِّمُ	تَعْلِيمٌ	to teach
قَدَّمَ 2	يُقَدِّمُ	تَقْدِيمٌ	to send forward, to bring forward
كَذَّبَ 2	يُكَذِّبُ	تَكْذِيبٌ	to deny, give the lie to
جَادَلَ 3	يُجَادِلُ	جِدَالٌ	to dispute, contend with
جَاهَدَ 3	يُجَاهِدُ	جِهَادٌ	to strive
قَاتَلَ 3	يُقَاتِلُ	قِتَالٌ	to fight, confound
أَرْسَلَ 4	يُرْسِلُ	إِرْسَالٌ	to send
أَنْزَلَ 4	يُنْزِلُ	إِنْزَالٌ	to send down
أَهْلَكَ 4	يُهْلِكُ	إِهْلَاكٌ	to destroy
تَذَكَّرَ 5	يَتَذَكَّرُ	تَذَكُّرٌ	to remember, bear in mind
تَوَكَّلَ 5	يَتَوَكَّلُ	تَوَكُّلٌ	to put one's trust in (ᶜ*alā*)
تَعَاوَنَ 6	يَتَعَاوَنُ	تَعَاوُنٌ	to co-operate, help one another
اِنْقَلَبَ 7	يَنْقَلِبُ	اِنْقِلَابٌ	return, be overturned

PERFECT	IMPERFECT	VERBAL NOUN	
اِتَّبَعَ 8	يَتَّبِعُ	اِتِّبَاعٌ	to follow
اِخْتَلَفَ 8	يَخْتَلِفُ	اِخْتِلَافٌ	to vary, differ
اِسْتَغْفَرَ 10	يَسْتَغْفِرُ	اِسْتِغْفَارٌ	to seek forgiveness
اِسْتَكْبَرَ 10	يَسْتَكْبِرُ	اِسْتِكْبَارٌ	to be haughty, insolent, proud

SINGULAR	PLURAL	
دِينٌ	أَدْيَانٌ	religion
سَاعَةٌ	سَاعَاتٌ	hour
مَاءٌ	مِيَاهٌ	water

EXERCISE FIFTEEN

1. عَلَّمَ ٱلْقُرْآنَ [55:2]
2. عَلَّمْتُكَ ٱلْكِتَابَ [5:110]
3. ذٰلِكَ بِمَا قَدَّمَتْ أَيْدِيكُمْ [3:182]
4. مَا قَدَّمَ وَأَخَّرَ [75:13]
5. كَذَّبُوا بِآيَاتِنَا [3:11]
6. كَذَّبَ بِٱلسَّاعَةِ [25:11]
7. جَاهَدُوا فِي سَبِيلِ ٱللّٰهِ [2:218]
8. جَاهَدَاكَ [29:8]
9. قَدْ جَادَلْتَنَا [11:32]
10. قَاتَلَهُمُ ٱللّٰهُ [9:30]

11. قَاتَلُوكُمْ فِي ٱلدِّينِ [60:9]

12. أَنْزَلْنَاهُ قُرْآنًا عَرَبِيًّا [12:2]

13. أَنْزَلَ مِنَ ٱلسَّمَآءِ مَآءً [2:22]

14. مَا أَنْزَلَ ٱللّٰهُ عَلَى بَشَرٍ مِنْ شَيْءٍ [6:91]

15. أَهْلَكْنَاهُمْ بِذُنُوبِهِمْ [6:6]

16. مَا أَهْلَكْنَا مِنْ قَرْيَةٍ إِلَّا وَلَهَا كِتَابٌ مَعْلُومٌ [15:4]

17. أَرْسَلَ رَسُولَهُ بِٱلْهُدَى [9:33]

18. أَرْسَلْنَا نُوحًا إِلَى قَوْمِهِ [11:25]

19. أَرْسَلْتَ إِلَيْنَا رَسُولًا [20:134]

20. تَوَكَّلْتُ عَلَى ٱللّٰهِ رَبِّي وَرَبِّكُمْ [11:56]

21. اِنْقَلَبَ عَلَى وَجْهِهِ [22:11]

22. اِنْقَلَبُوا إِلَى أَهْلِهِمُ [83:31]

23. نَصَرُوهُ وَٱتَّبَعُوا ٱلنُّورَ [7:157]

24. اِتَّبَعُوا ٱلْحَقَّ مِنْ رَبِّهِمْ [47:3]

25. اِخْتَلَفُوا فِي ٱلْكِتَابِ [2:176]

26. اِخْتَلَفَ ٱلْأَحْزَابُ مِنْ بَيْنِهِمْ [43:65]

27. وَٱسْتَغْفَرَ لَهُمُ ٱلرَّسُولُ [4:64]

28. فَٱسْتَغْفَرُوا لِذُنُوبِهِمْ [3:135]

29. وَٱسْتَكْبَرْتَ وَكُنْتَ مِنَ ٱلْكَافِرِينَ [39:59]

30. فَٱسْتَكْبَرُوا وَكَانُوا قَوْمًا مُجْرِمِينَ [7:133]

Lesson Sixteen
The Imperfect

The *muḍāriʿ* is usually known in English as the Imperfect, or, if one wishes to contrast it with the allied Subjunctive and Jussive moods, the Imperfect Indicative. The Imperfect stresses the incompleteness of an action or state. Standing on its own, it most frequently translates into an English present or future, though sometimes a verb in the imperfect may have a potential meaning. The Imperfect of *kataba* is as follows:

	Singular	Dual	Plural
3 m.	يَكْتُبُ	يَكْتُبَانِ	يَكْتُبُونَ
3 f.	تَكْتُبُ	تَكْتُبَانِ	يَكْتُبْنَ
2 m.	تَكْتُبُ	تَكْتُبَانِ	تَكْتُبُونَ
2 f.	تَكْتُبِينَ	تَكْتُبَانِ	تَكْتُبْنَ
1	أَكْتُبُ	–	نَكْتُبُ

Examples of the use of the Imperfect:

أَعْلَمُ مَا لَا تَعْلَمُونَ	I know what you do not know
يَظْلِمُونَ ٱلنَّاسَ	they wrong the people
تَجِدُ كُلُّ نَفْسٍ مَا عَمِلَتْ	every soul will find what it has done

The *muḍāriʿ* is used following the *māḍī* of another verb to show an action or state closely related to, or virtually simultaneous with, the first verb:

إِسْتَوَى عَلَى ٱلْعَرْشِ يُدَبِّرُ ٱلْأَمْرَ [A]	he sat on the throne directing the matter
جَاءَتْهُ [B] إِحْدَاهُمَا تَمْشِي [A]	one of the two of them came to him

IMPERFECT FORM NOTES

1. The Imperfect of *kataba* should be learned by heart from the table above. Once you have mastered the Imperfect of *kataba*, do the same with the Imperfect of the derived forms listed in Lesson 15. The prefixes, endings and suffixes of the derived forms work exactly like those of the first form, subject only to a variation of the vowel of the prefix, depending on which derived form is being used.
   The forms of the Imperfect are not as straightforward as the Perfect, for they involve a combination of prefixes, endings and suffixes, and two pairs of the forms (3 f.s. / 2 m.s. and 3 f.d. / 2 d.) are identical. One has to get used to this.
2. In verbs with the pattern *kataba*, *i.e.* with a *fatḥa* on the second radical in the *māḍī*, the vowel of the second radical of the *muḍāriᶜ* is a variable.
   In the majority of verbs of this pattern, the vowel is a *ḍamma* as in *yaktubu*. However, most verbs with one of the letters *hamza, ḥā', khā', ᶜayn, ghayn* or *hā'* as second or third radical take *fatḥa* as the vowel of the second radical in the Imperfect; but such common examples as *dakhala / yadkhulu* and *rajaᶜa / yarjiᶜu* are indications of the fallibility of this rule of thumb. As mentioned in Lesson 9, the best procedure is to learn the 3 m.s. Imperfect when you learn the 3 m.s. Perfect.
3. Verbs of the pattern of *shariba* take *fatḥa* in the Imperfect: *yashrabu*. This rule does not apply to verbs with an initial *wāw*.
4. Verbs of the pattern of *kabura* take *ḍamma* in the Imperfect.

[A] For these verbs see Lesson 30.
[B] For the verb *jā'a* 'to come' see Lesson 28.

5. This variability of the second radical vowel applies to the first form only. It does not apply to any of the derived forms. Note that when a suffix is added to the 3 m.p. and 2 m.p. the *nūn* remains:

يَسْمَعُونَكُمْ	they hear you
تَأْمُرُونَنَا	you order us

Beginners are tempted to assume that with a suffix this *nūn* will drop out. This is through a false analogy with what happens to sound masculine plural nouns. Dropping the *nūn* changes the mood (as you will see when the Subjunctive is dealt with in Lesson 17), and is thus impossible when the verb is an Imperfect Indicative.

THE IMPERFECT OF KĀNA

Also learn the *muḍāri*ᶜ of *kāna*, but remember that this is not used to express the present tense of the verb 'to be'. That must be done by means of a nominal sentence or using the Perfect of *kāna* as explained in Lesson 12. However, the imperfect of *kāna* is used for the future. See the section on *sa-* and *sawfa* below.

	SINGULAR	DUAL	PLURAL
3 m.	يَكُونُ	يَكُونَانِ	يَكُونُونَ
3 f.	تَكُونُ	تَكُونَانِ	يَكُنَّ
2 m.	تَكُونُ	تَكُونَانِ	تَكُونُونَ
2 f.	تَكُونِينَ	تَكُونَانِ	تَكُنَّ
1	أَكُونُ	–	نَكُونُ

NEGATIVE OF THE *muḍāri*ᶜ

The basic negative of the Imperfect is *lā*. However, *mā* is also found. The primary difference between them is that *lā* is a general negative, while *mā* negates a fact.

سَـ *sa-* AND سَوْفَ *sawfa*

The particles *sa-* (prefixed to the *muḍāri*ᶜ) and *sawfa* (an independent word preceding the *muḍāri*ᶜ) are used to indicate the future. They are not common, as the context usually gives enough indication of time. Note that *sa-* cannot be used with a negative and *sawfa lā* (the only correct combination) is very rare and not found in the Qur'ān.

سَيَكُونُ مِنْكُمْ مَرْضَى there will be sick people among you
سَوْفَ تَعْلَمُونَ you will know

Kāna WITH THE *muḍāri*ᶜ

The *māḍī* of *kāna* is used with the *muḍāri*ᶜ of a second verb to indicate a continuous past tense:

[2:75] كَانَ فَرِيقٌ مِنْهُمْ يَسْمَعُونَ كَلَامَ ٱللهِ
a party of them was listening to the word of God

[23:105] كُنْتُمْ بِهَا تُكَذِّبُونَ
you were denying it

VOCABULARY SIXTEEN

PERFECT	IMPERFECT	VERBAL NOUN	
أَبْصَرَ 4	يُبْصِرُ	إِبْصَارٌ	(+*bi-*) to see, observe
دَبَّرَ 2	يُدَبِّرُ	تَدْبِيرٌ	to manage, arrange
كَلَّمَ 2	يُكَلِّمُ	تَكْلِيمٌ	to speak to, address

SINGULAR	PLURAL	
حِكْمَةٌ		wisdom
زَكَاةٌ / زَكَوٰةٌ		alms

Singular	Plural	
صَلَاةٌ / صَلَوٰةٌ	صَلَوَاتٌ	prayer
عَرْشٌ		throne
فَرِيقٌ		party, company
قَدَمٌ (f.)	أَقْدَامٌ	foot
كَلَامٌ		speech, words, word
تَحْتَ		beneath

Exercise Sixteen

1. [16:89] نَبْعَثُ مِنْ كُلِّ أُمَّةٍ شَهِيدًا
2. [18:60] أَبْلُغَ مَجْمَعَ ٱلْبَحْرَيْنِ
3. [41:29] نَجْعَلْهُمَا تَحْتَ أَقْدَامِنَا
4. [23:33] يَأْكُلُ مِمَّا تَأْكُلُونَ مِنْهُ... وَيَشْرَبُ مِمَّا تَشْرَبُونَ
5. [19:27] (f.s.) تَحْمِلُهُ
6. [2:18] هُمْ لَا يَرْجِعُونَ
7. [13:23] يَدْخُلُونَ عَلَيْهِم مِنْ كُلِّ بَابٍ
8. [2:235] سَتَذْكُرُونَهُنَّ
9. [14:25] يَضْرِبُ ٱللَّهُ ٱلْأَمْثَالَ لِلنَّاسِ
10. [2:79] يَكْتُبُونَ ٱلْكِتَابَ بِأَيْدِيهِمْ
11. [11:64] يَأْخُذَكُمْ عَذَابٌ قَرِيبٌ
12. [19:55] كَانَ يَأْمُرُ أَهْلَهُ بِٱلصَّلَوٰةِ وَٱلزَّكَوٰةِ
13. [59:12] لَا يَخْرُجُونَ مَعَهُمْ

14. يَسْأَلُونَكَ عَنِ ٱلشَّهْرِ ٱلْحَرَامِ [2:217]

15. يَسْمَعُ كَلَامَ ٱللَّهِ [9:6]

16. يَعْلَمُ مَا تَكْسِبُ كُلُّ نَفْسٍ [13:42]

17. لَا يُكَلِّمُهُمُ ٱللَّهُ وَلَا يَنْظُرُ إِلَيْهِمْ [3:77]

18. يَنْصُرُونَكُمْ [26:93]

19. ٱللَّهُ شَهِيدٌ عَلَىٰ مَا تَعْمَلُونَ [3:98]

20. عَلَىٰ رَبِّهِمْ يَتَوَكَّلُونَ [8:2]

21. يَسْتَغْفِرُونَهُ وَٱللَّهُ غَفُورٌ رَحِيمٌ [5:74]

22. يُعَلِّمُكُمُ ٱلْكِتَابَ وَٱلْحِكْمَةَ [2:151]

23. لَا يَسْتَكْبِرُونَ [5:82]

24. لَا نُكَذِّبُ بِآيَاتِ رَبِّنَا [6:27]

25. تُجَاهِدُونَ فِي سَبِيلِ ٱللَّهِ بِأَمْوَالِكُمْ وَأَنْفُسِكُمْ [61:11]

26. يَتَذَكَّرُ أُولُوا ٱلْأَلْبَابِ [39:9]

27. سَأُنْزِلُ مِثْلَ مَا أَنْزَلَ ٱللَّهُ [6:93]

28. يُهْلِكُونَ أَنْفُسَهُمْ [6:26]

29. لَا يُقَاتِلُونَكُمْ [59:14]

30. سَوْفَ يُبْصِرُونَ [37:175]

Lesson Seventeen
Interrogatives

There are two interrogative particles that simply introduce a question. They are هَلْ *hal* and أَ *a-*. One peculiarity of *a-* is that if it is used with *wa-* or *fa-* it precedes that particle, giving *a-fa-* or *a-wa-* (not *fa-a-* or *wa-a-*).

أَلَهُمْ أَرْجُلٌ do they have feet?

أَفِي قُلُوبِهِمْ مَرَضٌ is there sickness in their hearts?

هَلْ أَنْتُمْ شَاكِرُونَ are you grateful?

هَلْ أَتَّبِعُكَ shall I follow you?

أَفَلَا تَسْمَعُونَ will you not hear?

أَوَلَا يَعْلَمُونَ do they not know?

Note that *a-lā* may be a negative and interrogative combined:

أَلَا تَأْكُلُونَ will you not eat?

or it may have the extended meaning 'indeed':

أَلَا لِلّٰهِ آلدِّينُ آلْخَالِصُ God indeed has the pure religion

The meaning will depend on the context, though when *a-lā* is followed by إِنَّ *inna* (see Lesson 19) it will always mean 'indeed'.

أَمْ *am* 'or' introduces an alternative in an interrogative question. It can be used only in interrogative sentences, and in the Qur'ān it is used only after *a-*. The general word for 'or' *aw* is used after *hal*.

Specific interrogative words that do not require a special construction are:

أَيْنَ *ayna*, 'where?'

أَيْنَ ٱلْمَفَرُّ where is the place of escape?

In the Qur'ān *ayna* is not preceded by *min* or *ilā* to produce 'whence' and 'whither', as we find elsewhere.

أَيْنَ تَذْهَبُونَ where are you going?

أَنَّى *annā*, 'whence?' and then **'how?'**

أَنَّى لَكِ هٰذَا whence does this [come] to you?

أَنَّى يُبْصِرُونَ how [can] they see?

أَيَّانَ *ayyāna*, 'when?'

أَيَّانَ يَوْمُ ٱلدِّينِ when is the Day of Judgement?

مَتَى *matā*, 'when?'

مَتَى نَصْرُ ٱللّٰهِ when is God's help?

كَيْفَ *kayfa*, 'how?'

كَيْفَ تَعْلَمُونَ how do you know?

كَيْفَ تَصْبِرُ how [can] you endure?

مَا *mā*, 'what?'

مَا أَصْحَابُ ٱلشِّمَالِ what are the companions of the left?

مَا ٱلْقَارِعَةُ what is the calamity?

The most striking examples of the interrogative *mā* are in the phrase مَا أَدْرَاكَ *mā adrā-ka* 'what has given you knowledge of. . . ?' which occurs thirteen times in early Meccan *sūras* (on the verb أَدْرَى *adrā* see Lesson 30).

If *dhā* is added to *mā* to give *mā-dhā* the meaning can only be interrogative:

مَاذَا يُنْفِقُونَ what do they spend?

مَاذَا تَأْمُرُونَ what do you order?

لِمَ *li-ma*, 'why?'

لِمَ تَلْبِسُونَ ٱلْحَقَّ بِٱلْبَاطِلِ why do you confound the truth with falsehood?

لِمَ تَكْفُرُونَ بِآيَاتِ ٱللّٰهِ why do you not believe in God's signs?

The shortened interrogative *-ma* with other prepositions, common elsewhere in Arabic, occurs only occasionally in the Qur'ān: بِمَ *bi-ma* and فِيمَ *fī-ma* . Note that the fuller form لِمَاذَا *li-mā-dhā* does not occur in the Qur'ān.

مَنْ *man*, 'who?'

مَنْ رَبُّكُمَا [20:49] who is the lord of the two of you?

مَنْ يَنْصُرُنِي [11:63] who will help me?

If *dhā* is added to *man* to give *man-dhā* the meaning can only be interrogative (as we have seen with *mā-dhā*). *Man-dhā* is, however, found in the Qur'ān only in a set phrase مَنْذَا ٱلَّذِي *man-dhā lladhī* 'who is there who. . . ?', which occurs a handful of times.

كَمْ *kam*, 'how many?'

The usual construction when *kam* is an interrogative is for it to take the accusative, like the number group 11 to 99. However, on the few occasions that it occurs as an interrogative in the Qur'ān the accusative is suppressed:

كَمْ لَبِثْتَ how long did you linger?

The context indicates that a reply with an accusative word such as *yawman* or *sanatan* is implied. In other places, *kam* is used in an exclamatory way and is followed by *min* and the genitive. كَأَيِّنْ *ka'ayyin*, a rare synonym of *kam*, is only used in this exclamatory fashion.

أَيٌّ *ayyun* 'which?'

In the Qur'ān *ayy* is always followed by a genitive or a suffix. It remains in the masculine regardless of the gender of the following noun:

أَيُّ شَيْءٍ what thing?

أَيُّ ٱلْفَرِيقَيْنِ which of the two parties?

فِي أَيِّ صُورَةٍ in what form?

أَيُّ آيَاتِ ٱللّٰهِ which of God's signs?

INDIRECT QUESTIONS

All the above interrogatives are also used to introduce indirect questions. So too is the conditional particle إِنْ *in* 'if' (on which see Lesson 36).

VOCABULARY SEVENTEEN

PERFECT	IMPERFECT	VERBAL NOUN	
شَكَرَ	يَشْكُرُ	شُكْرٌ	to thank, be thankful
صَبَرَ	يَصْبِرُ	صَبْرٌ	to be patient, endure
صَدَقَ	يَصْدُقُ	صِدْقٌ	to tell the truth
قَسَمَ	يَقْسِمُ	قِسْمٌ	to divide
عَقَلَ	يَعْقِلُ	عَقْلٌ	to understand
عَجِلَ	يَعْجَلُ	عَجَلٌ	to hasten to
اِسْتَعْجَلَ 10	يَسْتَعْجِلُ	اِسْتِعْجَالٌ	to hasten, seek to hasten
كَفَرَ	يَكْفُرُ	كُفْرٌ	to deny, not to believe in, to be an unbeliever
لَبَسَ	يَلْبِسُ	لَبْسٌ	to confound
أَسْمَعَ 4	يُسْمِعُ	إِسْمَاعٌ	to make hear
بَشَّرَ 2	يُبَشِّرُ	تَبْشِيرٌ	to bring good news/tidings
تَبَيَّنَ 5	يَتَبَيَّنُ	تَبَيُّنٌ	to become clear, be made clear
أَنْفَقَ 4	يُنْفِقُ	إِنْفَاقٌ	to spend

SINGULAR	PLURAL	
خُسْرَانٌ [from *khasira* 'to lose']		loss, ruin
حُكْمٌ		judgement
ذِكْرَى		remembrance, reminder

Singular	Plural	
مَفَرٌّ		refuge
قَارِعَةٌ		calamity
مَرَضٌ		illness
شِمَالٌ		left, left hand
يَمِينٌ	أَيْمَانٌ	right, right hand; oath
قَلْبٌ	قُلُوبٌ	heart
صُورَةٌ	صُوَرٌ	form
أَصَمُّ (f.) صَمَّاءُ	صُمٌّ	deaf
خَالِصٌ		pure
بَاطِلٌ		false

Exercise Seventeen

1. أَفَلَا تَتَذَكَّرُونَ [6:80]
2. سَنَنْظُرُ أَصَدَقْتَ أَمْ كُنْتَ مِنَ ٱلْكَاذِبِينَ [27:27]
3. أَفَنَجْعَلُ ٱلْمُسْلِمِينَ كَٱلْمُجْرِمِينَ [68:35]
4. مَتَىٰ هٰذَا ٱلْوَعْدُ [10:48]
5. أَنَّىٰ لَهُمُ ٱلذِّكْرَىٰ [44:13]
6. مَا أَصْحَابُ ٱلْيَمِينِ [56:27]
7. مَا أَدْرَاكَ مَا يَوْمُ ٱلدِّينِ [82:17]
8. فَهَلْ وَجَدْتُمْ مَا وَعَدَ رَبُّكُمْ [7:44]
9. هَلْ عِنْدَكُمْ مِنْ عِلْمٍ [6:148]

10. [2:77] أَوَلَا يَعْلَمُونَ

11. [17:94] أَبَعَثَ ٱللَّهُ بَشَرًا رَسُولًا

12. [6:62] أَلَا لَهُ ٱلْحُكْمُ

13. [10:14] نَنْظُرَ كَيْفَ تَعْمَلُونَ

14. [3:65] أَفَلَا تَعْقِلُونَ

15. [15:54] أَبَشَّرْتُمُونِي

16. [27:84] أَكَذَّبْتُمْ بِآيَاتِي

17. [43:32] أَهُمْ يَقْسِمُونَ رَحْمَةَ رَبِّكَ

18. [12:89] هَلْ عَلِمْتُمْ مَا فَعَلْتُمْ

19. [7:150] أَعَجِلْتُمْ أَمْرَ رَبِّكُمْ

20. [26:204] أَفَبِعَذَابِنَا يَسْتَعْجِلُونَ

21. [26:72] هَلْ يَسْمَعُونَكُمْ

22. [14:45] وَتَبَيَّنَ لَكُمْ كَيْفَ فَعَلْنَا بِهِمْ

23. [37:58] أَفَمَا نَحْنُ بِمَيِّتِينَ

24. [11:14] فَهَلْ أَنْتُمْ مُسْلِمُونَ

25. [39:15] أَلَا ذٰلِكَ هُوَ ٱلْخُسْرَانُ ٱلْمُبِينُ

26. [101:3] وَمَا أَدْرَاكَ مَا ٱلْقَارِعَةُ

27. [10:42] أَفَأَنْتَ تُسْمِعُ ٱلصُّمَّ

28. [4:21] كَيْفَ تَأْخُذُونَهُ

29. [10:2] أَكَانَ لِلنَّاسِ عَجَبًا

30. [88:17] أَفَلَا يَنْظُرُونَ إِلَى ٱلْإِبِلِ

Lesson Eighteen
The Subjunctive

The Subjunctive is closely related in form to the Imperfect Indicative, with the change of the final short vowel from *u* to *a*, and the dropping of the final *na* if it is preceded by a long vowel. These changes affect all numbers and persons except the 3 f.p. and the 2 f.p.

Learn the basic form of the Subjunctive from the table below.

	SINGULAR	DUAL	PLURAL
3 m.	يَكْتُبَ	يَكْتُبَا	يَكْتُبُوا
3 f.	تَكْتُبَ	تَكْتُبَا	يَكْتُبْنَ
2 m.	تَكْتُبَ	تَكْتُبَا	تَكْتُبُوا
2 f.	تَكْتُبِي	تَكْتُبَا	تَكْتُبْنَ
1	أَكْتُبَ	–	نَكْتُبَ

The Subjunctive in Arabic is used only after specific particles that require a subjunctive. With the exception of لَنْ *lan*, all these particles introduce subordinate clauses. In subordinate clauses the Subjunctive indicates an act or a state that is dependent on, and subsequent to, what precedes the subjunctive particle.

The most important of particles that take the Subjunctive are:

أَنْ *an* 'that' (very frequently translated in other words, such as 'to')

لِ *li*-and حَتَّى *ḥattā*'so that', 'until';

لِأَنْ *li-an*, كَيْ *kay* and لِكَيْ *likay*, which all mean 'so that', feature rarely in the Qur'ān.

لَنْ *lan* 'not'—a strong denial of the future (formed originally from لَا أَنْ *lā-an*).

The negative used with the Subjunctive after these subordinating particles is normally لَا *lā* , but see note 3 on أَنْ *an* on p. 115.

أَنْ لَا *an lā* normally becomes أَلَّا *allā*. لِ *li*-cannot be used with a negative.

EXAMPLES OF THE USE OF THE SUBJUNCTIVE:

[34:33] تَأْمُرُونَنَا أَنْ نَكْفُرَ بِٱللّٰهِ

you command us not to believe in God

[2:214] أَمْ حَسِبْتُمْ أَنْ تَدْخُلُوا ٱلْجَنَّةَ

do you think that you will enter Paradise?

[5:71] حَسِبُوا أَلَّا تَكُونَ فِتْنَةٌ

they thought that there would be no mischief

[10:67] جَعَلَ لَكُمُ ٱللَّيْلَ لِتَسْكُنُوا فِيهِ

he made the night for you to rest in

[5:22] لَنْ نَدْخُلَهَا حَتَّى يَخْرُجُوا مِنْهَا

we won't enter it till they leave it

It is important to note that the subjunctive particle requires the Subjunctive only in the verb that it governs or a verb that is made parallel to the first subjunctive by *wa-*, *fa-*, *aw* or *thumma*.

Take the first example above. Taking the text further, it runs:

[34:33] تَأْمُرُونَنَا أَنْ نَكْفُرَ بِٱللّٰهِ وَنَجْعَلَ لَهُ أَنْدَادًا

you command us not to believe in God
and establish rivals to him

Any verb that occurs in another clause within the subjunctive clause **will be in the indicative** unless it too is governed by a subjunctive particle, *e.g.*:

[11:87] أَصَلَاتُكَ تَأْمُرُكَ أَنْ نَتْرُكَ مَا يَعْبُدُ آبَاؤُنَا

does your prayer tell you that we should abandon what our forefathers have served?

7:129 has *an* and three subjunctives but then reverts to the indicative after *kayfa*:

عَسَىٰ رَبُّكُمْ أَنْ يُهْلِكَ عَدُوَّكُمْ وَيَسْتَخْلِفَكُمْ فِي ٱلْأَرْضِ
فَيَنْظُرَ كَيْفَ تَعْمَلُونَ [A]

it may be that your Lord will destroy your enemy and make you successors in the land to see how you act

The Subjunctive is used in these examples because the act or state mentioned in the subordinate clause is dependent on the main verb and subsequent to it in time. However, *an* may be followed by another tense, normally the perfect, if the verb governing it does not indicate any expectation or effect. This is normally the Perfect.

[11:69] مَا لَبِثَ أَنْ جَاءَ بِعِجْلٍ حَنِيذٍ

soon he came with a roast calf

[5:113] نَعْلَمُ أَنْ قَدْ صَدَقْتَنَا

we know that you have told us the truth

The same applies to *ḥattā* when it has the meaning 'until':

[10:93] مَا ٱخْتَلَفُوا حَتَّىٰ جَاءَهُمُ ٱلْعِلْمُ

they did not disagree until knowledge came to them

The Subjunctive of *kāna* conjugates as follows:

	SINGULAR	DUAL	PLURAL
3 m.	يَكُونَ	يَكُونَا	يَكُونُوا
3 f.	تَكُونَ	تَكُونَا	يَكُنَّ

[A] For the verb عَسَىٰ *ʿasā*see Lesson 37.

2 m.	تَكُونَ	تَكُونَا	تَكُونُوا
2 f.	تَكُونِي	تَكُونَا	تَكُنَّ
1	أَكُونَ	–	نَكُونَ

NOTES ON أَنْ *an*

1. It is common in Arabic for *an* clauses to be preceded by prepositions. Thus we find أَمَرَنِي أَنْ أَذْهَبَ *amara-nī an adhhaba* and أَمَرَنِي بِأَنْ أَذْهَبَ *amara-nī bi-an adhhaba*. The Arab grammarians point out that *an* clauses are the equivalent of *maṣdars*, and so أَمَرَنِي بِأَنْ أَذْهَبَ *amara-nī bi-an adhhaba* is the equivalent of أَمَرَنِي بِٱلذَّهَابِ *amara-nī bi-l-dhahābi*. All three mean 'he told me to go'. In the Qur'ān this use of prepositions with *an* clauses is rare: it is confined to ʿ*alā* (acting both in its own right and as the preposition taken by the participle قَادِرٌ *qādir* 'able to').

2. *An* is found in combination with both قَبْلَ *qabla* / مِنْ قَبْلِ *min qabli* and بَعْدَ *baʿda* / مِنْ بَعْدِ *min baʿdi* to form conjunctions meaning 'before' and 'after' respectively. Some examples have the Subjunctive and some the Perfect, *e.g.*:

[18:109] نَفِدَ ٱلْبَحْرُ قَبْلَ أَنْ تَنْفَدَ كَلِمَاتُ رَبِّي

the sea would be exhausted before the words of my Lord would be exhausted

[12:100] بَعْدَ أَنْ نَزَغَ ٱلشَّيْطَانُ بَيْنِي وَبَيْنَ إِخْوَتِي

after Satan caused dissension between me and my brothers

3. In some verses the negative used after *an* is *lan* and not *lā*.

[72:7] ظَنُّوا أَنْ لَنْ يَبْعَثَ ٱللَّهُ أَحَدًا

they thought that God would not raise anyone

There are further uses of *an*, dealt with in Lesson 37.

أَنَّ *anna*

The use of *an* with the perfect is relatively rare because there is a related particle which is normally used in factual statements. This is أَنَّ *anna*. It is essential to remember that while the two particles have some linkage in meaning **they differ totally in the construction they require**.

Anna takes an accusative, which must follow it **immediately** except in the one special case set out below. The accusative after *anna* may be a noun (or a pronoun like *hādhā*) or a pronominal suffix.

Examples:

[6:150] يَشْهَدُونَ أَنَّ ٱللَّهَ حَرَّمَ هٰذَا

they bear witness that God forbade this

[28:75] عَلِمُوا أَنَّ ٱلْحَقَّ لِلَّهِ

they will know that the truth belongs to God

[2:26] يَعْلَمُونَ أَنَّهُ ٱلْحَقُّ مِنْ رَبِّهِمْ

they know that it is the truth from their Lord

[59:17] كَانَ عَاقِبَتَهُمَا أَنَّهُمَا فِي ٱلنَّارِ

the consequence for both of them is that they will be in the fire

NOTES ON أَنَّ *anna*

1. Note that the rest of the sentence follows normal rules, as though the accusative after *anna* were a nominative. Under no circumstances can *anna* take a double accusative.
2. The only case in which a phrase can be placed between *anna* and its accusative is when the subordinate clause consists of an indefinite subject with a prepositional phrase as predicate.

In such a case the rules for prepositional predicate sentences have priority:

[69:49] نَعْلَمُ أَنَّ مِنْكُمْ مُكَذِّبِينَ

we know that some of you will deny the truth

It should be clear from the above sentences that the only requirement after *anna* is the following accusative. This accusative is essential, but, as set out in Note 1, the rest of the sentence follows the normal grammatical rules, as though the word in the accusative were a nominative.

3. *Anna* and the first person singular pronominal suffix produce two forms: *annī* and *anna-nī*. Likewise *anna* and the first person plural pronominal suffix produce *annā* and *anna-nā*.
4. The Qur'ān has *bi-anna* with the meaning 'because', *dhālika bi-anna*... 'that is because' being a common phrase:

[9:80] ذٰلِكَ بِأَنَّهُمْ كَفَرُوا بِٱللّٰهِ

that is because they disbelieve in God

[9:6] ذٰلِكَ بِأَنَّهُمْ قَوْمٌ لَا يَعْلَمُونَ

that is because they are a people who do not know

FURTHER NOTES ON أَنْ *an* AND أَنَّ *anna*

It is impossible to have the Subjunctive after *anna*, just as it is impossible to have an *anna* type accusative after *an*.

Though *an* and *anna* normally introduce indirect statements, it is sometimes the case that the clause introduced by *an* or *anna* turns out to be the subject of the sentence:

[2:280] وَأَنْ تَصَدَّقُوا خَيْرٌ لَكُمْ [A]

for you to remit [the debt] as alms is better for you

As a simple working rule remember:

an + subjunctive; *anna* + accusative.

[A] This is a shortened form of *tataṣaddaqū*—see Lesson 15.

This is of course a simplification, but if you stick to it you will get an important area of grammar correct.

VOCABULARY EIGHTEEN

PERFECT	IMPERFECT	VERBAL NOUN	
حَسِبَ	يَحْسَبُ	مَحْسِبَةٌ	to think, reckon
حَكَمَ	يَحْكُمُ	حُكْمٌ	to judge, decide
سَكَنَ	يَسْكُنُ	سُكُونٌ	to dwell, be at rest
طَمِعَ	يَطْمَعُ	طَمَعٌ	to desire
عَجَزَ	يَعْجِزُ	عَجْزٌ	to be unable
نَزَغَ	يَنْزَغُ	نَزْغٌ	to cause strife, dissension
نَفِدَ	يَنْفَدُ	نَفَادٌ	to be exhausted
حَرَّمَ 2	يُحَرِّمُ	تَحْرِيمٌ	to forbid, prohibit
نَزَّلَ 2	يُنَزِّلُ	تَنْزِيلٌ	to send down
أَنْذَرَ 4	يُنْذِرُ	إِنْذَارٌ	to warn
بَايَعَ 3	يُبَايِعُ	مُبَايَعَةٌ	to do allegiance to
أَدْخَلَ 4	يُدْخِلُ	إِدْخَالٌ	to cause to enter
ذَبَحَ	يَذْبَحُ	ذَبْحٌ	to sacrifice
أَسْخَطَ 4	يُسْخِطُ	إِسْخَاطٌ	to vex
أَشْرَكَ 4	يُشْرِكُ	إِشْرَاكٌ	to ascribe partners to
تَصَدَّقَ 5	يَتَصَدَّقُ	تَصَدُّقٌ	to give alms

SINGULAR	PLURAL	
بَقَرَةٌ		cow

Singular	Plural	
جَزَاءٌ		recompense
خَطِيئَةٌ	خَطِيئَاتٌ / خَطَايَا	sin
عِجْلٌ		calf
عَاقِبَةٌ		end, consequuence
لَحْمٌ		flesh
مَالٌ	أَمْوَالٌ	property
حَنِيذٌ		roast
وَسَطٌ		middle
غُرَابٌ		crow

Exercise Eighteen

1. يَسْأَلُكَ أَهْلُ ٱلْكِتَابِ أَنْ تُنَزِّلَ عَلَيْهِمْ كِتَابًا مِنَ ٱلسَّمَآءِ [4:153]
2. جَعَلْنَاكُمْ أُمَّةً وَسَطًا لِتَكُونُوا شُهَدَآءَ عَلَى ٱلنَّاسِ [2:143]
3. كَرِهُوا أَنْ يُجَاهِدُوا بِأَمْوَالِهِمْ وَأَنْفُسِهِمْ فِي سَبِيلِ ٱللهِ [9:81]
4. جَزَآؤُهُمْ أَنَّ عَلَيْهِمْ لَعْنَةَ ٱللهِ [3:87]
5. يُبَايِعْنَكَ عَلَى أَنْ لَا يُشْرِكْنَ بِٱللهِ شَيْئًا [60:12]
6. أَعَجَزْتُ أَنْ أَكُونَ مِثْلَ هٰذَا ٱلْغُرَابِ [5:31]
7. ذٰلِكَ بِأَنَّهُمُ ٱتَّبَعُوا مَا أَسْخَطَ ٱللهَ [47:28]
8. آيَتُكَ أَلَّا تُكَلِّمَ ٱلنَّاسَ ثَلَاثَ لَيَالٍ [19:10]
9. نَزَلَ بِهِ عَلَى قَلْبِكَ لِتَكُونَ مِنَ ٱلْمُنْذِرِينَ [26:193-4]
10. نَطْمَعُ أَنْ يُدْخِلَنَا رَبُّنَا مَعَ ٱلْقَوْمِ ٱلصَّالِحِينَ [5:84]

11. لَنْ يُؤَخِّرَ ٱللَّهُ نَفْسًا [63:11]

12. إِنَّ ٱللَّهَ يَأْمُرُكُمْ أَنْ تَذْبَحُوا بَقَرَةً [2:67]

13. هُوَ ٱلْحَقُّ مِنْ رَبِّكَ لِتُنْذِرَ قَوْمًا [32:3]

14. يُبَشِّرُ ٱلْمُؤْمِنِينَ أَنَّ لَهُمْ أَجْرًا كَبِيرًا [17:9]

15. جَعَلْنَا ٱللَّيْلَ لِيَسْكُنُوا فِيهِ [27:86]

16. هُوَ ٱلْقَادِرُ عَلَى أَنْ يَبْعَثَ عَلَيْكُمْ عَذَابًا [6:65]

17. تَبَيَّنَ لَهُمْ أَنَّهُمْ أَصْحَابُ ٱلْجَحِيمِ [A] [9:113]

18. تَبَيَّنَ لَهُ أَنَّهُ عَدُوٌّ لِلَّهِ [9:114]

19. وَكَتَبْنَا عَلَيْهِمْ فِيهَا أَنَّ ٱلنَّفْسَ بِٱلنَّفْسِ وَٱلْعَيْنَ بِٱلْعَيْنِ [5:45]

20. سَخَّرَ ٱلْبَحْرَ لِتَأْكُلُوا مِنْهُ لَحْمًا [16:14]

21. ذٰلِكَ جَزَآؤُهُمْ بِأَنَّهُمْ كَفَرُوا بِآيَاتِنَا [17:98]

22. إِنَّا نَطْمَعُ أَنْ يَغْفِرَ لَنَا رَبُّنَا خَطَايَانَا [26:51]

23. أَوَلَا يَذْكُرُ ٱلْإِنْسَانُ أَنَّا خَلَقْنَاهُ [19:67]

24. وَأَنْزَلَ مَعَهُمُ ٱلْكِتَابَ بِٱلْحَقِّ لِيَحْكُمَ بَيْنَ ٱلنَّاسِ [2:213]

25. هَلْ أَتَّبِعُكَ عَلَى أَنْ تُعَلِّمَنِي [18:66]

[A] *Al-Jaḥīmu* and *Jahannam* (p. 125) are two of the names for Hell.

Lesson Nineteen
Inna

Anna is only one of a number of particles that take an accusative, with the rest of the sentence or clause acting as though that accusative were a nominative. Of these the most important is إِنَّ *inna*—in fact, this is the word with which the construction originated. *Inna* is really a fossilized verb, which makes it easier to understand why the accusative is required.

Inna is commonly translated as 'indeed' or even 'verily', but neither rendering is adequate to give the effect of the word. In most cases it is best left untranslated.

Like *anna*, *inna* and the first person singular pronominal suffix produce two forms: *innī* and *inna-nī*; *inna* and the first person plural pronominal suffix produce *innā* and *inna-nā*.

Inna has three main functions:

a) to give emphasis (hence its translation as 'indeed')
b) to allow a change in word order, with the subject preceding the verb
c) to act as a slightly disjunctive 'marker'

The catch is that it may have one, two or all of these functions at once. Experience alone will tell you which.

Simple examples of the use of *inna*:

إِنَّ ٱللَّهَ مَعَ ٱلصَّابِرِينَ	God is with the patient
إِنَّهُمْ عِبَادُكَ	they are Your servants
إِنَّ خَلَقْنَاهُمْ مِنْ تُرَابٍ	We created them from dust
إِنَّ أَرْضِي وَاسِعَةٌ	My land is wide
إِنَّ مَعَ ٱلْعُسْرِ يُسْرًا	there is some ease with [all] the difficulty

Notes on the use of *inna*

1. It is common for the second half of a sentence introduced by *inna* to be prefixed by *la-*. In such cases it is immaterial whether the second half of the sentence is a predicate or a deferred subject.

إِنَّ رَبَّكَ لَذُو مَغْفِرَةٍ	your Lord is forgiving
إِنَّ فِي ذٰلِكَ لَآيَةً لَكُمْ	in that there is a sign for you

2. When *inna* has been followed by a pronominal suffix, one may still find that cluster followed by a nominative pronoun.

إِنَّكُمْ أَنْتُمُ ٱلظَّالِمُونَ	you are the wrong-doers
إِنَّكَ أَنْتَ ٱلْوَهَّابُ	you are the Forgiving

3. It is not uncommon for *inna* to have the pronominal suffix *-hu* attached to it and then for the rest of the sentence to move off in a completely different direction. In effect, the only role of the suffix in such circumstances is to meet the grammatical requirements of *inna*. This is also true of *anna*.

إِنَّهُ أَنَا ٱللّٰهُ ٱلْعَزِيزُ ٱلْحَكِيمُ	I am God, the Mighty and Decisive
إِنَّهُ لَا يُفْلِحُ ٱلظَّالِمُونَ	the wrong-doers will not prosper

THE USE OF *qāla*

The most striking use of the 'marker' function is after the verb *qāla* 'to say', the perfect of which was given in Lesson 12. The imperfect and subjunctive conjugate in the same way as those of *kāna*.

Imperfect

	SINGULAR	DUAL	PLURAL
3 m.	يَقُولُ	يَقُولَانِ	يَقُولُونَ
3 f.	تَقُولُ	تَقُولَانِ	يَقُلْنَ
2 m.	تَقُولُ	تَقُولَانِ	تَقُولُونَ
2 f.	تَقُولِينَ	تَقُولَانِ	تَقُلْنَ
1	أَقُولُ	–	نَقُولُ

Subjunctive

	SINGULAR	DUAL	PLURAL
3 m.	يَقُولَ	يَقُولَا	يَقُولُوا
3 f.	تَقُولَ	تَقُولَا	يَقُلْنَ
2 m.	تَقُولَ	تَقُولَا	تَقُولُوا
2 f.	تَقُولِي	تَقُولَا	تَقُلْنَ
1	أَقُولَ	–	نَقُولَ

Whereas other verbs in Arabic readily have indirect statements introduced by *an* or *anna*, this is not the case with *qāla*. In all normal circumstances it is followed by:

a) direct speech, not introduced by *inna*;
b) direct speech, introduced by *inna*;
c) indirect speech, also introduced by *inna*.

The third instance is rare in the Qur'ān.

Examples of *qāla* followed by *inna* and direct speech:

قَالَ إِنِّي سَقِيمٌ	he said, 'I am ill.'
قَالَ إِنَّ هٰؤُلَاءِ ضَيْفِي	he said, 'These are my guests.'

قَالُوا إِنَّا نَصَارَى they said, 'We are Christians.'

Examples of *qāla* followed immediately by direct speech without *inna*:

قَالَ ٱلْكَافِرُونَ هٰذَا سَاحِرٌ the unbelievers said, 'This is a sorcerer.'

قَالَتْ أَنَّى يَكُونُ لِي غُلَامٌ she said, 'How can I have a son?'

Very occasionally other verbs are followed by *inna* and direct speech, *e.g.*:

[36:16] رَبُّنَا يَعْلَمُ إِنَّا إِلَيْكُمْ مُرْسَلُونَ

our Lord knows we are sent to you

[63:1] نَشْهَدُ إِنَّكَ لَرَسُولُ ٱللّٰهِ

we bear witness that you are God's messenger

Vocabulary Nineteen

Perfect	Imperfect	Verbal noun	
جَمَعَ	يَجْمَعُ	جَمْعٌ	to gather, collect
غَفَلَ	يَغْفُلُ	غَفْلَةٌ	to be heedless, forget
3 خَادَعَ	يُخَادِعُ	خِدَاعٌ	to try to deceive
4 أَحْسَنَ	يُحْسِنُ	إِحْسَانٌ	to do good
4 أَفْلَحَ	يُفْلِحُ	إِفْلَاحٌ	to prosper
4 أَخْلَصَ	يُخْلِصُ	إِخْلَاصٌ	to be sincere

Singular	Plural	
تُرَابٌ		earth, dust
زَلْزَلَةٌ		earthquake
شَيْخٌ		old man

Singular	Plural	
ضَيْفٌ		guest; guests
عَدْلٌ		justice
عُسْرٌ		difficulty
غُلَامٌ		boy, son
نَعَمٌ	أَنْعَامٌ	animal, beast
يُسْرٌ		ease
سَقِيمٌ		sick, ill
أَصْفَرُ	صُفْرٌ / صَفْرَاءُ (f.)	yellow
مُنَافِقٌ		hypocrite
وَهَّابٌ		forgiving
بَشِيرٌ		bearer of good news/tidings

Exercise Nineteen

1. إِنَّا إِلَيْهِ رَاجِعُونَ [2:156]
2. إِنَّكَ جَامِعُ ٱلنَّاسِ [3:9]
3. إِنَّ كَذٰلِكَ نَفْعَلُ بِٱلْمُجْرِمِينَ [37:34]
4. قَالُوا إِنَّا إِلَى رَبِّنَا مُنْقَلِبُونَ [7:125]
5. إِنَّ ٱللّٰهَ يَأْمُرُ بِٱلْعَدْلِ وَٱلْإِحْسَانِ [16:90]
6. إِنَّ جَعَلْنَاكَ خَلِيفَةً فِي ٱلْأَرْضِ [38:26]
7. إِنَّ جَهَنَّمَ جَزَاؤُكُمْ [17:63]
8. إِنَّكَ لَمَجْنُونٌ [15:6]
9. إِنَّ ٱللّٰهَ غَفُورٌ رَحِيمٌ [2:173]

10. قَالَ ٱلْكَافِرُونَ إِنَّ هٰذَا لَسَاحِرٌ مُبِينٌ [10:2]

11. إِنَّ لَنْ نَدْخُلَهَا [5:22]

12. إِنَّ ٱللّٰهَ عَدُوٌّ لِلْكَافِرِينَ [2:98]

13. إِنَّا أَنْزَلْنَا إِلَيْكَ ٱلْكِتَابَ بِٱلْحَقِّ [4:105]

14. إِنَّ لَهُ أَبًا شَيْخًا كَبِيرًا [12:78]

15. إِنَّهُ مِنْ عِبَادِنَا ٱلْمُخْلَصِينَ [12:24]

16. إِنَّ هٰذَا لَشَيْءٌ عَجِيبٌ [11:72]

17. إِنَّ ٱلشَّيْطَانَ لِلْإِنْسَانِ عَدُوٌّ مُبِينٌ [12:5]

18. إِنَّهُ مِنَ ٱلصَّالِحِينَ [21:75]

19. إِنَّهُ بِمَا تَعْمَلُونَ بَصِيرٌ [11:112]

20. إِنَّ زَلْزَلَةَ ٱلسَّاعَةِ شَيْءٌ عَظِيمٌ [22:1]

21. إِنَّهَا بَقَرَةٌ صَفْرَاءُ [2:69]

22. إِنَّ ٱللّٰهَ عَلَىٰ كُلِّ شَيْءٍ قَدِيرٌ [2:148]

23. إِنِّي تَوَكَّلْتُ عَلَى ٱللّٰهِ [11:56]

24. إِنَّ كَثِيرًا مِنَ ٱلنَّاسِ عَنْ آيَاتِنَا لَغَافِلُونَ [10:92]

25. إِنَّ لَكُمْ فِي ٱلْأَنْعَامِ لَعِبْرَةً [23:21]

26. أَلَا إِنَّ لِلّٰهِ مَا فِي ٱلسَّمٰوَاتِ وَٱلْأَرْضِ [24:64]

27. إِنَّ ٱلْمُنَافِقِينَ يُخَادِعُونَ ٱللّٰهَ [4:142]

28. إِنَّا أَرْسَلْنَاكَ بِٱلْحَقِّ بَشِيرًا وَنَذِيرًا [35:24]

29. قَالُوا شَهِدْنَا عَلَىٰ أَنْفُسِنَا [6:130]

30. قَالُوا وَجَدْنَا آبَاءَنَا لَهَا عَابِدِينَ [21:53]

Lesson Twenty
The Jussive

Like the Subjunctive, the Jussive is closely related in form to the Imperfect Indicative. With the Jussive the final short vowel changes from the *u* of the Indicative and the *a* of the Subjunctive to a *sukūn*. However, when the following word begins with a prosthetic vowel the *sukūn* changes to a *kasra*. In other persons there is no difference between the forms of the Subjunctive and the Jussive. Learn the basic form of the Jussive from the table below.

	Singular	Dual	Plural
3 m.	يَكْتُبْ	يَكْتُبَا	يَكْتُبُوا
3 f.	تَكْتُبْ	تَكْتُبَا	يَكْتُبْنَ
2 m.	تَكْتُبْ	تَكْتُبَا	تَكْتُبُوا
2 f.	تَكْتُبِي	تَكْتُبَا	تَكْتُبْنَ
1	أَكْتُبْ	–	نَكْتُبْ

The Jussive of *kāna* is:

	Singular	Dual	Plural
3 m.	يَكُنْ	يَكُونَا	يَكُونُوا
3 f.	تَكُنْ	تَكُونَا	يَكُنَّ
2 m.	تَكُنْ	تَكُونَا	تَكُونُوا
2 f.	تَكُونِي	تَكُونَا	تَكُنَّ
1	أَكُنْ	–	نَكُنْ

In the Qur'ān there are occasions on which the forms of *yakun, takun, akun* and *nakun* become *yaku, taku, aku* and *naku*. These forms are common in poetry but rare elsewhere. The important thing is to be able to recognise them for the forms they are. There are no such problems with the jussive of *qāla*, which is:

	SINGULAR	DUAL	PLURAL
3 m.	يَقُلْ	يَقُولَا	يَقُولُوا
3 f.	تَقُلْ	تَقُولَا	يَقُلْنَ
2 m.	تَقُلْ	تَقُولَا	تَقُولُوا
2 f.	تَقُولِي	تَقُولَا	تَقُلْنَ
1	أَقُلْ	–	نَقُلْ

The Jussive has four uses:

1. It is used after the negative particle لَمْ *lam* 'not' (and the rare لَمَّا *lammā* 'not yet').

   In dealing with *lam* + the Jussive, grammarians normally say something akin to Wright's view that it 'invariably has the meaning *of mā* + the perfect' (*Grammar*, 2, 24). However, this is not true either of the Qur'ān or of early Arabic in general, where *lam* + the Jussive usually has a past meaning but sometimes a present meaning:

   [2:260] أَوَلَمْ تُؤْمِنْ
   do you not believe?

   [5:40] أَلَمْ تَعْلَمْ أَنَّ ٱللّٰهَ لَهُ مُلْكُ ٱلسَّمٰوَاتِ وَٱلْأَرْضِ
   do you not know that God has sovereignty over the heavens and the earth?

   [9:78] أَلَمْ يَعْلَمُوا أَنَّ ٱللّٰهَ يَعْلَمُ سِرَّهُمْ
   do they not know that God knows their secret?

   [17:111] لَمْ يَكُنْ لَهُ وَلِيٌّ
   he has no protector

2. After the negative *lā*, the Jussive is used to express prohibitions:

لَا تَحْزَنْ	do not be sad
لَا تُفْسِدُوا فِي ٱلْأَرْضِ	do not cause mischief in the earth
لَا تَكُونُوا أَوَّلَ كَافِرٍ	do not be the first infidel

3. After لِ *li-* , فَلْ *fal-* or وَلْ *wal-* , the Jussive is used to express indirect commands:

لِيُنْفِقْ ذُو سَعَةٍ مِنْ سَعَتِهِ	let the man of substance spend some of his substance
وَلْنَحْمِلْ خَطَايَاكُمْ	let us bear your sins
عَلَى ٱللّٰهِ فَلْيَتَوَكَّلِ ٱلْمُؤْمِنُونَ	let the believers trust in God

4. In conditional sentences (see Lesson 36).

Vocabulary Twenty

Perfect	Imperfect	Verbal noun	
حَزِنَ	يَحْزَنُ	حُزْنٌ	to be sad
عَرَفَ	يَعْرِفُ	مَعْرِفَةٌ	to know, recognize
قَرِبَ	يَقْرَبُ	قُرْبٌ	to come near, approach
نَقَضَ	يَنْقُضُ	نَقْضٌ	to break one's oath
أَفْسَدَ	يُفْسِدُ	فَسَادٌ	to cause mischief

Singular	Plural	
حُلُمٌ		puberty
سِرٌّ	أَسْرَارٌ	secret

Singular	Plural	
شَجَرَةٌ	شَجَرٌ	tree
كُفُوٌّ		equal
سَعَةٌ		wealth

Exercise Twenty

1. [2:6] لَمْ تُنْذِرْهُمْ
2. [2:151] يُعَلِّمُكُمْ مَا لَمْ تَكُونُوا تَعْلَمُونَ
3. [18:42] لَمْ أُشْرِكْ بِرَبِّي أَحَدًا
4. [17:111] لَمْ يَكُنْ لَهُ وَلِيٌّ
5. [22:70] أَلَمْ تَعْلَمْ أَنَّ ٱللَّهَ يَعْلَمُ مَا فِي ٱلسَّمَآءِ وَٱلْأَرْضِ
6. [25:2] لَمْ يَكُنْ لَهُ شَرِيكٌ فِي ٱلْمُلْكِ
7. [24:58] لَمْ يَبْلُغُوا ٱلْحُلُمَ
8. [24:40] لَمْ يَجْعَلِ ٱللَّهُ لَهُ نُورًا
9. [68:28] أَلَمْ أَقُلْ لَكُمْ
10. [46:35] لَا تَسْتَعْجِلْ
11. [48:27] فَعَلِمَ مَا لَمْ تَعْلَمُوا
12. [50:6] أَفَلَمْ يَنْظُرُوا إِلَى ٱلسَّمَآءِ فَوْقَهُمْ
13. [96:5] عَلَّمَ ٱلْإِنْسَانَ مَا لَمْ يَعْلَمْ
14. [71:25] فَلَمْ يَجِدُوا لَهُمْ مِنْ دُونِ ٱللَّهِ أَنْصَارًا
15. [90:8] أَلَمْ نَجْعَلْ لَهُ عَيْنَيْنِ

16. أَلَمْ نُهْلِكِ ٱلْأَوَّلِينَ [77:16]

17. لَمْ تَكُونُوا مُؤْمِنِينَ [37:29]

18. لَمْ يَسْمَعْهَا [31:7]

19. أَلَمْ يَعِدْكُمْ رَبُّكُمْ وَعْدًا حَسَنًا [20:86]

20. لَا تَقْرَبَا هَٰذِهِ ٱلشَّجَرَةَ [2:35]

21. لَمْ يَكُنْ لَهُ كُفُوًا أَحَدٌ [112:4]

22. لَا تَحْزَنِي [28:7]

23. لَا تَعْبُدِ ٱلشَّيْطَانَ [19:44]

24. لَا تَسْأَلْنِي عَنْ شَيْءٍ [18:70]

25. لَا تَكُنْ مَعَ ٱلْكَافِرِينَ [11:42]

26. لَا تَقْتُلُوا أَوْلَادَكُمْ [17:31]

27. لَا تَنْقُضُوا ٱلْأَيْمَانَ [16:91]

28. لَا تَدْخُلُوا مِنْ بَابٍ وَاحِدٍ [12:67]

Lesson Twenty-One
Laysa; idh; idhā; man

لَيْسَ *laysa*

You already know that *kāna* is not used in the Imperfect to give the sense of 'is'. However, there is a verb that is used to mean 'is not'. This is *laysa*. It has a present meaning (and only a present meaning), but its forms in the only tense that exists resemble those of a Perfect (of sorts):

	Singular	Dual	Plural
3 m.	لَيْسَ	لَيْسَا	لَيْسُو
3 f.	لَيْسَتْ	لَيْسَتَا	لَسْنَ
2 m.	لَسْتَ	لَسْتُمَا	لَسْتُمْ
2 f.	لَسْتِ	لَسْتُمَا	لَسْتُنَّ
1	لَسْتُ	–	لَسْنَا

The predicate of *laysa* is introduced either by *bi-* and the genitive or, less frequently, by the accusative. You have already seen this with the Ḥijāzī *mā* in Lesson 10. What appears to have happened is that in the Ḥijāz the usage of *mā* was assimilated to the usage of *laysa*.

أَلَيْسَ آللّٰهُ بِعَزِيزٍ	is not God mighty?
لَسْتُ عَلَيْكُمْ بِوَكِيلٍ	I am not a guardian over you
لَسْتَ مُرْسَلًا	you are not someone sent as a messenger

إِذْ *idh* AND إِذَا *idhā*

Idh and *idhā* are two closely related particles that developed from an obsolete noun *idh(un)* 'time'.

In general *idh* as a conjunction means 'when' or 'since'. The only exception to this is when it is used with *qabla* or *baʿda* to form compound conjuctions; *qabla idh* 'before' and *baʿda idh* 'after'.

Idh is most commonly followed by the perfect but imperfect and nominal sentences also occur. In the Qur'ān the ratio is 15:3:1, and *idh* almost always means 'when'. There are a couple of possible exceptions as well as a handful of examples in which *idh* is followed by *lam*, but these are unlikely to cause difficulties. Typical Qur'ānic examples are:

[15:52] إِذْ دَخَلُوا عَلَيْهِ

when they went in to see him

[3:153] إِذْ تُصْعِدُونَ

when you were climbing (the hill)

[6:93] إِذِ ٱلظَّالِمُونَ فِي غَمَرَاتِ ٱلْمَوْتِ

when the sinners are in death's pangs

In the Qur'ān the combination *wa-idh* at the beginning of a verse has a specific and highly idiomatic use to introduce a piece of narrative. The only convincing way that this can be rendered into English is to translate it as 'and [remember] when ...', unless it occurs in a series (e.g. in verses 2:49, 50, 51, 53, 54, 55) when the 'remember' is required only on the first occasion. This translation of *wa-idh* is confirmed by a handful of examples in which the Imperative 'remember' actually occurs. Here are a couple of examples:

[15:28] وَإِذْ قَالَ رَبُّكَ لِلْمَلَائِكَةِ

remember when your Lord said to the angels...

[33:7] وَإِذْ أَخَذْنَا مِنَ ٱلنَّبِيِّينَ مِيثَاقَهُمْ

remember when we took from the prophets their covenant...

Idhā has two functions:

1. As a conjunction meaning 'when', 'as often as', *idhā* is normally followed by the Perfect, though the Imperfect is sometimes found. Usually it implies a condition, and then its construction is normally that of a conditional sentence [see Lesson 36].
   A fuller form *idhā-mā* is also found from time to time, also with the construction of conditional sentences.
   One striking and somewhat unusual use of the conjuction *idhā* occurs in early Meccan *sūras*, where *idhā* is used in an exclamatory, almost oath-like way. *Sūra* 81, for example, starts with twelve examples of this, and *Sūra* 82 with four. In such cases the subject may precede the verb:

   [82:1] إِذَا ٱلسَّمَاءُ ٱنْفَطَرَتْ

   when the heavens are split asunder

2. If *idhā* is followed by a noun or pronoun, it acts as an interjection with the meaning 'lo', 'behold'. This is much less common than the conjunction *idhā*. In most examples of this usage, *idhā* is followed by a third person pronoun:

نَزَعَ يَدَهُ فَإِذَا هِيَ بَيْضَاءُ	he withdrew his hand and, behold, it was white
فَإِذَا هُمْ يَنْظُرُونَ	behold, they look on
إِذَا هُمْ يَسْخَطُونَ	behold, they are vexed

However, sometimes nouns follow *idhā* in this construction:

[24:48] إِذَا فَرِيقٌ مِنْهُمْ مُعْرِضُونَ

behold, a group of them turning away

مَنْ *man*

You have already read of the use of *mā* as a relative pronoun meaning 'that which' in Lesson 10 and of the use of *mā* and *man* as interrogative pronouns meaning 'what?' and 'who?' in Lesson 17. It will therefore come as no surprise to learn that *man* also operates as a relative pronoun 'he who', 'she who' or 'those who'. Under all normal circumstances, *man* is treated grammatically as a masculine singular, even when it refers to the feminine or the plural.

Examples of *man* as singular:

مَنْ وَجَدْنَا مَتَاعَنَا عِنْدَهُ	the one in whose possession we found our goods
أَتَجْعَلُ فِيهَا مَنْ يُفْسِدُ فِيهَا	will you place in it someone who will cause mischief in it?
اَلْبِرُّ مَنِ ٱتَّقَى	the pious man is the one who fears God

Examples of *man* as singular/plural:[A]

مَنْ كَفَرَ فَعَلَيْهِ كُفْرُهُ	whoever disbelieves bears the consequence of his unbelief
مَنْ عَمِلَ صَالِحًا فَلِنَفْسِهِ	whoever acts righteously it is to his own advantage

Examples of *man* as plural:

ذُرِّيَّةَ مَنْ حَمَلْنَا مَعَ نُوحٍ

the descendants of those whom we carried with Noah

لَا يَعْلَمُ مَنْ فِي ٱلسَّمَاوَاتِ وَٱلْأَرْضِ ٱلْغَيْبَ

those who are in the heavens and earth do not know the unseen

تُنْذِرُ مَنِ ٱتَّبَعَ ٱلذِّكْرَ

you warn those who follow the reminder

أَفَأَنْتَ تُنْقِذُ مَنْ فِي ٱلنَّارِ

can you rescue those who are in the fire?

[A] On the use of *fa-* in the following examples see Lesson 36.

Vocabulary Twenty-One

Perfect	Imperfect	Verbal noun	
رَكَضَ	يَرْكُضُ	رَكْضٌ	to run
صَعِدَ	يَصْعَدُ	صُعُودٌ	to ascend
زَيَّنَ 2	يُزَيِّنُ	تَزْيِينٌ	to cause to seem good
وَاعَدَ 3	يُواعِدُ	مُواعَدَةٌ	to make an agreement with
عَاهَدَ 3	يُعَاهِدُ	مُعَاهَدَةٌ	to make a covenant with
أَسْلَمَ 4	يُسْلِمُ	إِسْلَامٌ	to submit
أَخْطَأَ 4	يُخْطِئُ	إِخْطَاءٌ	to make a mistake
أَغْرَقَ 4	يُغْرِقُ	إِغْرَاقٌ	to drown
أَعْرَضَ 4	يُعْرِضُ	إِعْرَاضٌ	to turn away
اِنْفَطَرَ 7	يَنْفَطِرُ	اِنْفِطَارٌ	to be split
أَنْقَذَ 4	يُنْقِذُ	إِنْقَاذٌ	to save

Singular	Plural	
مَثْوًى		lodging
جِنٌّ		*Jinn*
حِزْبٌ	أَحْزَابٌ	party
ذُرِّيَّةٌ		seed, offspring, descendants
غَمْرَةٌ	غَمَرَاتٌ	pang
قَبْرٌ	قُبُورٌ	grave

Singular	Plural	
اَلْغَيْبُ		the unseen
جُنَاحٌ		sin
مِيثَاقٌ		covenant, pledge
قَاعِدٌ	قُعُودٌ	seated
مِصْرُ		Egypt
بِغَيْرِ		without

Exercise Twenty-One

1. [46:34] أَلَيْسَ هٰذَا بِٱلْحَقِّ
2. [42:11] لَيْسَ كَمِثْلِهِ شَيْءٌ
3. [48:11] يَقُولُونَ بِأَلْسِنَتِهِمْ مَا لَيْسَ فِي قُلُوبِهِمْ
4. [88:6] لَيْسَ لَهُمْ طَعَامٌ
5. [11:46] إِنَّهُ لَيْسَ مِنْ أَهْلِكَ
6. [29:68] أَلَيْسَ فِي جَهَنَّمَ مَثْوًى لِلْكَافِرِينَ
7. [33:5] لَيْسَ عَلَيْكُمْ جُنَاحٌ فِيمَا أَخْطَأْتُمْ
8. [6:122] لَيْسَ بِخَارِجٍ مِنْهَا
9. [43:51] أَلَيْسَ لِي مُلْكُ مِصْرَ
10. [85:6] إِذْ هُمْ عَلَيْهَا قُعُودٌ
11. [2:112] مَنْ أَسْلَمَ وَجْهَهُ لِلّٰهِ فَلَهُ أَجْرُهُ عِنْدَ رَبِّهِ
12. [29:40] وَمِنْهُمْ مَنْ أَغْرَقْنَا
13. [30:40] هَلْ مِنْ شُرَكَآئِكُمْ مَنْ يَفْعَلُ مِنْ ذٰلِكُمْ مِنْ شَيْءٍ

14. وَمِنَ ٱلْجِنِّ مَنْ يَعْمَلُ بَيْنَ يَدَيْهِ بِإِذْنِ رَبِّهِ [34:12]

15. مَا أَنْتَ بِمُسْمِعٍ مَنْ فِي ٱلْقُبُورِ [35:22]

16. مِنْهُمْ مَنْ عَاهَدَ ٱللَّهَ [9:75]

17. مِنَ ٱلْأَحْزَابِ مَنْ يُنْكِرُ بَعْضَهُ [13:36]

18. مِنَ ٱلنَّاسِ مَنْ يُجَادِلُ فِي ٱللَّهِ بِغَيْرِ عِلْمٍ [22:8]

19. إِذَا هُمْ مِنْهَا يَرْكُضُونَ [21:12]

20. فَإِذَا هُمْ فَرِيقَانِ [27:45]

21. إِذَا أَنْتُمْ بَشَرٌ [30:20]

22. إِذَا فَرِيقٌ مِنْهُمْ بِرَبِّهِمْ يُشْرِكُونَ [30:33]

23. وَإِذْ زَيَّنَ لَهُمُ ٱلشَّيْطَانُ أَعْمَالَهُمْ [8:48]

24. وَإِذْ وَاعَدْنَا مُوسَى أَرْبَعِينَ لَيْلَةً [2:51]

Lesson Twenty-Two
Verbs with a *hamza* as one of their Radicals

The basic rules for the spelling of *hamza* were set out in the Introduction to the Arabic alphabet (p. 1). To recapitulate:

1. At the beginning of a word the bearer of *hamza* is *alif.*
2. When *hamza* follows a short vowel or *sukūn* the bearer is determined by the vowel immediately before and the vowel immediately after the *hamza* in the following order of precedence: *kasra, ḍamma, fatḥa* (*sukūn* can have no precedence[A]), *i.e.*:
   a) if there is a *kasra* in either place, the bearer is *yā'* without dots;
   b) if there is no *kasra* in either place, but there is a *ḍamma* in either place, the bearer is *wāw*;
   c) if neither *kasra* nor *ḍamma* occur, the bearer will be an *alif.*
3. After a long vowel *hamza* does not have a bearer:
   a) if it is the final letter;
   b) if the vowel following the *hamza* is *fatḥa.*
4. In other cases the bearer of the *hamza* that follows a long vowel is determined by the vowel coming after the *hamza.*

   Rules 3 and 4 are illustrated clearly by the following examples:

friends		أَصْدِقَاءُ
His friends		
	nom.	أَصْدِقَاؤُهُ
	acc.	أَصْدِقَاءَهُ
	gen.	أَصْدِقَائِهِ

[A] Unless the *sukūn* is followed by *hamza* as final radical, in which case there is no bearer.

5. *hamza* followed by *ā* is written *alif madda* آ.
   Rules with which you will not yet be familiar are:
6. At the beginning of a word *fatḥa*, when followed by *hamza* plus *sukūn*, becomes a *madda*.
7. In theory prosthetic *kasra* when followed by *hamza* plus *sukūn* becomes إي and prosthetic *ḍamma* + *hamza* + *sukūn* becomes أُو. However, after another vowel reversion takes place. This happens most often with verb forms, including verbal nouns, particularly in the 8th form. However, it is not a feature that appears in the Qur'ān. The only regular 8th forms that occur are those of أَمَرَ *amara* [Imperfect 28:20, Imperative 65:6] and of أَمِنَ *amina* [Perfect passive 2:283]. That of أَخَذَ *akhadha*, which occurs over 120 times, acts as though it were an assimilated verb (see Lesson 24), producing إِتَّخَذَ *ittakhadha*, as would have been normal in the Ḥijāz.
8. In the Imperfect of third radical *hamza* verbs, final *hamza* preceded by *fatḥa* and followed by *ḍamma* retains *alif* as its bearer, *e.g.*: يَقْرَأُ.
9. The *maṣdar* of the 2nd form of third-radical *hamza* verbs is based on the pattern *taf'ilatun*, *e.g.* تَبْرِئَةٌ *tabri'atun* from بَرَّأَ *barra'a*.

You have already been introduced to some of the most important verbs with *hamza* as one of their radicals: *akhadha, akala, amara* and *sa'ala*. The vocabulary that follows includes all the remaining verbs that have *hamza* as one of their radicals and sound letters as the other two and that occur in the Qur'ān with reasonable frequency. By far the most important of them is the 4th form آمَنَ *āmana*, 'to believe', the active participle of which is *mu'minun*, 'a believer'.

It will not be possible to introduce you to verbs that have *hamza* as one radical and a *wāw* or a *yā'* as one of the other two until hollow and defective verbs are dealt with (see Lessons 28 and 30). They include some of the most common verbs in the Qur'ān:

جَاءَ *jā'a*, أَتَى *atā*, رَأَى *ra'ā*, شَاءَ *shā'a*, سَاءَ *sā'a*; and the fourth form آتَى *ātā*.

ADVERBS IN -*u*

Arabic has one genuine adverbial ending: final *ḍamma*. Most of the words in which it occurs are nouns that have developed a prepositional form. Thus from *qabla*, *ba'da*, *taḥta* and *fawqa* there is an adverbial form قَبْلُ *qablu*, بَعْدُ *ba'du*, تَحْتُ *taḥtu* and فَوْقُ *fawqu*. These adverbial forms are invariable. 'Beforehand' may be *qablu* or *min qablu* and so on. The adverbial form قَطُّ *qaṭṭu*, 'ever', common elsewhere in Arabic, does not occur in the Qur'ān.

Vocabulary Twenty-Two

Perfect	Imperfect	Verbal noun	
آثَرَ 4	يُؤْثِرُ	إِيثَارٌ	to prefer
أَذِنَ	يَأْذَنُ	إِذْنٌ	to permit, allow
اِسْتَأْذَنَ 10	يَسْتَأْذِنُ	اِسْتِئْذَانٌ	to seek permission
أَمِنَ	يَأْمَنُ	أَمْنٌ	to be secure; to trust in
آمَنَ 4	يُؤْمِنُ	إِيمَانٌ	to believe
آنَسَ 4	يُؤْنِسُ	إِينَاسٌ	to see, perceive
تَسَاءَلَ 6	يَتَسَاءَلُ	تَسَاؤُلٌ	to ask one another
قَرَأَ	يَقْرَأُ	قُرْآنٌ	to recite
نَبَّأَ 2	يُنَبِّئُ	تَنْبِئَةٌ	to inform, tell
أَنْبَأَ 4	يُنْبِئُ	إِنْبَاءٌ	to inform, tell
أَنْشَأَ 4	يُنْشِئُ	إِنْشَاءٌ	to raise, create, produce, grow

PERFECT	IMPERFECT	VERBAL NOUN	
بَرِحَ	يَبْرَحُ	بَرَحٌ	to leave
أَقْبَلَ 4	يُقْبِلُ	إِقْبَالٌ	to advance
كَمَا			like (conjunction)
مِثْلَ			like (preposition)

EXERCISE TWENTY-TWO

1. [37:27] أَقْبَلَ بَعْضُهُمْ عَلَى بَعْضٍ يَتَسَآءَلُونَ
2. [17:71] أُولَآئِكَ يَقْرَؤُونَ كِتَابَهُمْ
3. [26:199] قَرَأَهُ عَلَيْهِمْ
4. [20:109] أَذِنَ لَهُ ٱلرَّحْمٰنُ
5. [12:80] لَنْ أَبْرَحَ ٱلْأَرْضَ حَتَّى يَأْذَنَ لِي أَبِي
6. [2:186] سَأَلَكَ عِبَادِي عَنِّي
7. [51:12] يَسْأَلُونَ أَيَّانَ يَوْمُ ٱلدِّينِ
8. [33:63] يَسْأَلُكَ ٱلنَّاسُ عَنِ ٱلسَّاعَةِ
9. [6:98] أَنْشَأَكُمْ مِنْ نَفْسٍ وَاحِدَةٍ
10. [56:72] أَأَنْتُمْ أَنْشَأْتُمْ شَجَرَتَهَا أَمْ نَحْنُ ٱلْمُنْشِئُونَ
11. [23:42] أَنْشَأْنَا مِنْ بَعْدِهِمْ قُرُونًا آخَرِينَ
12. [19:55] كَانَ يَأْمُرُ أَهْلَهُ بِٱلصَّلَوٰةِ وَٱلزَّكَوٰةِ
13. [2:285] آمَنَ بِٱللّٰهِ وَمَلَآئِكَتِهِ وَكُتُبِهِ وَرُسُلِهِ
14. [23:47] أَنُؤْمِنُ لِبَشَرَيْنِ مِثْلِنَا

15. [16:72] أَفَبِٱلْبَاطِلِ يُؤْمِنُونَ وَبِنِعْمَةِ ٱللَّهِ هُمْ يَكْفُرُونَ
16. [87:16] تُؤْثِرُونَ ٱلْحَيَوٰةَ ٱلدُّنْيَا
17. [12:91] قَدْ آثَرَكَ ٱللَّهُ عَلَيْنَا
18. [2:33] أَنْبَأَهُمْ بِأَسْمَآئِهِمْ
19. [6:108] فَيُنَبِّئُهُمْ بِمَا كَانُوا يَعْمَلُونَ
20. [10:18] أَتُنَبِّئُونَ ٱللَّهَ بِمَا لَا يَعْلَمُ
21. [66:3] مَنْ أَنْبَأَكَ هٰذَا
22. [9:83] فَٱسْتَأْذَنُوكَ لِلْخُرُوجِ
23. [20:10] إِنِّي آنَسْتُ نَارًا
24. [3:49] أُنَبِّئُكُمْ بِمَا تَأْكُلُونَ

Lesson Twenty-Three
Relative Sentences

You have already seen how the two main relative pronouns, *mā* and *man*, are used. It is now time to look at the way the relative اَلَّذِي *alladhī* is used. *Alladhī* can be used as a pronoun, in which case it acts like *mā* or *man*. However, it is basically an adjective, and its adjectival use needs careful attention.

Alladhī declines in a way that is similar to that of the demonstratives. The singular and plural do not decline, but the dual does:

	m.s.	f.s.
	اَلَّذِي	اَلَّتِي

	m.d.	f.d.
nom.	اَللَّذَانِ	اَللَّتَانِ
acc., gen.	اَللَّذَيْنِ	اَللَّتَيْنِ

m.p.	f.p.
اَلَّذِينَ	اَللَّائِي, اَللَّاتِي اَللَّوَاتِي

The masculine dual forms occur only once each in the Qur'ān, whilst the feminine dual forms do not occur at all. Note that in the dual and in the feminine plural forms the *lām* is written twice, as opposed to once elsewhere.

The first element of اَلَّذِي *alladhī* is the definite article. This means that *alladhī* can **be used only with a definite antecedent**. The form of *alladhī* that is used is determined by the antecedent in **number, gender** and **case**. In the Qur'ān you cannot actually see that this is so for case, as the two dual examples, the only ones in which case is clearly shown, are both examples of pronominal usage and thus are their own antecedent. Two non-Qur'ānic examples that have the same meaning but different word order will show how *alladhī* works:

a) لَا يَرْجِعُ ٱلرَّجُلَانِ ٱللَّذَانِ نَصَرَانِي

the two men who helped me will not return

In this example a negative verb (*lā yarji'u*) is followed by a definite subject/antecedent in the nominative together with its relative adjective, which agrees with it in number, gender and case (*l-rajulāni lladhāni*), then the relative sentence (*naṣarā-nī*). It is important to note that *lladhāni* is not part of the relative sentence.

b) إِنَّ ٱلرَّجُلَيْنِ ٱللَّذَيْنِ نَصَرَانِي لَا يَرْجِعَانِ

The second sentence has the same meaning, but it starts with the particle *inna* followed by the definite subject/antecedent in the accusative together with its relative adjective, which agrees with it in number, gender and case (*l-rajulayni lladhayni*), then the same relative sentence (*naṣarā-nī*), and finally the verb of the main sentence with its negative (*lā yarjiʿāni*). Once again it should be noted that the relative adjective is not part of the relative sentence.

If the relative sentence is changed from 'who helped me' to 'whom I helped', the sentences become:

c) لَا يَرْجِعُ ٱلرَّجُلَانِ ٱللَّذَانِ نَصَرْتُهُمَا

d) إِنَّ ٱلرَّجُلَيْنِ ٱللَّذَيْنِ نَصَرْتُهُمَا لَا يَرْجِعَانِ

The analysis given above again applies, but this time the relative sentence *naṣartu-humā* has an explicit pronoun referring back to the antecedent. With *naṣarā-nī* in (a) and (b) the pronoun is implicit in the verb. This referring pronoun is an essential part of the relative sentence. In fact, there are two things to be remembered about the relative sentence: (i) it must normally be a complete sentence in itself; (ii) it must normally contain a referring pronoun, whether this is explicit or implicit.

Now look at the sentences with an indefinite subject substituted for the definite one:

(a) لَا يَرْجِعُ رَجُلَانِ نَصَرَانِي

(b) إِنَّ رَجُلَيْنِ نَصَرَانِي لَا يَرْجِعَانِ

two men who helped me will not return

(c) لَا يَرْجِعُ رَجُلَانِ نَصَرْتُهُمَا

(d) إِنَّ رَجُلَيْنِ نَصَرْتُهُمَا لَا يَرْجِعَانِ

two men whom I helped will not return

The following rules govern the above sentences:

1. The relative adjective is used only with a definite antecedent, with which it agrees in number, gender and case; it has no role in the relative sentence.
2. The relative sentence is normally a complete sentence in itself.
3. The relative sentence must contain a pronoun that refers to the antecedent.

Exceptions of which you must be aware are:

a) Sentences in which the antecedent is definite but the relative adjective is not used.
The commonly accepted rule that this should occur only when a noun is used in a generalized way (see Wright, 2, 318) is not true of early Arabic, where the relative adjective is quite often omitted:

كَمَثَلِ ٱلْحِمَارِ يَحْمِلُ أَسْفَارًا

[62:5 'like the donkey that carries books'] fits the rule.

ذَٰلِكَ ٱلْكِتَابُ لَا رَيْبَ فِيهِ

[2:2 'this is the book in which there is no doubt'] and

اَلتَّابُوتُ فِيهِ سَكِينَةٌ

[2:248 'the ark in which there is an assurance'] do not.

b) Sentences in which the relative sentence is not a complete sentence:
Where a subject can be implied from a relative pronoun or adjective and where the predicate is a prepositional phrase, or, more rarely, an adverb:

[73:20] اَلَّذِينَ مَعَكَ
those who are with you

[22:46] اَلْقُلُوبُ ٱلَّتِي فِي ٱلصُّدُورِ
their hearts which are in their breasts

c) Sentences in which the referring pronoun is omitted from the relative sentence. This is common with *mā*, much less so with *alladhī*, but cf.:

[4:136] اَلْكِتَابُ ٱلَّذِي أَنْزَلَ ٱللّٰهُ [for أَنْزَلَهُ]
the scripture which God has sent down

[19:61] جَنَّاتُ عَدْنٍ ٱلَّتِي وَعَدَ ٱلرَّحْمٰنُ عِبَادَهُ [for وَعَدَهَا]
gardens of Eden which the Merciful has promised His servants

[40:28] بَعْضُ ٱلَّذِي يَعِدُكُمْ [for يَعِدُكُمُوهُ]
some of what he promises you

[10:104] اَلَّذِينَ تَعْبُدُونَ [for تَعْبُدُونَهُمْ]
those whom you worship

[4:81] اَلَّذِي تَقُولُ [for تَقُولُهُ]
what you say

Vocabulary Twenty-Three

Perfect	Imperfect	Verbal noun	
حَبِطَ	يَحْبَطُ	حُبُوطٌ	to be useless
سَخَّرَ 2	يُسَخِّرُ	تَسْخِيرٌ	to subject
مَتَّعَ 2	يُمَتِّعُ	تَمْتِيعٌ	to let enjoy; make provision for

PERFECT	IMPERFECT	VERBAL NOUN	
أَقْرَضَ 4	يُقْرِضُ	قَرْضٌ	to lend, make a loan
أَنْعَمَ 4	يُنْعِمُ	إِنْعَامٌ	to bless, be gracious
تَفَرَّقَ 5	يَتَفَرَّقُ	تَفَرُّقٌ	to be divided
تَبَارَكَ 6	يَتَبَارَكُ	تَبَارُكٌ	to be blessed

SINGULAR	PLURAL	
أَصْلٌ	أُصُولٌ	root
بَأْسٌ		might
تَابُوتٌ		ark
حَبٌّ	حُبُوبٌ	grain
حَجَرٌ	حِجَارَةٌ	stone
حَدِيدٌ		iron
حِمَارٌ	حَمِيرٌ	donkey
خَضِرٌ		green crop
رِجْسٌ		abomination
رَيْبٌ		doubt
	أَسْفَارٌ	books
سَكِينَةٌ		tranquillity, reassurance
سِيمَا		sign
فَتًى	فِتْيَةٌ	youth
وَقُودٌ		fuel
سَمِينٌ	سِمَانٌ	fat

Exercise Twenty-Three

1. [2:40] نِعْمَتِيَ ٱلَّتِي أَنْعَمْتُ عَلَيْكُمْ
2. [52:14] هٰذِهِ ٱلنَّارُ ٱلَّتِي كُنْتُمْ بِهَا تُكَذِّبُونَ
3. [2:24] اَلنَّارُ ٱلَّتِي وَقُودُهَا ٱلنَّاسُ وَٱلْحِجَارَةُ
4. [6:151] لَا تَقْتُلُوا ٱلنَّفْسَ ٱلَّتِي حَرَّمَ ٱللّٰهُ
5. [7:196] إِنَّ وَلِيِّيَ ٱللّٰهُ ٱلَّذِي نَزَّلَ ٱلْكِتَابَ
6. [16:14] هُوَ ٱلَّذِي سَخَّرَ ٱلْبَحْرَ لِتَأْكُلُوا مِنْهُ
7. [25:41] أَهٰذَا ٱلَّذِي بَعَثَ ٱللّٰهُ رَسُولًا
8. [26:82] اَلَّذِي أَطْمَعُ أَنْ يَغْفِرَ لِي خَطِيئَتِي يَوْمَ ٱلدِّينِ
9. [2:245] مَنْذَا ٱلَّذِي يُقْرِضُ ٱللّٰهَ قَرْضًا حَسَنًا
10. [67:1] تَبَارَكَ ٱلَّذِي بِيَدِهِ ٱلْمُلْكُ
11. [59:2] هُوَ ٱلَّذِي أَخْرَجَ ٱلَّذِينَ كَفَرُوا
12. [32:7] أَحْسَنَ كُلَّ شَيْءٍ خَلَقَهُ
13. [3:22] أُولَٰئِكَ ٱلَّذِينَ حَبِطَتْ أَعْمَالُهُمْ فِي ٱلدُّنْيَا وَٱلْآخِرَةِ
14. [3:105] لَا تَكُونُوا كَٱلَّذِينَ تَفَرَّقُوا وَٱخْتَلَفُوا
15. [17:9] يُبَشِّرُ ٱلْمُؤْمِنِينَ ٱلَّذِينَ يَعْمَلُونَ ٱلصَّالِحَاتِ أَنَّ لَهُمْ أَجْرًا كَبِيرًا
16. [10:100] يَجْعَلُ ٱلرِّجْسَ عَلَى ٱلَّذِينَ لَا يَعْقِلُونَ
17. [13:43] وَيَقُولُ ٱلَّذِينَ كَفَرُوا لَسْتَ مُرْسَلًا
18. [37:64] إِنَّهَا شَجَرَةٌ تَخْرُجُ فِي أَصْلِ ٱلْجَحِيمِ

19. إِنَّا نُبَشِّرُكَ بِغُلَامٍ ٱسْمُهُ يَحْيَى [19:7]

20. سَبْعُ بَقَرَاتٍ سِمَانٍ يَأْكُلُهُنَّ سَبْعٌ عِجَافٌ [12:43]

21. إِنَّ فِي ذٰلِكَ لَآيَاتٍ لِقَوْمٍ يَعْقِلُونَ [13:4]

22. إِنَّهُمْ فِتْيَةٌ آمَنُوا بِرَبِّهِمْ [18:13]

23. سُورَةٌ أَنْزَلْنَاهَا [24:1]

24. فَأَخْرَجْنَا مِنْهُ خَضِرًا نُخْرِجُ مِنْهُ حَبًّا [6:99]

25. عَلَى ٱلْأَعْرَافِ رِجَالٌ يَعْرِفُونَ كُلًّا بِسِيمَاهُمْ [7:46]

26. كَانَ مِنْ قَوْمٍ بَيْنَكُمْ وَبَيْنَهُمْ مِيثَاقٌ [4:92]

27. أَنْزَلْنَا ٱلْحَدِيدَ فِيهِ بَأْسٌ شَدِيدٌ وَمَنَافِعُ لِلنَّاسِ [57:25]

28. أُمَمٌ سَنُمَتِّعُهُمْ [11:48]

Lesson Twenty-Four
Assimilated Verbs

A. VERBS WITH *wāw* AS FIRST RADICAL

Verbs with *wāw* as their first radical are common, and many of them are important. Three of these, وَجَدَ *wajada*, وَقَعَ *waqaʿa* and وَعَدَ *waʿada*, have already been included in earlier lessons. As *wāw* is a weak radical, it is subject to some change. There are three points to be remembered:

1. The most characteristic feature of verbs beginning with *wāw* is that almost all of them lose the *wāw* in the Imperfect active (but not the passive, see Lesson 33):

   (وَقَعَ) يَقَعُ (وَعَدَ) يَعِدُ (وَجَدَ) يَجِدُ

2. The *wāw* changes to a *yā'* in the *maṣdars* of the 4th and 10th forms and in some *maṣdar mīmī* forms. It is only these latter that occur in the Qur'ān:

   (و ع د) مِيعَادٌ (و ث ق) مِيثَاقٌ
   (و ز ن) مِيزَانٌ (و ر ث) مِيرَاثٌ

3. The *wāw* is changed into a *tā'* in the 8th form. There are only a couple of verbs in the Qur'ān that show this change: اِتَّكَأَ *ittaka'a* 'to recline on', which is rare, and اِتَّقَى *ittaqā* 'to protect oneself, guard against, be god-fearing', which is common. As *ittaqā* is also a defective verb, it will not be dealt with until Lesson 30.
   There are two verbs with *wāw* as their first radical that in general do not occur in the Perfect but only in the imperfect tenses and the Imperative. These are يَدَعُ *yadaʿu*

and يَذَرُ *yadharu*. *Yadaʿu* occurs only once in the Imperative, once in the 2nd form, and twice in the 10th form passive participle/noun of place. *Yadharu*, on the other hand, occurs twenty-odd times in the imperfect tenses and twenty-odd in the Imperative. In the rest of Arabic *yadaʿu* is much the more common. Both mean 'to let', 'to allow', 'leave alone'.

B. VERBS WITH *yā'* AS FIRST RADICAL

Verbs with *yā'* as their first radical have fewer changes (and are less common) than those with *wāw*. There are two basic changes:

1. In the Imperfect passive of the first form and in the Imperfect and the participles of the 4th form the *yā'* changes to *wāw*.
2. The *yā'* is changed into a *tā'* in the 8th form (as with assimilated verbs beginning with *wāw*).

There are only a handful of verbs in the Qur'ān from roots beginning with *yā'*. The only one to show any mutation is أَيْقَنَ *ayqana* 'to be certain', in all the Qur'ānic forms of which (3/2 m.pl. Imperfect and active participle) the *yā'* is transformed to *wāw*.

Vocabulary Twenty-Four

Perfect	Imperfect	Verbal noun	
	يَذَرُ		to let, allow
وَرِثَ	يَرِثُ	إِرْثٌ	to inherit
وَزَرَ	يَزِرُ	وِزْرٌ	to carry a burden
وَسِعَ	يَسَعُ	وُسْعٌ	to be wide; encompass
وَصَفَ	يَصِفُ	وَصْفٌ	to describe
وَصَلَ	يَصِلُ	وُصُولٌ	to arrive
وَضَعَ	يَضَعُ	وَضْعٌ	to put down

Perfect	Imperfect	Verbal noun	
وَعَظَ	يَعِظُ	عِظَةٌ/وَعْظٌ	to exhort, admonish
وَهَبَ	يَهِبُ	هِبَةٌ	to give
اِتَّخَذَ 8	يَتَّخِذُ	اِتِّخَاذٌ	to take, adopt
يَئِسَ	يَيْئَسُ	يَأْسٌ	to despair
أَيْقَنَ 4	يُوقِنُ	إِيقَانٌ	to be certain
بَطَلَ	يَبْطُلُ	بَطْلٌ	to be worthless

Singular	Plural	
صَنَمٌ	أَصْنَامٌ	idol
فَرْدٌ	أَفْرَادٌ	individual, alone
وَازِرَةٌ		soul bearing a burden
مِيزَانٌ	مَوَازِينُ	balance

Exercise Twenty-Four

1. إِنَّا نَحْنُ نَرِثُ ٱلْأَرْضَ وَمَنْ عَلَيْهَا [19:40]
2. يَرِثُهَا عِبَادِيَ ٱلصَّالِحُونَ [21:105]
3. أَتَذَرُ مُوسَى وَقَوْمَهُ لِيُفْسِدُوا فِي ٱلْأَرْضِ [7:127]
4. لَا تَذَرْنِي فَرْدًا [21:89]
5. لَا تَزِرُ وَازِرَةٌ وِزْرَ أُخْرَى [6:164]
6. وَسِعَ رَبِّي كُلَّ شَيْءٍ عِلْمًا [6:80]
7. وَتَصِفُ أَلْسِنَتُهُمُ ٱلْكَذِبَ [16:62]

8. مِمَّا تَصِفُونَ [21:18]

9. فَلَا يَصِلُونَ إِلَيْكُمَا [28:35]

10. لَنْ يَصِلُوا إِلَيْكَ [11:81]

11. وَضَعَ ٱلْمِيزَانَ [55:7]

12. نَضَعُ ٱلْمَوَازِينَ لِيَوْمِ ٱلْقِيَامَةِ [21:47]

13. إِنَّ ٱللَّهَ وَعَدَكُمْ وَعْدَ ٱلْحَقِّ [14:22]

14. أَلَمْ يَعِدْكُمْ رَبُّكُمْ وَعْدًا حَسَنًا [20:86]

15. أَعِظُكُمْ بِوَاحِدَةٍ [34:46]

16. يَعِظُكُمُ ٱللَّهُ [24:17]

17. وَقَعَ ٱلْحَقُّ وَبَطَلَ مَا كَانُوا يَعْمَلُونَ [7:118]

18. وَهَبْنَا لَهُمْ مِنْ رَحْمَتِنَا [19:50]

19. وَهَبَ لِي رَبِّي حُكْمًا [26:21]

20. أُولَٰٓئِكَ يَئِسُوا مِنْ رَحْمَتِي [29:23]

21. يَئِسُوا مِنَ ٱلْآخِرَةِ [60:13]

22. هُمْ بِٱلْآخِرَةِ هُمْ يُوقِنُونَ [27:3]

23. كَانُوا بِآيَاتِنَا يُوقِنُونَ [27:82]

24. أَتَتَّخِذُ أَصْنَامًا آلِهَةً [6:74]

25. يَتَّخِذَ مِنْكُمْ شُهَدَآءَ [3:140]

26. يَتَّخِذُونَ ٱلْكَافِرِينَ أَوْلِيَآءَ [4:139]

Lesson Twenty-Five
The Elative

The Elative is the form used in Arabic to express the comparative and superlative.

THE FORM

The basic form is أَفْعَلُ *afʿalu*, *e.g.*:

أَكْرَمُ from كَرِيمٌ

أَحْسَنُ from حَسَنٌ

أَسْفَلُ from سَافِلٌ

If the two last radicals are the same, contraction takes place:

أَشَدُّ from شَدِيدٌ

أَعَزُّ from عَزِيزٌ

أَقَلُّ from قَلِيلٌ

If the last radical is *wāw* or *yā'*, that radical becomes *alif maqṣūra* in the elative form:

أَزْكَى from زَكِيٌّ

أَبْقَى from بَاقٍ

In general, an elative cannot be formed from:

a) a passive participle;
b) a derived form participle;
c) a word that has the same form of the elative;
d) a noun.

To express the elative of such a word, a compound phrase must be used. This consists of an elative meaning 'more', such as *aktharu, ashaddu, aʿẓamu*, together with an appropriate noun in the indefinite accusative singular. If a derived form participle is concerned, it is the appropriate *maṣdar* that is used. In the Qur'ān we find examples of only (b) and (d).

أَشَدُّ حُبًّا more loving [2:165]

أَعْظَمُ أَجْرًا more rewarding [73:20]

This compound construction must also be used if one needs to express the idea of 'less' or 'least'. There is only one clear example in the Qur'ān:

أَقَلُّ عَدَدًا less numerous [72:24]

'Better/best' is expressed by the noun *khayr* 'good', and 'worse/worst' by the noun *sharr*, 'bad, evil'. Both words can have their ordinary meaning or an elative meaning, depending on the construction and, sometimes, on the context.

It should be noted that elative forms sometimes convey only an intensive meaning 'very…', etc. Thus *al-ḥajju al-akbaru* [9:3] means 'the great pilgrimage'. This is particularly common with *aʿlamu*, which normally means 'well-aware'.

THE CONSTRUCTIONS

a) Comparative

The form does not change for number or gender, but it does for case.

'Than' is expressed by *min*.

إِثْمُهُمَا أَكْبَرُ مِنْ نَفْعِهِمَا their sin is greater than their benefit

(acc.) أَصْغَرَ مِنْ ذٰلِكَ smaller than that

هِيَ أَحْسَنُ it is better

نَحْنُ أَحَقُّ بِٱلْمُلْكِ مِنْهُ	we are more deserving of sovereignty than him
اَللّٰهُ خَيْرٌ وَأَبْقَى	God is better and more enduring
هُوَ شَرٌّ لَهُمْ	it is worse for them

If comparison is made to a word that has already occurred in the sentence, there are two possible ways of referring to it, either by the appropriate pronominal suffix after *min* or by a clause after *mimmā* ('than that which'). There is very little trace of this in the Qur'ān. The nearest to the first way has *anfusi-him* in the place of a simple suffix:

[33:6] اَلنَّبِيُّ أَوْلَى بِٱلْمُؤْمِنِينَ مِنْ أَنْفُسِهِمْ

the Prophet is closer to the believers than they are themselves

An example of the second way is:

[30:9] عَمَرُوهَا أَكْثَرَ مِمَّا عَمَرُوهَا

they built it up more than they had already built it up

b) Superlative

The two main constructions are:

1. the elative plus an indefinite genitive singular (this is much less common in the Qur'ān than elsewhere):

فِي أَحْسَنِ تَقْوِيمٍ	in the finest form
(acc.) أَكْثَرَ شَيْءٍ جَدَلًا	the most contentious thing

2. the elative plus a definite genitive plural, collective, suffix, etc.:

أَكْثَرُ ٱلنَّاسِ	most of the people
أَوْهَنُ ٱلْبُيُوتِ	the frailest house

أَدْنَى ٱلْأَرْضِ	the nearest part of the earth
هُوَ خَيْرُ ٱلنَّاصِرِينَ	he is the best helper

In these two constructions, the elative form again does not change for number or gender. (It acts like a noun rather than an adjective.)

(acc.) أَوَّلَ مَرَّةٍ	the first time
أَوَّلُ ٱلْمُؤْمِنِينَ	the first of the believers OR the first believers

The elative can also be used adjectivally to express the superlative:

اَلْعَذَابُ ٱلْأَكْبَرُ	the greatest punishment
اَلْأُفُقُ ٱلْأَعْلَى	the highest horizon

This construction, which gives no problems when translating from Arabic, gives rise to problems when one is translating into Arabic, as it can properly be used only with masculine words [though present-day usage will eventually destroy this rule]. There is a special form for the feminine superlative adjective: فُعْلَى *fuʿlā*; and this feminine form is found with only a very limited number of adjectives. The Qur'ān has a greater proportion of these feminine elative forms than one would expect from their incidence elsewhere in Arabic. Even so there are only nine of them, and one, اَلدُّنْيَا *al-dunyā* , has a specialised usage (اَلدَّارُ ٱلدُّنْيَا *al-dār al-dunyā* 'the lowest world', *i.e.* 'this world') in the majority of its occurrences.

اَلْعُرْوَةُ ٱلْوُثْقَى	the firmest handle
اَلصَّلَاةُ ٱلْوُسْطَى	the middle prayer
آيَاتُ رَبِّهِ ٱلْكُبْرَى	the greatest signs of his Lord

Vocabulary Twenty-Five

Perfect	Imperfect	Verbal noun	
عَمَرَ	يَعْمُرُ	عَمْرٌ	to build, build up
8 اِسْتَمَعَ	يَسْتَمِعُ	اِسْتِمَاعٌ	to listen to

Singular	Plural	
أُفُقٌ	آفَاقٌ	horizon
بَرٌّ	أَبْرَارٌ	pious, god-fearing
بَطْشٌ		might
جَدَلٌ		contention
خُلْدٌ		eternity
رَازِقٌ	s.p.	provider of sustenance
شِقَاقٌ		dissension
عَدَدٌ		number
عَدَاوَةٌ		enmity
عُدْوَةٌ		side of a valley
عُرْوَةٌ		handle
مُسْتَقَرٌّ		abode
قَسْوَةٌ		hardness
تَقْوِيمٌ		form
مَقِيلٌ		noon resting-place
أَبْقَى		more lasting

SINGULAR

[from حَقِيقٌ]	أَحَقُّ	more deserving
[from دَانٍ]	أَدْنَى / (f.) دُنْيَا	lowest, nearest
[from رَذِيلٌ]	أَرْذَلُ	worst
[from زَكِيٌّ]	أَزْكَى	purer
[from سَافِلٌ]	أَسْفَلُ	lower
	أَقْصَى / (f.) قُصْوَى	further, furthest
[from كَرِيمٌ]	أَكْرَمُ	nobler
	ٱلْوُثْقَى	firmest
[from تَقِيٌّ]	أَتْقَى	more pious
	أَوْلَى	nearer
	أَوْهَنُ	frailest
	خَيْرٌ	good, better, best
	شَرٌّ	bad, worse, worst

EXERCISE TWENTY-FIVE

1. [4:153] سَأَلُوا مُوسَىٰ أَكْبَرَ مِنْ ذَٰلِكَ
2. [34:35] نَحْنُ أَكْثَرُ أَمْوَالًا وَأَوْلَادًا
3. [2:140] ءَأَنْتُمْ أَعْلَمُ أَمِ ٱللَّهُ
4. [16:41] أَجْرُ ٱلْآخِرَةِ أَكْبَرُ
5. [2:74] هِيَ كَٱلْحِجَارَةِ أَوْ أَشَدُّ قَسْوَةً

6. كَلِمَةُ ٱلَّذِينَ كَفَرُوا ٱلسُّفْلَى وَكَلِمَةُ ٱللهِ هِيَ ٱلْعُلْيَا [9:40]

7. إِنَّ أَكْرَمَكُمْ عِنْدَ ٱللهِ أَتْقَاكُمْ [49:13]

8. اِتَّبَعَكَ ٱلْأَرْذَلُونَ [26:111]

9. أَيُّكُمْ أَحْسَنُ عَمَلًا [11:7]

10. أَذٰلِكَ خَيْرٌ أَمْ جَنَّةُ ٱلْخُلْدِ [25:15]

11. اَللهُ خَيْرٌ وَأَبْقَى [20:73]

12. مَنْ أَضَلُّ مِمَّنْ هُوَ فِي شِقَاقٍ بَعِيدٍ [41:52]

13. فَٱللهُ أَوْلَى بِهِمَا [4:135]

14. أَكْثَرُهُمْ لَا يَعْقِلُونَ [5:103]

15. أَشَدُّ ٱلنَّاسِ عَدَاوَةً [5:82]

16. أَنْتُمْ بِٱلْعُدْوَةِ ٱلدُّنْيَا وَهُمْ بِٱلْعُدْوَةِ ٱلْقُصْوَى [8:42]

17. فَمَنْ أَظْلَمُ مِمَّنْ كَذَّبَ بِآيَاتِ ٱللهِ [6:157]

18. هَلْ أُنَبِّئُكُمْ بِشَرٍّ مِنْ ذٰلِكَ [5:60]

19. لَهُ ٱلْأَسْمَاءُ ٱلْحُسْنَى [17:110]

20. اَللهُ أَعْلَمُ بِمَا فِي أَنْفُسِهِمْ [11:31]

21. أَصْحَابُ ٱلْجَنَّةِ يَوْمَئِذٍ خَيْرٌ مُسْتَقَرًّا وَأَحْسَنُ مَقِيلًا [25:24]

22. وَمَا عِنْدَ ٱللهِ خَيْرٌ لِلْأَبْرَارِ [3:198]

23. هُوَ خَيْرُ ٱلرَّازِقِينَ [23:72]

24. رَبُّكُمْ أَعْلَمُ بِمَا لَبِثْتُمْ [18:19]

25. ذٰلِكَ أَزْكَى لَهُمْ [24:30]

26. [40:57] خَلْقُ ٱلسَّمَاوَاتِ وَٱلْأَرْضِ أَكْبَرُ مِنْ خَلْقِ ٱلنَّاسِ
وَلَٰكِنَّ أَكْثَرَ ٱلنَّاسِ لَا يَعْلَمُونَ

27. [39:18] يَسْتَمِعُونَ ٱلْقَوْلَ وَيَتَّبِعُونَ أَحْسَنَهُ

28. [56:85] نَحْنُ أَقْرَبُ إِلَيْهِ مِنْكُمْ

Lesson Twenty-Six
Doubled Verbs

Doubled verbs are those in which the second and third radicals are the same. The presence of the same two letters leads to some variations from the sound verbs. Two rules cover these changes:

1. When both the first and the third radicals have vowels, the short vowel on the second radical drops out and the second and third radicals combine, *e.g.* رَدَّ *radda* , مَسَّ *massa* , ضَلَّ *ḍalla*, etc.
2. When the third radical has a vowel and the first does not, the vowel of the second radical moves back to the first, *e.g.* يَمُرُّ *yamurru*, نُمِدُّ *numiddu*, يَصُدُّ *yaṣuddu*, etc.

The crucial point is that for contraction to take place the third radical must have a vowel. If the third radical has *sukūn* no contraction can take place. Thus the vowel of the second radical will reappear if the vowel of the third radical disappears through conjugation: رَدَدْتُ *radadtu* , مَسِسْتُ *masistu* , ضَلَلْتُ *ḍalaltu*, etc. Nor can there be contraction if the second radical has a long vowel, *e.g. mardūdun.*

JUSSIVE FORMS OF DOUBLE VERBS

In the seventh century there were two forms of Jussive for those persons of the doubled verb that take *sukūn* on the final consonant, *i.e.* forms analogous to *yaktub*, etc. The first is the same form that one finds with a sound verb, يَمْسَسْ *yamsas* (from *massa*), يُشَاقِقْ *yushāqiq* (from the 3rd form *shāqqa*), يُحْبِبْ *yuḥbib* (from *aḥabba*), يُضْلِلْ *yuḍlil* (from *aḍalla*), يَرْتَدِدْ *yartadid* (from *irtadda*), etc. Alternatively, contraction of the kind mentioned above can take place, with the doubled letter taking a final *kasra* (*e.g.* يَرْتَدِّ

yartaddi, also from *irtadda*). The forms without contraction are more common in the Qur'ān, as seems to have been the case in the Ḥijāz in general.

Vocabulary Twenty-Six

Perfect	Imperfect	Verbal noun	
أَحَبَّ 4	يُحِبُّ	حُبٌّ	to love
حَاجَّ 3	يُحَاجُّ	حِجَاجٌ	to argue about (*fī*)
أَحَلَّ 4	يُحِلُّ	إِحْلَالٌ	to make lawful, permit
رَدَّ	يَرُدُّ	رَدٌّ	to return, restore
صَدَّ	يَصُدُّ	صَدٌّ	to block
ضَرَّ	يَضُرُّ	ضُرٌّ	to harm
اِضْطَرَّ 8	يَضْطَرُّ	اِضْطِرَارٌ	to force, compel
ضَلَّ	يَضِلُّ	ضَلَالٌ	to stray, err
أَضَلَّ 4	يُضِلُّ	إِضْلَالٌ	to cause to stray
ظَنَّ	يَظُنُّ	ظَنٌّ	to think
عَدَّ	يَعُدُّ	عَدٌّ	to count
أَعَدَّ 4	يُعِدُّ	إِعْدَادٌ	to prepare, make ready
قَصَّ	يَقُصُّ	قَصَصٌ	to tell
مَرَّ	يَمُرُّ	مَرٌّ	to pass
مَسَّ	يَمَسُّ	مَسٌّ	to touch
نَفَعَ	يَنْفَعُ	نَفْعٌ	to benefit

SINGULAR	PLURAL	
بَيْعٌ		trading
رِبًا (with article اَلرِّبَوٰا)		usury
	أَشْرَارٌ	evil men (pl.)
نَبَأٌ	أَنْبَاءٌ	news
أَلِيمٌ		painful

EXERCISE TWENTY-SIX

1. [2:275] أَحَلَّ ٱللّٰهُ ٱلْبَيْعَ وَحَرَّمَ ٱلرِّبَوٰا
2. [9:37] يُحِلُّونَهُ عَامًا وَيُحَرِّمُونَهُ عَامًا
3. [2:217] يُقَاتِلُونَكُمْ حَتَّى يَرُدُّوكُمْ عَنْ دِينِكُمْ
4. [28:13] فَرَدَدْنَاهُ إِلَى أُمِّهِ
5. [17:83] مَسَّهُ ٱلشَّرُّ
6. [10:12] مَسَّ ٱلْإِنْسَانَ ٱلضُّرُّ
7. [18:13] نَحْنُ نَقُصُّ عَلَيْكَ نَبَأَهُمْ بِٱلْحَقِّ
8. [4:164] قَدْ قَصَصْنَاهُمْ عَلَيْكَ مِنْ قَبْلُ
9. [23:106] كُنَّا قَوْمًا ضَالِّينَ
10. [38:26] يَضِلُّونَ عَنْ سَبِيلِ ٱللّٰهِ
11. [14:27] وَيُضِلُّ ٱللّٰهُ ٱلظَّالِمِينَ
12. [16:25] يُضِلُّونَكُمْ بِغَيْرِ عِلْمٍ
13. [17:101] فَقَالَ لَهُ فِرْعَوْنُ إِنِّي لَأَظُنُّكَ يَا مُوسَى مَسْحُورًا

14. ظَنَنْتُمْ أَنَّ ٱللَّهَ لَا يَعْلَمُ كَثِيرًا مِمَّا تَعْمَلُونَ [41:22]

15. مَا لَا يَنْفَعُنَا وَلَا يَضُرُّنَا [6:71]

16. لَا تَضُرُّونَهُ شَيْئًا [11:57]

17. ثُمَّ أَضْطَرُّهُ إِلَى عَذَابِ ٱلنَّارِ [2:126]

18. أَعَدَّ لِلْكَافِرِينَ عَذَابًا أَلِيمًا [33:8]

19. أَعَدَّ ٱللَّهُ لَهُمْ جَنَّاتٍ [9:89]

20. كُنَّا نَعُدُّهُمْ مِنَ ٱلْأَشْرَارِ [38:62]

21. إِنَّ يَوْمًا عِنْدَ رَبِّكَ كَأَلْفِ سَنَةٍ مِمَّا تَعُدُّونَ [22:47]

22. إِنَّ ٱللَّهَ لَا يُحِبُّ ٱلْمُفْسِدِينَ [28:77]

23. فَلِمَ تُحَاجُّونَ فِي مَا لَيْسَ لَكُمْ بِهِ عِلْمٌ [3:66]

24. أَتُحَاجُّونَنَا فِي ٱللَّهِ [2:139]

25. إِنَّهُمْ لَيَصُدُّونَهُمْ عَنِ ٱلسَّبِيلِ [43:37]

26. كَأَيِّنْ مِنْ آيَةٍ فِي ٱلسَّمَاوَاتِ وَٱلْأَرْضِ يَمُرُّونَ عَلَيْهَا [12:105]

Lesson Twenty-Seven
Exceptive Sentences with *illā*

The main exceptive particle *illā* was mentioned briefly in Lesson 10, and occasional examples have been given since then. However, *illā* is a pervasive word (it occurs over 600 times in the Qur'ān), and the rules for its use need to be understood.

When *illā* follows a positive sentence, the exception is put in the accusative case:

شَرِبُوا مِنْهُ إِلَّا قَلِيلًا مِنْهُمْ	they drank from it—except a few of them
سَجَدُوا إِلَّا إِبْلِيسَ	they prostrated themselves, except Iblis
كُلُّ شَيْءٍ هَالِكٌ إِلَّا وَجْهَهُ	everything will perish except His face

However, exceptions to positive sentences are a small proportion of the total. More often, *illā* is used to introduce exceptions to negative sentences, particularly where the negative and the exceptive combine to give the meaning 'only'.

In all normal cirsumstances the exception to a negative goes into the logical case. The same applies to interrogative sentences that imply negation. Before turning to Qur'ānic examples, let us look at six non-Qur'ānic examples, three of which show what or who it is to which the exception is made, and three of which do not:

مَا ذَهَبَ أَحَدٌ إِلَّا زَيْدٌ	no one left, except Zayd
مَا سَمِعْتُ أَحَدًا إِلَّا زَيْدًا	I didn't hear anyone, except Zayd
مَا مَرَرْتُ بِأَحَدٍ إِلَّا بِزَيْدٍ	I didn't pass by anyone, except Zayd

With *aḥad* omitted the sentences run:

مَا ذَهَبَ إِلَّا زَيْدٌ	only Zayd left
مَا سَمِعْتُ إِلَّا زَيْدًا	I heard only Zayd
مَا مَرَرْتُ إِلَّا بِزَيْدٍ	I passed only Zayd

When the exception is of a totally different kind from the term to which the exception is made, only the accusative can be used for the exception:

مَا شَرِبَ ٱلْقَوْمُ إِلَّا حِمَارًا	none of the people drank, but a donkey did

It is also possible for the exception to take the form of a clause (with or without *wa-* or *qad* or *an* to introduce it) or a prepositional phrase.

Before giving some Qur'ānic examples, it is necessary to introduce the archaic negative particle إِنْ *in*, 'not'. The negative *in* is relatively common in the Qur'ān: there are well over 100 examples. All but a handful of these are in exceptive sentences with *illā* introducing the exception:

إِنْ هٰذَا إِلَّا سِحْرٌ مُبِينٌ	this is simply manifest magic
إِنْ يُهْلِكُونَ إِلَّا أَنْفُسَهُمْ	they destroy only themselves
إِنِ ٱلْحُكْمُ إِلَّا لِلّٰهِ	judgement belongs to God alone

OTHER EXAMPLES

[5:75] مَا ٱلْمَسِيحُ ٱبْنُ مَرْيَمَ إِلَّا رَسُولٌ

the Anointed One, the son of Mary, was only a prophet

[6:59] مَا تَسْقُطُ مِنْ وَرَقَةٍ إِلَّا يَعْلَمُهُ ٱللّٰهُ

no leaf falls without God knowing it

[11:105] لَا [A] تَكَلَّمُ نَفْسٌ إِلَّا بِإِذْنِهِ
no soul shall speak except with His permission

[26:208] وَمَا أَهْلَكْنَا مِنْ قَرْيَةٍ إِلَّا لَهَا مُنْذِرُونَ
We have not destroyed any settlement without it having had warners

[45:25] مَا كَانَ حُجَّتَهُمْ إِلَّا أَنْ قَالُوا
their only argument is to say, ...

[2:80] لَنْ تَمَسَّنَا ٱلنَّارُ إِلَّا أَيَّامًا مَعْدُودَةً
The fire will touch us only for a few days

Vocabulary Twenty-Seven

Perfect	Imperfect	Verbal noun	
سَجَدَ	يَسْجُدُ	سُجُودٌ	to prostrate oneself
سَحَرَ	يَسْحِرُ	سِحْرٌ	to bewitch
سَقَطَ	يَسْقُطُ	سُقُوطٌ	to fall
عَبَدَ	يَعْبُدُ	عِبَادَةٌ	to serve, worship
غَفَرَ	يَغْفِرُ	مَغْفِرَةٌ	to forgive
5 تَنَزَّلَ	يَتَنَزَّلُ	تَنَزُّلٌ	to descend
هَلَكَ	يَهْلِكُ	هَلَاكٌ	to perish
وَضَعَ	يَضَعُ	وَضْعٌ	to give birth to (sentence 21)

Singular	Plural	
إِفْكٌ		lie
(f.) أُنْثَى	إِنَاثٌ	female

[A] For the dropping of the prefix see Lesson 16.

Singular	Plural	
بَشِيرٌ		bringer of good tidings
حُجَّةٌ	s.p.	proof
دَابَّةٌ	دَوَابُّ	beast
رِزْقٌ		sustenance
قَدَرٌ		measure
لِسَانٌ	أَلْسِنَةٌ	tongue
اَلْمَسِيحُ		the Anointed One
وَرَقَةٌ	وَرَقٌ	leaf
خَاطِئٌ	s.p.	sinner

Exercise Twenty-Seven

1. [3:135] مَنْ يَغْفِرُ ٱلذُّنُوبَ إِلَّا ٱللّٰهُ
2. [4:142] لَا يَذْكُرُونَ ٱللّٰهَ إِلَّا قَلِيلًا
3. [7:184] إِنْ هُوَ إِلَّا نَذِيرٌ مُبِينٌ
4. [10:36] مَا يَتَّبِعُ أَكْثَرُهُمْ إِلَّا ظَنًّا
5. [11:36] لَنْ يُؤْمِنَ مِنْ قَوْمِكَ إِلَّا مَنْ قَدْ آمَنَ
6. [11:104] مَا نُؤَخِّرُهُ إِلَّا لِأَجَلٍ مَعْدُودٍ
7. [12:81] مَا شَهِدْنَا إِلَّا بِمَا عَلِمْنَا
8. [14:4] مَا أَرْسَلْنَا مِنْ رَسُولٍ إِلَّا بِلِسَانِ قَوْمِهِ
9. [15:85] مَا خَلَقْنَا ٱلسَّمَاوَاتِ وَٱلْأَرْضَ وَمَا بَيْنَهُمَا إِلَّا بِٱلْحَقِّ
10. [14:11] إِنْ نَحْنُ إِلَّا بَشَرٌ مِثْلُكُمْ

11. [34:20] فَٱتَّبَعُوهُ إِلَّا فَرِيقًا مِنَ ٱلْمُؤْمِنِينَ

12. [12:106] مَا يُؤْمِنُ أَكْثَرُهُمْ بِٱللّٰهِ إِلَّا وَهُمْ مُشْرِكُونَ

13. [11:109] مَا يَعْبُدُونَ إِلَّا كَمَا يَعْبُدُ آبَآؤُهُمْ

14. [15:21] مَا نُنَزِّلُهُ إِلَّا بِقَدَرٍ مَعْلُومٍ

15. [16:43] مَا أَرْسَلْنَا مِنْ قَبْلِكَ إِلَّا رِجَالًا

16. [17:47] يَقُولُ ٱلظَّالِمُونَ إِنْ تَتَّبِعُونَ إِلَّا رَجُلًا مَسْحُورًا

17. [19:64] مَا نَتَنَزَّلُ إِلَّا بِأَمْرِ رَبِّكَ

18. [25:44] إِنْ هُمْ إِلَّا كَٱلْأَنْعَامِ

19. [29:14] لَبِثَ فِيهِمْ أَلْفَ سَنَةٍ إِلَّا خَمْسِينَ عَامًا

20. [29:43] مَا يَعْقِلُهَا إِلَّا ٱلْعَالِمُونَ

21. [41:47] مَا تَحْمِلُ مِنْ أُنْثَى وَلَا تَضَعُ إِلَّا بِعِلْمِهِ

22. [17:58] إِنْ مِنْ قَرْيَةٍ إِلَّا نَحْنُ مُهْلِكُوهَا قَبْلَ يَوْمِ ٱلْقِيَامَةِ

23. [69:37] لَا يَأْكُلُهُ إِلَّا ٱلْخَاطِئُونَ

24. [34:43] مَا هٰذَا إِلَّا إِفْكٌ

25. [3:144] مَا مُحَمَّدٌ إِلَّا رَسُولٌ

26. [11:6] مَا مِنْ دَابَّةٍ فِي ٱلْأَرْضِ إِلَّا عَلَى ٱللّٰهِ رِزْقُهَا

Lesson Twenty-Eight
Hollow Verbs

Hollow verbs are those with *wāw* or *yā'* as their middle radical. There are three distinct types:

1. those whose middle radical is *wāw* and whose original vowel pattern was that of *kataba*;
2. those whose middle radical is *yā'* and whose original vowel pattern was that of *kataba*;
3. those whose original vowel pattern was that of *shariba*. (It is immaterial what the middle radical is. The only place where it may show up is the *maṣdar*.)

FIRST FORM

Because of the importance of *qāla* and *kāna*, the two most common verbs in Arabic, you have already been introduced to the first form of type 1.

For type 2 a *kasra* takes the place of the *ḍamma* that comes between the first and third radicals in contracted forms; and an *ī* replaces the *ū* in the long vowel that comes between the first and third radicals in the imperfect tenses.

Learning a table is, however, more effective than applying substitution rules:

Perfect

	SINGULAR	DUAL	PLURAL
3 m.	سَارَ	سَارَا	سَارُوا
3 f.	سَارَتْ	سَارَتَا	سِرْنَ
2 m.	سِرْتَ	سِرْتُمَا	سِرْتُمْ
2 f.	سِرْتِ	سِرْتُمَا	سِرْتُنَّ
1	سِرْتُ	–	سِرْنَا

Imperfect

	SINGULAR	DUAL	PLURAL
3 m.	يَسِيرُ	يَسِيرَانِ	يَسِيرُونَ
3 f.	تَسِيرُ	تَسِيرَانِ	يَسِرْنَ
2 m.	تَسِيرُ	تَسِيرَانِ	تَسِيرُونَ
2 f.	تَسِيرِينَ	تَسِيرَانِ	تَسِرْنَ
1	أَسِيرُ	–	نَسِيرُ

Subjunctive

	SINGULAR	DUAL	PLURAL
3 m.	يَسِيرَ	يَسِيرَا	يَسِيرُوا
3 f.	تَسِيرَ	تَسِيرَا	يَسِرْنَ
2 m.	تَسِيرَ	تَسِيرَا	تَسِيرُوا
2 f.	تَسِيرِي	تَسِيرَا	تَسِرْنَ
1	أَسِيرَ	–	نَسِيرَ

Jussive

	SINGULAR	DUAL	PLURAL
3 m.	يَسِرْ	يَسِيرَا	يَسِيرُوا
3 f.	تَسِرْ	تَسِيرَا	يَسِرْنَ
2 m.	تَسِرْ	تَسِيرَا	تَسِيرُوا
2 f.	تَسِيرِي	تَسِيرَا	تَسِرْنَ
1	أَسِرْ	–	نَسِرْ

Type 3 is identical with type 2 in the Perfect: خِفْتُ *khiftu*, خِفْنَا *khifnā*, etc. from خَافَ *khāfa* (for an original *khawifa*). However, in the Imperfect type 3 has *ā* instead of the *ū* of type 1 and the *ī* of type 2: يَخَافُ *yakhāfu*, etc.; and when this long vowel is shortened, one gets a *fatḥa*: يَخَفْنَ *yakhafna*, تَخَفْنَ *takhafna*. Once again tables are a clearer guide:

Perfect

	SINGULAR	DUAL	PLURAL
3 m.	خَافَ	خَافَا	خَافُوا
3 f.	خَافَتْ	خَافَتَا	خِفْنَ
2 m.	خِفْتَ	خِفْتُمَا	خِفْتُمْ
2 f.	خِفْتِ	خِفْتُمَا	خِفْتُنَّ
1	خِفْتُ	–	خِفْنَا

Imperfect

	SINGULAR	DUAL	PLURAL
3 m.	يَخَافُ	يَخَافَانِ	يَخَافُونَ
3 f.	تَخَافُ	تَخَافَانِ	يَخَفْنَ
2 m.	تَخَافُ	تَخَافَانِ	تَخَافُونَ
2 f.	تَخَافِينَ	تَخَافَانِ	تَخَفْنَ
1	أَخَافُ	–	نَخَافُ

Subjunctive

	Singular	Dual	Plural
3 m.	يَخَافَ	يَخَافَا	يَخَافُوا
3 f.	تَخَافَ	تَخَافَا	يَخَفْنَ
2 m.	تَخَافَ	تَخَافَا	تَخَافُوا
2 f.	تَخَافِي	تَخَافَا	تَخَفْنَ
1	أَخَافَ	–	نَخَافَ

Jussive

	Singular	Dual	Plural
3 m.	يَخَفْ	يَخَافَا	يَخَافُوا
3 f.	تَخَفْ	تَخَافَا	يَخَفْنَ
2 m.	تَخَفْ	تَخَافَا	تَخَافُوا
2 f.	تَخَافِي	تَخَافَا	تَخَفْنَ
1	أَخَفْ	–	نَخَفْ

DERIVED FORMS

Four of the derived forms (2nd, 3rd, 5th and 6th forms) act like sound verbs with the *wāw* or *yā'* appearing as an ordinary radical (*zawwaja, bāyaʿa, rāwada, tabayyana, tafāwata,* etc.). The other four derived forms that we deal with (4th, 7th, 8th and 10th forms) have hollow forms which are the same for all three types of hollow verbs.

Perfect

In the Perfect the same shortening is found for all four forms, 4th, 7th, 8th and 10th: the vowel before the third radical is a *fatḥa*: أَرَدْتُمْ *aradtum* from أَرَادَ *arāda*, اِسْتَطَعْنَا from اِسْتَطَاعَ, etc.

Imperfect etc.

In the imperfect tenses, in the *maṣdars* and in the participles, the forms fall into pairs. The 4th and 10th forms undergo one set of changes, and the 7th and 8th forms another:

4th and 10th forms The Imperfects are similar to that of سَارَ *sāra*, يَسِيرُ *yasīru* : يُرِيدُ *yurīdu* from أَرَادَ *arāda*; يَسْتَطِيعُ *yastaṭī'u* from اِسْتَطَاعَ *istaṭā'a*.

The *maṣdars* show no real sign of the weak radical and have a compensatory *tā' marbūṭa* instead: إِرَادَةٌ *irādatun* and اِسْتِطَاعَةٌ *istiṭā'atun* . The Qur'ān also has the form إِقَامٌ *iqāmun* instead of the normal إِقَامَةٌ *iqāmatun* as the *maṣdar* of أَقَامَ *aqāma*.

The participles are clearly differentiated:

active: مُجِيبٌ *mujībun*, مُسْتَقِيمٌ *mustaqīmun*;
passive: مُطَاعٌ *muṭā'un*, مُسْتَنَارٌ *mustanārun*.

7th and 8th forms These forms are very rare in the Qur'ān. (The 7th form is rare in general).

The Imperfects are similar to that of خَافَ *khāfa* , يَخَافُ *yakhāfu*: يَنْهَارُ *yanhāru* from اِنْهَارَ *inhāra* ; يَكْتَالُ *yaktālu* from اِكْتَالَ *iktāla* (1p. Jussive نَكْتَلْ *naktal*).

The *maṣdars* show the weak radical as *yā'*, regardless of what the middle radical is: اِنْهِيَارٌ *inhiyārun*; اِكْتِيَالٌ *iktiyālun*.

There is only one form for both the active and passive participles: مُنْهَارٌ *munhārun* , مُكْتَالٌ *muktālun* .

There are a number of important hollow verbs in addition to *kāna* and *qāla*. They include some doubly defective verbs, which have *hamza* as the final radical. The three you will come across most frequently are جَاءَ *jā'a* , شَاءَ *shā'a* and سَاءَ *sā'a* . These are given in the vocabulary. You should note that إِسْتَجَابَ *istajāba* is used more frequently than أَجَابَ *ajāba* for 'to answer'. In later Arabic *ajāba* is the more common.

Vocabulary Twenty-Eight

Perfect	Imperfect	Verbal noun	
سَارَ	يَسِيرُ	سَيْرٌ	to journey
خَافَ	يَخَافُ	خَوْفٌ	to fear
جَاءَ	يَجِيءُ		to come
زَادَ	يَزِيدُ	زِيَادَةٌ	to increase
شَاءَ	يَشَاءُ		to wish
سَاءَ	يَسُوءُ	سُوءٌ	to be bad
أَرَادَ 4	يُرِيدُ	إِرَادَةٌ	to want
أَطَاعَ 4	يُطِيعُ	إِطَاعَةٌ	to obey
إِسْتَطَاعَ 10 [A]	يَسْتَطِيعُ	إِسْتِطَاعَةٌ	to be able
قَامَ	يَقُومُ	قِيَامٌ	to stand, rise
أَقَامَ 4	يُقِيمُ	(إِقَامَةٌ) إِقَامٌ	to perform, uphold
مَاتَ [B]	يَمُوتُ	مَوْتٌ	to die
ذَاقَ	يَذُوقُ	ذَوْقٌ	to taste

[A] This verb—exceptionally—sometimes drops the *tā'* of the 10th form prefix, producing *isṭāʿū*, *yasṭiʿ*, and *tasṭiʿ*

[B] Though *māta* has a *wāw* as its middle radical, the contracted forms of the Perfect normally have a *kasra*: *mittu* etc.

PERFECT	IMPERFECT	VERBAL NOUN	
أَحَاطَ 4	يُحِيطُ	إِحَاطَةٌ	to surround, comprehend
أَصَابَ 4	يُصِيبُ	إِصَابَةٌ	to smite, befall
اِسْتَجَابَ 10	يَسْتَجِيبُ	جَوَابٌ	to answer
أَجَابَ 4	يُجِيبُ	جَوَابٌ	to answer
صَرَفَ	يَصْرِفُ	صَرْفٌ	to turn, turn away (trans.)
أَبْدَلَ 4	يُبْدِلُ	إِبْدَالٌ	to give in exchange

بَرْدٌ	cold (noun)
بَيِّنَةٌ	clear proof
كَيْدٌ	plotting, wiles
وَبَالٌ	mischief
وَزْنٌ	weight
بِٱلْأَمْسِ	yesterday

EXERCISE TWENTY-EIGHT

1. لَا تَخَافِي وَلَا تَحْزَنِي [28:7]
2. أَفَلَمْ يَسِيرُوا فِي ٱلْأَرْضِ [40:82]
3. سَاءَتْ مُسْتَقَرًّا [25:66]
4. سَاءَ مَا كَانُوا يَعْمَلُونَ [58:15]
5. مَا تَشَاؤُونَ إِلَّا أَنْ يَشَاءَ ٱللّٰهُ [76:30]

6. [12:56] نُصِيبُ بِرَحْمَتِنَا مَنْ نَشَاءُ

7. [9:90] سَيُصِيبُ ٱلَّذِينَ كَفَرُوا مِنْهُمْ عَذَابٌ أَلِيمٌ

8. [10:74] جَاؤُوهُمْ بِٱلْبَيِّنَاتِ

9. [7:70] أَجِئْتَنَا لِنَعْبُدَ ٱللَّهَ وَحْدَهُ

10. [28:19] أَتُرِيدُ أَنْ تَقْتُلَنِي كَمَا قَتَلْتَ نَفْسًا بِٱلْأَمْسِ

11. [53:29] لَمْ يُرِدْ إِلَّا ٱلْحَيَوٰةَ ٱلدُّنْيَا

12. [18:81] أَرَدْنَا أَنْ يُبْدِلَهُمَا رَبُّهُمَا خَيْرًا مِنْهُ

13. [11:20] مَا كَانُوا يَسْتَطِيعُونَ ٱلسَّمْعَ

14. [2:285] قَالُوا سَمِعْنَا وَأَطَعْنَا

15. [47:26] سَنُطِيعُكُمْ فِي بَعْضِ ٱلْأَمْرِ

16. [30:25] وَمِنْ آيَاتِهِ أَنْ تَقُومَ ٱلسَّمَاءُ

17. [4:102] فَلْتَقُمْ طَآئِفَةٌ مِنْهُمْ مَعَكَ

18. [18:105] لَا نُقِيمُ لَهُمْ يَوْمَ ٱلْقِيَامَةِ وَزْنًا

19. [78:24] لَا يَذُوقُونَ فِيهَا بَرْدًا وَلَا شَرَابًا

20. [65:9] ذَاقَتْ وَبَالَ أَمْرِهَا

21. [42:26] يَسْتَجِيبُ ٱلَّذِينَ آمَنُوا وَعَمِلُوا ٱلصَّالِحَاتِ

22. [12:34] فَٱسْتَجَابَ لَهُ رَبُّهُ فَصَرَفَ عَنْهُ كَيْدَهُنَّ

23. [28:65] يَقُولُ مَا ذَا أَجَبْتُمُ ٱلْمُرْسَلِينَ

24. [27:22] أَحَطْتُ بِمَا لَمْ تُحِطْ بِهِ

Lesson Twenty-Nine
The Vocative

In the Qur'ān the vocative is normally introduced by the simple particle *yā* or the compound one *yā ayyuhā*. The constructions taken by the two particles are somewhat different.

يَا *yā*

yā must be followed by a noun that does not have the article. The noun may have a pronominal suffix or a following genitive.

If *yā* is followed by a simple noun, the noun is in the nominative, **without** *tanwīn*:

يَا أَرْضُ O earth

يَا سَمَاءُ O heaven

يَا صَالِحُ O Ṣaliḥ

Forms such as *yā ʿīsā, yā mūsā, yā bushrā* are regarded as falling within this rule, though there is of course no visible change.

If *yā* is followed by a noun with a pronominal suffix or with a following genitive, the noun is in the accusative. The use of *tanwīn* is of course impossible.

يَا أَهْلَ ٱلْكِتَابِ O people of the book

يَا أُولِي ٱلْأَلْبَابِ O men of understanding

يَا بَنِيَّ O my sons

When the *yā* is followed by a noun with the first person singular pronominal suffix, it is usual for the long vowel of the suffix to be shortened, although this does not always occur.

يَا رَبِّ My Lord!

يَا قَوْمِ My people!
يَا عِبَادِ My servants!

يَا أَيُّهَا *yā ayyuhā*

yā ayyuhā is followed either by a noun or an adjective with the article:

يَا أَيُّهَا ٱلنَّاسُ O people
يَا أَيُّهَا ٱلنَّمْلُ O ants
يَا أَيُّهَا ٱلْعَزِيزُ O Mighty One
يَا أَيُّهَا ٱلنَّبِيُّ O prophet

or by a definite clause:

ٱلَّذِينَ آمَنُوا those who believe

which becomes:

يَا أَيُّهَا ٱلَّذِينَ آمَنُوا O you who believe

There are a handful of other phrases such as *alladhīna hādū* 'those who are Jews' and *alladhīna kafarū* 'those who disbelieve', but they are rarely found. The only singular phrase is in 15:6:

قَالُوا يَا أَيُّهَا ٱلَّذِي نُزِّلَ عَلَيْهِ ٱلذِّكْرُ إِنَّكَ لَمَجْنُونٌ

> they said, 'You to whom the reminder has been sent down, you are possessed by the *Jinn*'

OMISSION OF THE VOCATIVE PARTICLE

It is quite common for there to be no particle before *rabbi* and *rabba-nā*:

رَبَّنَا Our Lord!

Otherwise omission is relatively rare. There are, however, some good examples in *Sūra* 12. The first two are with the name *Yūsuf*. Verse 29 simply has the name in the nominative and then the rest of the sentence:

[12:29] يُوسُفُ أَعْرِضْ عَنْ هٰذَا

O Joseph, turn away from this

In verse 46 the name is followed by an adjective preceded by *ayyuhā*:

[12:46] يُوسُفُ أَيُّهَا ٱلصِّدِّيقُ

O Joseph, you man of truth!

Verse 101 has a compound phrase, with an accusative vocative:

فَاطِرَ ٱلسَّمَوَاتِ وَٱلْأَرْضِ O Creator of the heavens and the earth

اَللّٰهُمَّ *allāhumma*

Allāhumma as the vocative of *allāh* occurs five times: 3:26; 5:114; 8:32; 10:10; and 39:46.

An anomalous vocative *yā abati*, from *ab*, is found eight times: 12:4; 12:100; 19:42; 19:43; 19:44; 19:45; 28:26 and 37:102. [The corresponding form from *umm* does not occur.]

Vocabulary Twenty-Nine

Perfect	Imperfect	Verbal noun	
سَارَعَ 3	يُسَارِعُ	سِرَاعٌ	to vie in; race
أَبْلَغَ 4	يُبْلِغُ	إِبْلَاغٌ	to convey
أَكْثَرَ 4	يُكْثِرُ	إِكْثَارٌ	to multiply, make much of
اِعْتَذَرَ 8	يَعْتَذِرُ	اِعْتِذَارٌ	to make excuses
فَطَرَ	يَفْطُرُ	فَطْرٌ	to create

Singular

رَهْطٌ	kin; person
صِدِّيقٌ	truthful
كَلِمَةٌ	word
لِبَاسٌ	clothing; garment
نَمْلٌ	ants (collective)
رِسَالَةٌ	message, letter
مَائِدَةٌ	table
أَبَدًا	ever

Exercise Twenty-Nine

1. [2:54] قَالَ مُوسَى لِقَوْمِهِ يَا قَوْمِ إِنَّكُمْ ظَلَمْتُمْ
2. [3:45] يَا مَرْيَمُ إِنَّ ٱللّٰهَ يُبَشِّرُكِ بِكَلِمَةٍ مِنْهُ
3. [5:24] يَا مُوسَى إِنَّا لَنْ نَدْخُلَهَا أَبَدًا
4. [7:26] يَا بَنِي آدَمَ قَدْ أَنْزَلْنَا عَلَيْكُمْ لِبَاسًا
5. [11:46] قَالَ يَا نُوحُ إِنَّهُ لَيْسَ مِنْ أَهْلِكَ
6. [3:70] يَا أَهْلَ ٱلْكِتَابِ لِمَ تَكْفُرُونَ بِآيَاتِ ٱللّٰهِ
7. [38:26] يَا دَاوُودُ إِنَّا جَعَلْنَاكَ خَلِيفَةً فِي ٱلْأَرْضِ
8. [29:56] يَا عِبَادِيَ ٱلَّذِينَ آمَنُوا إِنَّ أَرْضِي وَاسِعَةٌ
9. [5:68] يَا أَهْلَ ٱلْكِتَابِ لَسْتُمْ عَلَى شَيْءٍ
10. [5:112] يَا عِيسَى ٱبْنَ مَرْيَمَ هَلْ يَسْتَطِيعُ رَبُّكَ أَنْ يُنَزِّلَ عَلَيْنَا مَائِدَةً

11. [7:61] يَا قَوْمِ لَيْسَ بِي ضَلَالَةٌ

12. [7:79] قَالَ يَا قَوْمِ لَقَدْ أَبْلَغْتُكُمْ رِسَالَةَ رَبِّي

13. [3:99] يَا أَهْلَ ٱلْكِتَابِ لِمَ تَصُدُّونَ عَنْ سَبِيلِ ٱللهِ مَنْ آمَنَ

14. [11:51] يَا قَوْمِ لَا أَسْأَلُكُمْ عَلَيْهِ أَجْرًا

15. [19:42] يَا أَبَتِ لِمَ تَعْبُدُ مَا لَا يَسْمَعُ

16. [11:92] يَا قَوْمِ أَرَهْطِي أَعَزُّ عَلَيْكُمْ مِنَ ٱللهِ

17. [11:78] يَا قَوْمِ هٰؤُلَاءِ بَنَاتِي

18. [7:104] قَالَ مُوسَى يَا فِرْعَوْنُ إِنِّي رَسُولٌ مِنْ رَبِّ ٱلْعَالَمِينَ

19. [11:32] قَالُوا يَا نُوحُ قَدْ جَادَلْتَنَا فَأَكْثَرْتَ جِدَالَنَا

20. [4:174] يَا أَيُّهَا ٱلنَّاسُ قَدْ جَاءَكُمْ بُرْهَانٌ مِنْ رَبِّكُمْ

21. [5:41] يَا أَيُّهَا ٱلرَّسُولُ لَا يَحْزُنْكَ ٱلَّذِينَ يُسَارِعُونَ فِي ٱلْكُفْرِ

22. [35:15] يَا أَيُّهَا ٱلنَّاسُ أَنْتُمُ ٱلْفُقَرَاءُ إِلَى ٱللهِ

23. [61:2] يَا أَيُّهَا ٱلَّذِينَ آمَنُوا لِمَ تَقُولُونَ مَا لَا تَفْعَلُونَ

24. [66:7] يَا أَيُّهَا ٱلَّذِينَ كَفَرُوا لَا تَعْتَذِرُوا ٱلْيَوْمَ

Lesson Thirty
Defective Verbs

There are three types of defective verbs:

1. verbs of the *kataba* pattern with *wāw* as their final radical, *e.g.* *rajā*;
2. verbs of the *kataba* pattern with *yā'* as their final radical, *e.g.* *ramā*;
3. verbs of the *shariba* pattern with either *wāw* or *yā'* as their final radical, *e.g* *raḍiya, baqiya* and *nasiya.*

As there are no defective verbs that are as common as *kāna* or *qāla*, it is not possible to introduce them gradually. However, they are easier to deal with than hollow verbs. Many of the forms of the Perfect, Imperfect and Subjunctive do not differ from those of the sound verb, but care is needed with the Jussive, where the final radical often appears only as a short vowel.

VERBS OF THE *kataba* PATTERN WITH *wāw* AS FINAL RADICAL

Perfect

	SINGULAR	DUAL	PLURAL
3 m.	رَجَا	رَجَوَا	رَجَوْا
3 f.	رَجَتْ	رَجَتَا	رَجَوْنَ
2 m.	رَجَوْتَ	رَجَوْتُمَا	رَجَوْتُمْ
2 f.	رَجَوْتِ	رَجَوْتُمَا	رَجَوْتُنَّ
1	رَجَوْتُ	–	رَجَوْنَا

Imperfect

	SINGULAR	DUAL	PLURAL
3 m.	يَرْجُو	يَرْجُوَانِ	يَرْجُونَ
3 f.	تَرْجُو	تَرْجُوَانِ	يَرْجُونَ
2 m.	تَرْجُو	تَرْجُوَانِ	تَرْجُونَ
2 f.	تَرْجِينَ	تَرْجُوَانِ	تَرْجُونَ
1	أَرْجُو	–	نَرْجُو

Subjunctive

	SINGULAR	DUAL	PLURAL
3 m.	يَرْجُوَ	يَرْجُوَا	يَرْجُوا
3 f.	تَرْجُوَ	تَرْجُوَا	يَرْجُونَ
2 m.	تَرْجُوَ	تَرْجُوَا	تَرْجُوا
2 f.	تَرْجِي	تَرْجُوَا	تَرْجُونَ
1	أَرْجُوَ	–	نَرْجُوَ

Jussive

	SINGULAR	DUAL	PLURAL
3 m.	يَرْجُ	يَرْجُوَا	يَرْجُوا
3 f.	تَرْجُ	تَرْجُوَا	يَرْجُونَ
2 m.	تَرْجُ	تَرْجُوَا	تَرْجُوا
2 f.	تَرْجِي	تَرْجُوَا	تَرْجُونَ
1	أَرْجُ	–	نَرْجُ

VERBS OF THE *kataba* PATTERN WITH *yā'* AS FINAL RADICAL

Perfect

	SINGULAR	DUAL	PLURAL
3 m.	رَمَى	رَمَيَا	رَمَوْا
3 f.	رَمَتْ	رَمَتَا	رَمَيْنَ
2 m.	رَمَيْتَ	رَمَيْتُمَا	رَمَيْتُمْ
2 f.	رَمَيْتِ	رَمَيْتُمَا	رَمَيْتُنَّ
1	رَمَيْتُ	–	رَمَيْنَا

Imperfect

	SINGULAR	DUAL	PLURAL
3 m.	يَرْمِي	يَرْمِيَانِ	يَرْمُونَ
3 f.	تَرْمِي	تَرْمِيَانِ	يَرْمِينَ
2 m.	تَرْمِي	تَرْمِيَانِ	تَرْمُونَ
2 f.	تَرْمِينَ	تَرْمِيَانِ	تَرْمِينَ
1	أَرْمِي	–	نَرْمِي

Subjunctive

	SINGULAR	DUAL	PLURAL
3 m.	يَرْمِيَ	يَرْمِيَا	يَرْمُوا
3 f.	تَرْمِيَ	تَرْمِيَا	يَرْمِينَ
2 m.	تَرْمِيَ	تَرْمِيَا	تَرْمُوا
2 f.	تَرْمِي	تَرْمِيَا	تَرْمِينَ
1	أَرْمِيَ	–	نَرْمِيَ

Jussive

	Singular	Dual	Plural
3 m.	يَرْمِ	يَرْمِيَا	يَرْمُوا
3 f.	تَرْمِ	تَرْمِيَا	يَرْمِينَ
2 m.	تَرْمِ	تَرْمِيَا	تَرْمُوا
2 f.	تَرْمِي	تَرْمِيَا	تَرْمِينَ
1	أَرْمِ	–	نَرْمِ

Verbs of the *shariba* pattern

Perfect

	Singular	Dual	Plural
3 m.	بَقِيَ	بَقِيَا	بَقُوا
3 f.	بَقِيَتْ	بَقِيَتَا	بَقِينَ
2 m.	بَقِيتَ	بَقِيتُمَا	بَقِيتُمْ
2 f.	بَقِيتِ	بَقِيتُمَا	بَقِيتُنَّ
1	بَقِيتُ	–	بَقِينَا

Imperfect

	Singular	Dual	Plural
3 m.	يَبْقَى	يَبْقَيَانِ	يَبْقَوْنَ
3 f.	تَبْقَى	تَبْقَيَانِ	يَبْقَيْنَ
2 m.	تَبْقَى	تَبْقَيَانِ	تَبْقَوْنَ
2 f.	تَبْقَيْنَ	تَبْقَيَانِ	تَبْقَيْنَ
1	أَبْقَى	–	نَبْقَى

Subjunctive

	Singular	Dual	Plural
3 m.	يَبْقَى	يَبْقَيَا	يَبْقَوْا
3 f.	تَبْقَى	تَبْقَيَا	يَبْقَيْنَ
2 m.	تَبْقَى	تَبْقَيَا	تَبْقَوْا
2 f.	تَبْقَيْ	تَبْقَيَا	تَبْقَيْنَ
1	أَبْقَى	–	نَبْقَى

Jussive

	Singular	Dual	Plural
3 m.	يَبْقَ	يَبْقَيَا	يَبْقَوْا
3 f.	تَبْقَ	تَبْقَيَا	يَبْقَيْنَ
2 m.	تَبْقَ	تَبْقَيَا	تَبْقَوْا
2 f.	تَبْقَيْ	تَبْقَيَا	تَبْقَيْنَ
1	أَبْقَ	–	نَبْقَ

DERIVED FORMS

In the Perfect **all** the derived forms conjugate like *ramā*, regardless of which type the verb is in the first form. In the imperfect tenses they also conjugate like *ramā*, apart from the 5th and 6th forms, which conjugate like the imperfect tenses of *baqiya*.

The basic forms are:

Form	Perfect	Imperfect	Subjunctive	Jussive
2	لَقَّى	يُلَقِّي	يُلَقِّيَ	يُلَقِّ
3	لَاقَى	يُلَاقِي	يُلَاقِيَ	يُلَاقِ
4	أَلْقَى	يُلْقِي	يُلْقِيَ	يُلْقِ
5	تَلَقَّى	يَتَلَقَّى	يَتَلَقَّى	يَتَلَقَّ
6	تَرَاضَى	يَتَرَاضَى	يَتَرَاضَى	يَتَرَاضَ
7	اِنْقَضَى	يَنْقَضِي	يَنْقَضِيَ	يَنْقَضِ
8	اِلْتَقَى	يَلْتَقِي	يَلْتَقِيَ	يَلْتَقِ
10	اِسْتَعْلَى	يَسْتَعْلِي	يَسْتَعْلِيَ	يَسْتَعْلِ

Note that the *maṣdar* of the 2nd form of defective verbs, like that of the 2nd form of third radical *hamza* verbs, is based on the form *tafᶜilatun*. Thus the *maṣdar* of سَمَّى *sammā* is تَسْمِيَةٌ *tasmiyatun* .

As with hollow verbs, some of the most important defective verbs have two weak radicals. They include أَتَى *atā* and its 4th form آتَى *ātā*, وَفَى *wafā*and its 4th form أَوْفَى *awfā*, وَلِيَ *waliya* and its 2nd and 5th forms وَلَّى *wallā*and تَوَلَّى *tawallā* , and اِتَّقَى *ittaqā*, the 8th form of وَقَى *waqā*.

Verbs with two final weak radicals are treated as though the middle radical is sound. They conjugate like *ramā* or *baqiya*. On this basis the triply weak أَوَى *awā* is no different from *atā*.

Special attention should be paid to the very common verb رَأَى *ra'ā*, 'to see'. The Perfect is regular and conjugates like *rama*. However, in the Imperfect the *hamza* disappears: يَرَى *yarā*, يَرَوْنَ *yarawna*, نَرَى *narā*, etc. The same loss of *hamza* occurs in both the Perfect and the Imperfect of the 4th form.

VOCABULARY THIRTY

PERFECT	IMPERFECT	VERBAL NOUN	
أَتَى	يَأْتِي	إِتْيَانٌ	to come
آتَى 4	يُؤْتِي	إِيتَاءٌ	to give
رَأَى	يَرَى	رَأْيٌ	to see
جَزَى	يَجْزِي	جَزَاءٌ	to requite
دَعَا	يَدْعُو	دُعَاءٌ	to call, pray
رَجَا	يَرْجُو	رَجَاءٌ	to hope
قَضَى	يَقْضِي	قَضَاءٌ	to determine
مَشَى	يَمْشِي	مَشْيٌ	to walk
هَدَى	يَهْدِي	هُدًى	to guide
بَقِيَ	يَبْقَى	بَقَاءٌ	to remain
خَشِيَ	يَخْشَى	خَشْيَةٌ	to fear
لَقِيَ	يَلْقَى	لِقَاءٌ	to meet
نَسِيَ	يَنْسَى	نَسْيٌ	to forget
سَمَّى 2	يُسَمِّي	تَسْمِيَةٌ	to name
صَلَّى 2	يُصَلِّي	صَلَاةٌ	to pray
نَادَى 3	يُنَادِي	نِدَاءٌ	to call out to
أَلْقَى 4	يُلْقِي	إِلْقَاءٌ	to throw
أَعْطَى 4	يُعْطِي	إِعْطَاءٌ	to give
أَوْفَى 4	يُوفِي	إِيفَاءٌ	to fulfil, give in full
تَوَلَّى 5	يَتَوَلَّى	تَوَلٍّ	to turn away; to take on oneself

Perfect	Imperfect	Verbal noun	
اِتَّقى 8	يَتَّقِي	اِتِّقَاءٌ	to protect oneself, to be god-fearing
شَعَرَ	يَشْعُرُ	شُعُورٌ	to feel, perceive
أَنْجَى 4	يُنْجِي	إِنْجَاءٌ	to rescue

Singular	Plural	
طِينٌ		clay
رُعْبٌ		terror
سُوقٌ (f.)	اَسْوَاقٌ	market
ثُمَّ		then
بَغْتَةً		suddenly

Exercise Thirty

1. أَتَتْ بِهِ قَوْمَهَا [19:27]
2. تَأْتِيهُمُ آلسَّاعَةُ بَغْتَةً وَهُمْ لَا يَشْعُرُونَ [12:107]
3. كَمْ آتَيْنَاهُمْ مِنْ آيَةٍ بَيِّنَةٍ [2:211]
4. يُقِيمُونَ ٱلصَّلَوٰةَ وَيُؤْتُونَ ٱلزَّكَوٰةَ [5:55]
5. إِنِّي أَرَاكَ وَقَوْمَكَ فِي ضَلَالٍ مُبِينٍ [6:74]
6. أَفَرَأَيْتُمُ ٱلْمَاءَ ٱلَّذِي تَشْرَبُونَ [56:68]
7. أُولَآئِكَ يَرْجُونَ رَحْمَةَ ٱللهِ [2:218]
8. إِنِّي دَعَوْتُ قَوْمِي لَيْلًا وَنَهَارًا [71:5]
9. وَسَيَجْزِي ٱللهُ ٱلشَّاكِرِينَ [3:144]

10. خَلَقَكُمْ مِنْ طِينٍ ثُمَّ قَضَى أَجَلًا [6:2]

11. يَمْشُونَ عَلَى ٱلْأَرْضِ [25:63]

12. يَأْكُلُ ٱلطَّعَامَ وَيَمْشِي فِي ٱلْأَسْوَاقِ [25:7]

13. ٱلْيَوْمَ نَنْسَاهُمْ كَمَا نَسُوا لِقَآءَ يَوْمِهِمْ هَذَا [7:51]

14. لَا يَخْشَوْنَ أَحَدًا إِلَّا ٱللَّهَ [33:39]

15. هُوَ سَمَّاكُمُ ٱلْمُسْلِمِينَ [22:78]

16. فَنَادَتْهُ ٱلْمَلَآئِكَةُ وَهُوَ قَآئِمٌ يُصَلِّي [3:39]

17. هَدَيْنَاهُمْ إِلَى صِرَاطٍ مُسْتَقِيمٍ [6:87]

18. إِنَّ ٱللَّهَ لَا يَهْدِي مَنْ هُوَ كَاذِبٌ كَفَّارٌ [39:3]

19. أَلْقَى عَصَاهُ [7:107]

20. سَنُلْقِي فِي قُلُوبِ ٱلَّذِينَ كَفَرُوا ٱلرُّعْبَ [3:151]

21. أَنْجَيْنَا ٱلَّذِينَ آمَنُوا وَكَانُوا يَتَّقُونَ [27:53]

22. أَوْفَى بِعَهْدِهِ وَٱتَّقَى [3:76]

23. أَفَرَأَيْتَ ٱلَّذِي تَوَلَّى وَأَعْطَى قَلِيلًا [53:34]

24. تَوَلَّى عَنْهُمْ وَقَالَ يَا قَوْمِ لَقَدْ أَبْلَغْتُكُمْ رِسَالَاتِ رَبِّي [7:93]

25. ثُمَّ يَتَوَلَّى فَرِيقٌ مِنْهُمْ وَهُمْ مُعْرِضُونَ [3:23]

Lesson Thirty-One
Ordinal and Other Numbers

In addition to the cardinal numbers set out in Lesson 14, the Qur'ān has examples of three other kinds of numerals: ordinals, fractions and distributives. The use of distributives is very limited, but there is a fair scattering of the ordinals [first to sixth, and eighth] and fractions [a half, a third, a quarter, a fifth, a sixth, an eighth, a tenth]. General tables for the ordinals up to 'tenth', the fractions up to 'one tenth' and the distributives up to 'four each' are set out below.[A]

Ordinals

You have already been fully introduced to the only ordinal that needs care: *awwalu*, *ūlā* f., 'first', normally with the definite article. This operates effectively as an elative. The other ordinals from 'second' to 'tenth' are adjectives of the pattern *fāʿilun*. In the case of 'second' the final weak radical produces *thānin*, which declines like *wālin*; with 'sixth' the basic radicals *s-d-s*, not apparent in the cardinal forms, appear in full; and with 'eighth' there is no sign of the *-in* ending of the cardinal. Ordinal numbers between 'two' and 'ten' agree in number, gender and case with the noun to which they are attached:

	masc.	fem.
first	اَلْأَوَّلُ	اَلْأُولَى
second	ثَانٍ	ثَانِيَةٌ
third	ثَالِثٌ	ثَالِثَةٌ

[A] For ordinals above 'tenth' and for other rare numerical forms see Wright, *Arabic Grammar*, I, pp. 262–264.

fourth	رَابِعٌ	رَابِعَةٌ
fifth	خَامِسٌ	خَامِسَةٌ
sixth	سَادِسٌ	سَادِسَةٌ
seventh	سَابِعٌ	سَابِعَةٌ
eighth	ثَامِنٌ	ثَامِنَةٌ
ninth	تَاسِعٌ	تَاسِعَةٌ
tenth	عَاشِرٌ	عَاشِرَةٌ

Fractions

Apart from نِصْفٌ *nisfun*, 'half', which is not linked to any other part of the numerical system, the basic form for fractions is فُعُلٌ *fuᶜulun* / فُعْلٌ *fuᶜlun* .

In addition, there is a form *mifᶜālun*, which is found with a quarter and a tenth only, the form *miᶜshārun* '1/10' occurring in 34:45. All the other fractions that occur in the Qur'ān are of the *fuᶜulun* form. (In later Arabic *fuᶜlun* is much the more common form.)

1/2	نِصْفٌ	
1/3	ثُلُثٌ	
1/4	رُبُعٌ	مِرْبَاعٌ
1/5	خُمُسٌ	
1/6	سُدُسٌ	
1/7	سُبُعٌ	
1/8	ثُمُنٌ	
1/9	تُسُعٌ	
1/10	عُشُرٌ	مِعْشَارٌ

Distributives

The two distributive forms are *fu'ālu* and *maf'alu*. Both are to be found in the phrase مَثْنَى وَثُلَاثَ وَرُبَاعَ *mathnā wa-thulātha wa-rubā'a* 'two, three or four each' that occurs in 4:3 and 35:1. *mathnā* also occurs with *furādā*, 'singly', in 34:46.

Vocabulary Thirty-One

In addition to the numerals in the lesson you will need the following words:

Perfect	Imperfect	Verbal noun	
أَرَى 4	يُرِي		to show
رَضِيَ	يَرْضَى	رِضْوَانٌ / مَرْضَاةٌ	to be pleased with (+ 'an)
اِبْتَغَى 8	يَبْتَغِي	اِبْتِغَاءٌ	to seek
كَفَى	يَكْفِي	كِفَايَةٌ	to be sufficient

Singular	Plural	
زَوْجٌ	أَزْوَاجٌ	spouse
	صُحُفٌ	sheets
كَلْبٌ	كِلَابٌ	dog
نَجْوَى		secret conference

Idioms Note the construction كَفَى بِٱللّٰهِ حَسِيبًا *kafā bi-llāhi ḥasīban* 'there is sufficiency in God as a reckoner' i.e. 'God is sufficient as a reckoner'. There are further examples in sentences 22 and 23 below.

Exercise Thirty-One

1. [4:11] لِكُلِّ وَاحِدٍ مِنْهُمَا ٱلسُّدُسُ
2. [58:7] مَا يَكُونُ مِنْ نَجْوَى ثَلَاثَةٍ إِلَّا هُوَ رَابِعُهُمْ
3. [18:22] رَابِعُهُمْ كَلْبُهُمْ
4. [4:12] لَكُمُ ٱلرُّبُعُ مِمَّا تَرَكْنَ
5. [4:11] لِأُمِّهِ ٱلثُّلُثُ
6. [4:11] لَهُنَّ ثُلُثَا مَا تَرَكَ
7. [5:73] لَقَدْ كَفَرَ ٱلَّذِينَ قَالُوا إِنَّ ٱللَّهَ ثَالِثُ ثَلَاثَةٍ
8. [43:81] أَنَا أَوَّلُ ٱلْعَابِدِينَ
9. [2:41] لَا تَكُونُوا أَوَّلَ كَافِرٍ بِهِ
10. [87:18] إِنَّ هَٰذَا لَفِي ٱلصُّحُفِ ٱلْأُولَىٰ
11. [77:16] أَلَمْ نُهْلِكِ ٱلْأَوَّلِينَ
12. [17:5] جَآءَ وَعْدُ أُولَاهُمَا
13. [18:22] وَيَقُولُونَ سَبْعَةٌ وَثَامِنُهُمْ كَلْبُهُمْ
14. [4:12] لَهُنَّ ٱلثُّمُنُ مِمَّا تَرَكْتُمْ
15. [34:45] مَا بَلَغُوا مِعْشَارَ مَا آتَيْنَاهُمْ
16. [73:20] إِنَّ رَبَّكَ يَعْلَمُ أَنَّكَ تَقُومُ أَدْنَىٰ مِنْ ثُلُثَيِ ٱللَّيْلِ وَنِصْفَهُ وَثُلُثَهُ
17. [4:12] لَكُمْ نِصْفُ مَا تَرَكَ أَزْوَاجُكُمْ
18. [58:22] رَضِيَ ٱللَّهُ عَنْهُمْ وَرَضُوا عَنْهُ
19. [79:20] فَأَرَاهُ ٱلْآيَةَ ٱلْكُبْرَىٰ

20. كَذَٰلِكَ يُرِيهِمُ ٱللَّهُ أَعْمَالَهُمْ [2:167]

21. أَوَلَمْ يَكْفِهِمْ أَنَّا أَنْزَلْنَا عَلَيْكَ ٱلْكِتَابَ [29:51]

22. كَفَىٰ بِٱللَّهِ وَلِيًّا [4:45]

23. كَفَىٰ بِٱللَّهِ شَهِيدًا بَيْنَنَا وَبَيْنَكُمْ [10:29]

24. لَيْسَ عَلَيْكُمْ جُنَاحٌ أَنْ تَبْتَغُوا فَضْلًا مِنْ رَبِّكُمْ [2:198]

Lesson Thirty-Two
The Imperative

The Imperative occurs in the second person only. It is used for commands, and only for commands—it cannot be used with a negative. As you have already been shown in Lesson 20, prohibitions (negative commands) are expressed by *lā* and the Jussive.

The Imperative is formed directly from the second person of the Jussive, by dropping the prefix *ta-* or *tu-*.

a) If the letter that follows that prefix has its own vowel, that is all there is to process:

Imperative	2 Jussive
قُلْ	تَقُلْ
كُونِي	تَكُونِي
قُولُوا	تَقُولُوا
ذَرُوا	تَذَرُوا
قِ	تَقِ
قَدِّرْ	تُقَدِّرْ
قَدِّمُوا	تُقَدِّمُوا
جَاهِدُوا	تُجَاهِدُوا
تَوَكَّلْ	تَتَوَكَّلْ
تَوَقَّ	تَتَوَقَّ

The only exception to this rule is with the 4th form doubled and hollow verbs. This is dealt with in the section on the 4th form below.

b) If the letter that follows the prefix does not have its own vowel, a vowel must be added. In most cases this will be a temporary *hamzat al-waṣl* (in the 1st, 7th, 8th and 10th forms), but the 4th form takes the permanent *hamzat al-qaṭᶜ*.

1st Form

If the vowel of the second radical is *ḍamma*, the added vowel is *ḍamma*; if it is *fatḥa* or *kasra*, the added vowel is *kasra*:

Imperative	2 Jussive
أُكْتُبْ	تَكْتُبْ
اِرْجِعُوا	تَرْجِعُوا
اِذْهَبَا	تَذْهَبَا
اِشْرَبِي	تَشْرَبِي

4th Form

The prefix *tu-* is replaced by *a-* (*hamzat al-qaṭᶜ* and *fatḥa*), regardless of the presence or absence of a vowel on the first radical:

Imperative	2 Jussive
أَدْخِلْ	تُدْخِلْ
أَنْذِرُوا	تُنْذِرُوا
أَلْقِ	تُلْقِ
أَقِمْ	تُقِمْ
أَقِيمُوا	تُقِيمُوا
أَعِدُّوا	تُعِدُّوا

8th and 10th Forms

With these forms *ta-* is replaced by a temporary *kasra*:

Imperative	2 Jussive
اِنْتَصِرْ	تَنْتَصِرْ
اِتَّخِذُوا	تَتَّخِذُوا
اِتَّقُوا	تَتَّقُوا
اِسْتَغْفِرْ	تَسْتَغْفِرْ
اِسْتَفْتِ	تَسْتَفْتِ
اِسْتَقِيمُوا	تَسْتَقِيمُوا

Special Forms

Three verbs that have *hamza* as their initial radical—*akhadha*, *akala*, *amara*—lose the *hamza* in the imperative:

Imperative	2 Jussive
خُذْ	تَأْخُذْ
خُذُوا	تَأْخُذُوا
كُلِي	تَأْكُلِي
كُلَا	تَأْكُلَا
مُرْ	تَأْمُرْ

By a quirk of Qur'ānic orthography, مُرْ *mur*, which occurs with *wa-* in *wa-mur* is written with a redundant *alif*, *hamza*, *sukūn* before the *mīm*: وَأْمُرْ. Tradition is the only justification for this. The verb سَأَلَ *sa'ala* has both forms that retain the *hamza* (اِسْأَلُوا *is'alū* and

فَٱسْأَلْ *fa-s'al* etc.) and one that drops the *hamza* (سَلْ *sal*). The latter is what one would expect in the Ḥijāz.

The 4th form verb *ātā* has some imperative forms that have an initial *hā'* instead of *hamza*. In the Qur'ān only the masculine plural form هَاتُوا *hātū*is to be found.

Vocabulary Thirty-Two

Perfect	Imperfect	Verbal noun	
بَدَأَ	يَبْدَأُ	بَدْءٌ	to begin
رَزَقَ	يَرْزُقُ	رِزْقٌ	to give sustenance to
سَرَقَ	يَسْرِقُ	سَرِقٌ	to steal
هَجَرَ	يَهْجُرُ	هِجْرٌ	to forsake, leave
5 تَمَتَّعَ	يَتَمَتَّعُ	تَمَتُّعٌ	to enjoy, enjoy oneself

Singular	Plural	
سُورَةٌ	سُوَرٌ	*sura*
قِبْلَةٌ		direction, *qibla*
قُوَّةٌ	قُوًى	power, force
كَيْلٌ		measure
آلٌ		family

Exercise Thirty-Two

1. أَعْرِضْ عَنْهُمْ وَتَوَكَّلْ عَلَى ٱللّٰهِ [4:81]
2. خُذُوا مَا آتَيْنَاكُمْ بِقُوَّةٍ وَٱذْكُرُوا مَا فِيهِ [2:63]
3. اُسْكُنْ أَنْتَ وَزَوْجُكَ ٱلْجَنَّةَ وَكُلَا مِنْهَا [2:35]

4. [20:132] وَمُرْ أَهْلَكَ بِٱلصَّلَوٰةِ وَٱصْطَبِرْ عَلَيْهَا

5. [57:7] آمِنُوا بِٱللّٰهِ وَرَسُولِهِ

6. [4:138] بَشِّرِ ٱلْمُنَافِقِينَ بِأَنَّ لَهُمْ عَذَابًا أَلِيمًا

7. [12:29] اِسْتَغْفِرِي لِذَنْبِكِ

8. [10:87] اِجْعَلُوا بُيُوتَكُمْ قِبْلَةً وَأَقِيمُوا ٱلصَّلَاةَ

9. [35:6] إِنَّ ٱلشَّيْطَانَ لَكُمْ عَدُوٌّ فَٱتَّخِذُوهُ عَدُوًّا

10. [71:1] أَنْذِرْ قَوْمَكَ مِنْ قَبْلِ أَنْ يَأْتِيَهُمْ عَذَابٌ أَلِيمٌ

11. [9:119] اِتَّقُوا ٱللّٰهَ وَكُونُوا مَعَ ٱلصَّادِقِينَ

12. [2:126] رَبِّ ٱجْعَلْ هٰذَا بَلَدًا آمِنًا وَٱرْزُقْ أَهْلَهُ مِنَ ٱلثَّمَرَاتِ

13. [4:59] رُدُّوهُ إِلَى ٱللّٰهِ وَٱلرَّسُولِ

14. [46:4] أَرُونِي مَا ذَا خَلَقُوا مِنَ ٱلْأَرْضِ

15. [74:2] قُمْ فَأَنْذِرْ

16. [39:8] قُلْ تَمَتَّعْ بِكُفْرِكَ قَلِيلًا إِنَّكَ مِنْ أَصْحَابِ ٱلنَّارِ

17. [29:30] قَالَ رَبِّ ٱنْصُرْنِي عَلَى ٱلْقَوْمِ ٱلْمُفْسِدِينَ

18. [12:88] أَوْفِ لَنَا ٱلْكَيْلَ وَتَصَدَّقْ عَلَيْنَا

19. [41:40] اِعْمَلُوا مَا شِئْتُمْ إِنَّهُ بِمَا تَعْمَلُونَ بَصِيرٌ

20. [27:56] أَخْرِجُوا آلَ لُوطٍ مِنْ قَرْيَتِكُمْ

21. [2:23] فَأْتُوا بِسُورَةٍ مِنْ مِثْلِهِ وَٱدْعُوا شُهَدَآءَكُمْ

22. [16:32] يَقُولُونَ سَلَامٌ عَلَيْكُمُ ٱدْخُلُوا ٱلْجَنَّةَ بِمَا كُنْتُمْ تَعْمَلُونَ

23. [3:32] قُلْ أَطِيعُوا ٱللّٰهَ وَٱلرَّسُولَ

24. [73:10] اِصْبِرْ عَلَى مَا يَقُولُونَ وَٱهْجُرْهُمْ هَجْرًا جَمِيلًا

25. [29:20] قُلْ سِيرُوا فِي ٱلْأَرْضِ فَٱنْظُرُوا كَيْفَ بَدَأَ ٱلْخَلْقَ

Lesson Thirty-Three
The Passive

The Passive is much less common than the Active. Early Arabic, in particular, does not allow the Passive to be used with the agent. Thus one will always find the equivalent of 'the thunderbolt took them' rather than 'they were taken by the thunderbolt'. On the other hand, the use of impersonal passive verbs produces a series of third person masculine singular passive forms from intransitive verbs or those, like *aḥāṭa bi-* or *ghaḍiba ʿalā*, whose object is governed by a preposition. The Passive is formed by using a different set of vowels from those used in the Active. Conjugation is precisely the same as that of the Active. The basic forms for the Passive of *qabila* are:

Form	Perfect	Imperfect	Subjunctive	Jussive
1	قُبِلَ	يُقْبَلُ	يُقْبَلَ	يُقْبَلْ
2	قُبِّلَ	يُقَبَّلُ	يُقَبَّلَ	يُقَبَّلْ
3	قُوبِلَ	يُقَابَلُ	يُقَابَلَ	يُقَابَلْ
4	أُقْبِلَ	يُقْبَلُ	يُقْبَلَ	يُقْبَلْ
5	تُقُبِّلَ	يُتَقَبَّلُ	يُتَقَبَّلَ	يُتَقَبَّلْ
6	تُقُوبِلَ	يُتَقَابَلُ	يُتَقَابَلَ	يُتَقَابَلْ
7	أُنْقُبِلَ	يُنْقَبَلُ	يُنْقَبَلَ	يُنْقَبَلْ
8	أُقْتُبِلَ	يُقْتَبَلُ	يُقْتَبَلَ	يُقْتَبَلْ
10	أُسْتُقْبِلَ	يُسْتَقْبَلُ	يُسْتَقْبَلَ	يُسْتَقْبَلْ

Note that there is no variation in the vowel of the second radical of the first form in the Passive.

DOUBLED VERBS

There are no special problems. Contraction takes place as in the Active. Thus from the verb رَدَّ *radda* there are such passive forms as رُدَّتْ *ruddat*, رُدِدْتُ *rudidtu*, رُدُّوا *ruddū*, تُرَدُّ *turaddu*, يُرَدُّونَ *yuraddūna*, نُرَدُّ *nuraddu*, etc.

There are a handful of examples of the 8th form Passive أُضْطُرَّ *uḍṭurra*, which, as elsewhere in Arabic, is more common in the Passive than the Active.

ASSIMILATED VERBS

Note that first radical *wāw* is retained in the imperfect passive of the first form, unlike the active where the *wāw* normally disappears in the imperfect tenses.

وَجَدَ *wajada*

imperfect active: يَجِدُ *yajidu* imperfect passive: يُوجَدُ *yūjadu*

HOLLOW VERBS

Hollow verb passives are generally rare in Arabic, and the only examples in the Qur'ān are the 1st and 4th form passives. (7th, 8th and 10th form examples are to be found in other texts.)

Form	Perfect	Imperfect	Subjunctive	Jussive
1	قِيلَ	يُقَالُ	يُقَالَ	يُقَلْ
4	أُحِيطَ	يُحَاطُ	يُحَاطَ	يُحَطْ

As mentioned above, the forms *uḥīṭa* and *yuḥāṭa* are impersonal, as are جِيءَ *jī'a* (from جَاءَ *jā'a*) and, probably, سِيءَ *sī'a* (from سَاءَ *sā'a*).

In the Perfect of these forms, the long vowel *ī* remains in those persons in which *ā* is found in the active. When contraction takes place, *ī* becomes *i*. Thus the 2 m.s. of *qīla* is قِلْتَ *qilta*. The imperfect tenses conjugate like the imperfect tenses of *khāfa*.

DEFECTIVE VERBS

Form	Perfect	Imperfect	Subjunctive	Jussive
1	جُزِيَ	يُجْزَى	يُجْزَى	يُجْزَ
3	نُودِيَ	يُنَادَى	يُنَادَى	يُنَادَ
4	أُوتِيَ	يُؤْتَى	يُؤْتَى	يُؤْتَ
5	تُوُفِّيَ	يُتَوَفَّى	يُتَوَفَّى	يُتَوَفَّ

All these forms conjugate like *nasiya*.

The Qur'ān has a greater incidence of passives of defective verbs than of hollow verbs, but only three are relatively common: the 4th form *ātā*; the 4th form *awḥā*; and the 1st form *jazā*. Otherwise there is a scattering of 1st, 3rd, 4th and 5th form passives, and the occasional 8th form passive participle (e.g. the plural of مُصْطَفًى). Other derived form passives, though found elsewhere in Arabic, need not detain us here. It is worth noting that there are a couple of examples of *yurā*, the imperfect passive of *ra'ā*, and one of *yuraw*, which is the 3 m.p. subjunctive of *arā*.

The Impersonal Passive

The impersonal passive is expressed by the 3 m.s. It is usually easy to spot:

قُضِيَ بَيْنَهُمْ	there was judgement between them
اُسْتُهْزِئَ بِهِ	there was mockery of him
يُكْشَفُ عَنْ سَاقٍ	there is uncovering of a leg (metaphorical for fighting taking place)

It should be noted that the impersonal use extends to the passive participle. First, two non-Quranic examples:

اَلْمَغْضُوبُ عَلَيْهِ	the man against whom there is anger

اَلْمَغْضُوبُ عَلَيْهَا the woman against whom there is anger

Hence we get in the *Fātiḥa* the genitive phrase:

اَلْمَغْضُوبِ عَلَيْهِمْ those against whom there is anger

Vocabulary Thirty-Three

Perfect	Imperfect	Verbal noun	
غَضِبَ	يَغْضَبُ	غَضَبٌ	to be angry with (+ ʿ*alā*)
وَفَّى 2	يُوَفِّي	تَوْفِيَةٌ	to pay, repay
تَوَفَّى 5	يَتَوَفَّى	تَوَفٍّ	to take
أَوْحَى 4	يُوحِي	إِيحَاءٌ	to inspire
نَفَخَ	يَنْفُخُ	نَفْخٌ	to blow
بَلَّغَ 2	يُبَلِّغُ	تَبْلِيغٌ	to convey
اِسْتَهْزَأَ 10	يَسْتَهْزِئُ	اِسْتِهْزَاءٌ	to mock (+ *bi-*)

Singular	
بَلَاغٌ	message, conveyance
صُورٌ	trumpet

Exercise Thirty-Three

1. أُخْرِجُوا مِنْ دِيَارِهِمْ [3:195]
2. أُخِذُوا مِنْ مَكَانٍ قَرِيبٍ [34:51]
3. مَا أُوتِيتُمْ مِنَ آلْعِلْمِ إِلَّا قَلِيلًا [17:85]

4. [6:124] لَنْ نُؤْمِنَ حَتَّى نُؤْتَى مِثْلَ مَا أُوتِيَ رُسُلُ ٱللّٰهِ
5. [39:69] جِيءَ بِٱلنَّبِيِّينَ وَٱلشُّهَدَآءِ وَقُضِيَ بَيْنَهُمْ
6. [48:16] سَتُدْعَوْنَ إِلَى قَوْمٍ أُولِي بَأْسٍ شَدِيدٍ
7. [10:27] أُغْشِيَتْ وُجُوهُهُمْ قِطَعًا مِنَ ٱللَّيْلِ
8. [2:281] ثُمَّ تُوَفَّى كُلُّ نَفْسٍ مَا كَسَبَتْ وَهُمْ لَا يُظْلَمُونَ
9. [23:83] لَقَدْ وُعِدْنَا نَحْنُ وَآبَآؤُنَا هٰذَا مِنْ قَبْلُ
10. [46:35] يَرَوْنَ مَا يُوعَدُونَ
11. [20:48] أُوحِيَ إِلَيْنَا أَنَّ ٱلْعَذَابَ عَلَى مَنْ كَذَّبَ وَتَوَلَّى
12. [21:41] لَقَدِ ٱسْتُهْزِئَ بِرُسُلٍ مِنْ قَبْلِكَ
13. [6:47] هَلْ يُهْلَكُ إِلَّا ٱلْقَوْمُ ٱلظَّالِمُونَ
14. [29:46] قُولُوا آمَنَّا بِٱلَّذِي أُنْزِلَ إِلَيْنَا
15. [41:16] هُمْ لَا يُنْصَرُونَ
16. [2:279] لَا تَظْلِمُونَ وَلَا تُظْلَمُونَ
17. [40:40] يُرْزَقُونَ فِيهَا بِغَيْرِ حِسَابٍ
18. [12:65] هٰذِهِ بِضَاعَتُنَا رُدَّتْ إِلَيْنَا
19. [6:121] لَا تَأْكُلُوا مِمَّا لَمْ يُذْكَرِ ٱسْمُ ٱللّٰهِ عَلَيْهِ
20. [10:52] هَلْ تُجْزَوْنَ إِلَّا بِمَا كُنْتُمْ تَكْسِبُونَ
21. [14:52] هٰذَا بَلَاغٌ لِلنَّاسِ وَلِيُنْذَرُوا بِهِ
22. [41:44] أُولَآئِكَ يُنَادَوْنَ مِنْ مَكَانٍ بَعِيدٍ
23. [3:184] قَدْ كُذِّبَ رُسُلٌ مِنْ قَبْلِكَ جَاءُوا بِٱلْبَيِّنَاتِ
24. [46:23] أُبَلِّغُكُمْ مَا أُرْسِلْتُ بِهِ

25. يُنْفَخُ فِي ٱلصُّورِ [6:73]

26. اِتَّقُوا ٱلنَّارَ ٱلَّتِي أُعِدَّتْ لِلْكَافِرِينَ [3:131]

27. ظَنُّوا أَنَّهُمْ أُحِيطَ بِهِمْ [10:22]

28. إِنَّ هٰذَا لَشَيْءٌ يُرَادُ [38:6]

Lesson Thirty-Four
More about Nouns

Iḍāfa CLAUSES

In Lesson 7 attention was drawn in passing to the fact that the second element of an *iḍāfa* may sometimes be a clause rather than the normal noun or pronoun. Now that the full range of verbs has been introduced, it is appropriate to look at these *iḍāfa* clauses, the most common usages of which are temporal. The majority of Qur'ānic examples in which a verb provides the second element of an *iḍāfa* involve *yawm* or *ḥīn*:

[5:119] هَٰذَا يَوْمُ يَنْفَعُ ٱلصَّادِقِينَ صِدْقُهُمْ

this is the day when the truthful will benefit from their truthfulness

[15:36] إِلَى يَوْمِ يُبْعَثُونَ

till the day when they are raised

[19:15] يَوْمَ وُلِدَ

the day he was born

[68:42] يَوْمَ يُكْشَفُ عَنْ سَاقٍ

on the day when [the] leg shall be bared

[25:42] حِينَ يَرَوْنَ ٱلْعَذَابَ

when they see the torment

[5:101] حِينَ يُنَزَّلُ ٱلْقُرْآنُ

when the Recitation is being sent down

ذُو *dhū*, أَبٌ *ab*, أَخٌ *akh*, فَمٌ *fam*

The noun *dhū* (accusative *dhā*, genitive *dhī*- found only with a following genitive) was mentioned briefly in Lesson 7.

A few other nouns have long final vowels when they are the first element in an *iḍāfa* construction. The most important of these words are common in the Qur'ān, and have already been partially introduced: *ab* and *akh*. Both originally had a *wāw* as the third radical. When these words are the first element in an *iḍāfa* they have the following forms:

nom.	acc.	gen.
أَبُو ٱلْوَلَدِ	أَبَا ٱلْوَلَدِ	أَبِي ٱلْوَلَدِ
أَبُوهُ	أَبَاهُ	أَبِيهِ
أَخُو ٱلْبِنْتِ	أَخَا ٱلْبِنْتِ	أَخِي ٱلْبِنْتِ
أَخُوهَا	أَخَاهَا	أَخِيهَا

In the Qur'ān *ab* and *akh* normally occur only with suffixes:

abū-humā, abā-nā, abī-kum; akhū-ka, akhā-hum, akhī-hi

There are three exceptions: *abā aḥadin* [33:40], *abī lahabin* [111:1] and *akhā ʿādin* [46:21]. The rarity of such examples does not reflect usage outside the Qur'ān, where the use of *abū* in proper names, for example, is widespread.

The dual of *ab* is أَبَوَانِ *abawāni* / أَبَوَيْنِ *abawayni* (with the sense of 'parents'); and that of *akh* is *akhawāni* / *akhawayni*.

The most awkward noun in this little group is فَمٌ *fam*, 'mouth', which has the following forms as the first element of an *iḍāfa* (here with the suffix *-hu* as the second element):

	nom.	acc.	gen.
(regular)	فَمُهُ	فَمَهُ	فَمِهِ
OR			
(irregular)	فُوهُ	فَاهُ	فِيهِ

The only one of these forms found in the Qur'ān is *fā-hu* [13:14], though the plural, which is أَفْوَاهٌ *afwāhun*, occurs a dozen times.

The Improper Genitive

The improper genitive occurs in two types of phrases:

1. Where an adjective is followed by a genitive that restricts its meaning:

وَاسِعُ ٱلْمَغْفِرَةِ	[53:32]	wide in forgiveness
سَرِيعُ ٱلْحِسَابِ	[3:19]	swift to the reckoning
شَدِيدُ ٱلْعَذَابِ	[2:165]	severe in punishment
شَدِيدُ ٱلْمِحَالِ	[13:13]	mighty in wrath
غَلِيظَ ٱلْقَلْبِ	[3:159]	hard-hearted

2. Where the genitive comes after the participle of a transitive verb and takes the place of an object in the accusative:

كُلُّ نَفْسٍ ذَائِقَةُ ٱلْمَوْتِ	[3:185]	every soul will taste death
(acc.) هَدْيًا بَالِغَ ٱلْكَعْبَةِ	[5:95]	an offering getting to the Ka'ba
(acc.) مُقِيمَ ٱلصَّلَوٰةِ	[14:40]	performing prayer
(gen.) مُتَّخِذِي أَخْدَانٍ	[5:5]	taking 'companions'

Such genitives are termed 'improper' because they have no grammatical influence on the governing word, other than causing it to drop *tanwīn*, even though they modify its meaning. The governing word many therefore take the definite article. This is rare in early Arabic but has gradually become more common. In the Qur'ān we find:

(acc.) ٱلْمُقِيمِي ٱلصَّلَوٰةِ [22:35] those performing prayer

(in contrast to وَٱلْمُقِيمِينَ ٱلصَّلَوٰةَ [4:162], with the same meaning)

Ghayr AND ITS DERIVATIVES

Ghayrun is in the first instance a noun, used with a following genitive, to mean 'something different from' or 'other than...' or 'another...':

غَيْرَ ٱلْإِسْلَامِ	[3:85]	other than Islam
غَيْرَ ٱلْحَقِّ	[5:77]	anything but the truth
غَيْرَ سَبِيلِ ٱلْمُؤْمِنِينَ	[4:115]	[a way] other than that of the believers

If the second element of the *iḍāfa* is indefinite, the *iḍāfa* phrase will have the sense of an indefinite adjectival phrase, and be treated as such grammatically:

أَجْرٌ غَيْرُ مَمْنُونٍ	[41:8]	an unbroken reward
عَمَلٌ غَيْرُ صَالِحٍ	[11:46]	an unrighteous deed

In such cases it is the second term in the *iḍāfa* that will link back in gender and number either to the noun to which the phrase as appended or to the subject:

غَيْرَ مُشْرِكِينَ بِهِ [22:31] not associating anything with him

[links back to the imperative *ijtanibū* in the previous verse]

غَيْرُ مُعْجِزِي ٱللَّهِ [9:2] not frustrating God

[refers back to *anna-kum* that immediately precedes it]

جَنَّاتٍ مَعْرُوشَاتٍ وَغَيْرَ مَعْرُوشَاتٍ	[6:141]	gardens [both] trellised and untrellised
إِنَّهُمْ غَيْرُ مَلُومِينَ	[23:6]	they are not blameworthy

In the Qur'ān it is extremely rare for the second term to be definite, though there is a well-known example from the *Fātiḥa*:

غَيْرِ ٱلْمَغْضُوبِ عَلَيْهِمْ [1:7]

[the suffix -*him* refers back to *alladhīna*; see also Lesson 33]

If repetition of the negative idea occurs, *ghayr* is not repeated but *wa-lā* is used instead:

غَيْرَ بَاغٍ وَلَا عَادٍ	[2:173]	not outraging nor transgressing

The accusative *ghayra* is also used as a preposition, meaning 'without'. The compound forms *bi-ghayri* (see Lesson 21) and *min ghayri* are also common. With these prepositions, too, repetition is by use of *wa-lā*:

بِغَيْرِ عِلْمٍ وَلَا هُدًى وَلَا كِتَابٍ مُنِيرٍ [22:8]

without knowledge or guidance or an illuminating scripture

Vocabulary Thirty-Four

Perfect	Imperfect	Verbal noun	
بَسَطَ	يَبْسُطُ	بَسْطٌ	to spread,extend
خَتَمَ	يَخْتِمُ	خَتْمٌ	to seal
سَبَقَ	يَسْبِقُ	سَبْقٌ	to precede
فَتَنَ	يَفْتِنُ	فِتْنَةٌ	to tempt, afflict, stir up
فَرَّ	يَفِرُّ	فِرَارٌ	to flee
كَشَفَ	يَكْشِفُ	كَشْفٌ	to uncover, remove, relieve

Perfect	Imperfect	Verbal noun	
وُلِدَ	يُولَدُ	[passive]	to be born
تَبَّ			to wither, perish
بَغَى	يَبْغِي	بَغْيٌ	to outrage; to seek
عَدَا	يَعْدُو	عَدْوٌ	to transgress, turn away, run
4 أَصْلَحَ	يُصْلِحُ	إِصْلَاحٌ	to put right
4 أَعْجَزَ	يُعْجِزُ	إِعْجَازٌ	to frustrate

Singular	Plural	
اِمْرُؤٌ		man
حَكَمٌ		arbiter
سَاقٌ (f.)	سُوقٌ	leg
عِقَابٌ		punishment, requital
عَمَدٌ		columns, supports
فَمٌ	أَفْوَاهٌ	mouth
مِحَالٌ		wrath, anger
هَدْيٌ		offering
	أَخْدَانٌ	companions
سَرِيعٌ		quick, swift
غَلِيظٌ		thick, rough, hard
مَعْرُوشٌ		in trellises
مَلُومٌ [from لَامَ, يَلُومُ]		blamed, blameworthy
مَمْنُونٌ		broken, cut

غَيْرٌ other than

غَيْرَ without

Exercise Thirty-Four

1. [24:24] يَوْمَ تَشْهَدُ عَلَيْهِمْ أَلْسِنَتُهُمْ
2. [10:28] يَوْمَ نَحْشُرُهُمْ جَمِيعًا
3. [9:36] يَوْمَ خَلَقَ ٱلسَّمَوَاتِ وَٱلْأَرْضَ
4. [50:42] يَوْمَ يَسْمَعُونَ ٱلصَّيْحَةَ
5. [51:13] يَوْمَ هُمْ عَلَى ٱلنَّارِ يُفْتَنُونَ
6. [6:73] يَوْمَ يُنْفَخُ فِي ٱلصُّورِ
7. [80:34] يَوْمَ يَفِرُّ ٱلْمَرْءُ مِنْ أَخِيهِ
8. [28:23] أَبُونَا شَيْخٌ كَبِيرٌ
9. [111:1] تَبَّتْ يَدَا أَبِي لَهَبٍ
10. [12:81] اِرْجِعُوا إِلَى أَبِيكُمْ فَقُولُوا يَا أَبَانَا إِنَّ ٱبْنَكَ سَرَقَ
11. [37:85] قَالَ لِأَبِيهِ وَقَوْمِهِ مَا ذَا تَعْبُدُونَ
12. [19:28] مَا كَانَ أَبُوكَ ٱمْرَأَ سَوْءٍ
13. [18:80] كَانَ أَبَوَاهُ مُؤْمِنَيْنِ
14. [7:27] أَخْرَجَ أَبَوَيْكُمْ مِنَ ٱلْجَنَّةِ
15. [26:106] قَالَ لَهُمْ أَخُوهُمْ نُوحٌ أَلَا تَتَّقُونَ
16. [23:45] أَرْسَلْنَا مُوسَى وَأَخَاهُ هَارُونَ بِآيَاتِنَا
17. [12:64] هَلْ آمَنُكُمْ عَلَيْهِ إِلَّا كَمَا أَمِنْتُكُمْ عَلَى أَخِيهِ

18. [49:10] فَأَصْلِحُوا بَيْنَ أَخَوَيْكُمْ

19. [53:32] إِنَّ رَبَّكَ وَاسِعُ ٱلْمَغْفِرَةِ

20. [8:52] إِنَّ ٱللّٰهَ قَوِيٌّ شَدِيدُ ٱلْعِقَابِ

21. [36:40] وَلَا ٱللَّيْلُ سَابِقُ ٱلنَّهَارِ

22. [6:93] اَلْمَلَائِكَةُ بَاسِطُو أَيْدِيهِمْ

23. [36:65] اَلْيَوْمَ نَخْتِمُ عَلَى أَفْوَاهِهِمْ

24. [24:27] يَا أَيُّهَا ٱلَّذِينَ آمَنُوا لَا تَدْخُلُوا بُيُوتًا غَيْرَ بُيُوتِكُمْ

25. [6:114] أَفَغَيْرَ ٱللّٰهِ أَبْتَغِي حَكَمًا

26. [68:3] إِنَّ لَكَ لَأَجْرًا غَيْرَ مَمْنُونٍ

27. [19:33] اَلسَّلَامُ عَلَيَّ يَوْمَ وُلِدْتُّ وَيَوْمَ أَمُوتُ

Lesson Thirty-Five
More on the Accusative

The Particle *iyyā-*

iyyā- is a particle which is normally found only with a pronominal suffix attached to it. The particle and suffix indicate the accusative (though the particle and the 1 s. suffix produce *iyyā-ya*).

It tends to be used in the Qur'ān to enable the object to be placed in front of the verb for emphasis. The best known example of this is in the *Fātiḥa*:

[1:5] إِيَّاكَ نَعْبُدُ وَإِيَّاكَ نَسْتَعِينُ

You we worship, You we turn to for help

In that verse the accusative is not repeated. It is more common for the suffix to be repeated with the verb for further emphasis:

[16:51] فَإِيَّايَ فَٱرْهَبُونِ

Me, be in awe of Me

Otherwise it is used for a second pronominal object:

[17:31] نَحْنُ نَرْزُقُهُمْ وَإِيَّاكُمْ

We provide sustenance for them and for you

[60:1] يُخْرِجُونَ ٱلرَّسُولَ وَإِيَّاكُمْ

they drive out the messenger and you

[9:114] وَعَدَهَا إِيَّاهُ

he promised it to him

When it follows *inna* it indicates the subject, as in:

وَإِنَّا أَوْ إِيَّاكُمْ لَعَلَى هُدًى [34:24]

we or you are rightly guided

It is also used after *illā*:

لَا تَعْبُدُوا إِلَّا إِيَّاهُ [12:40] serve Him only

There is no Qur'ānic example of the usage found elsewhere in Arabic, in which *iyyā-*. . . *wa-iyyā* has the sense of 'beware'.

THE ACCUSATIVE OF ABSOLUTE NEGATION

In this usage, known in Arabic as لَا لِنَفْيِ ٱلْجِنْسِ *lā li-nafyi l-jinsi*, the negative *lā* is followed immediately by a noun in the accusative without *tanwīn*. The most famous example occurs at the beginning of the *shahāda*:

لَا إِلَاهَ إِلَّا ٱللهُ there is no god but God

There are examples throughout the Qur'ān, e.g.:

لَا رَيْبَ فِيهِ	[2:2]	there is no doubt about it
لَا مَرَدَّ لَهُ	[13:11]	there is no turning it back
لَا كَاشِفَ لَهُ	[6:17]	there is no one to remove it

THE COGNATE ACCUSATIVE

In this usage, known in Arabic as the *mafʿūl muṭlaq*, a verb may take its own *maṣdar* (or sometimes the *maṣdar* of a verb with the same or a similar meaning) to add greater force to the verb or to extend its meaning. In its simplest form we find:

عَدَّهُمْ عَدًّا [19:94] he has numbered them [exactly]

إِذَا رُجَّتِ ٱلْأَرْضُ رَجًّا [56:4] when the earth shall be shaken

Sometimes the *maṣdar* is repeated for greater emphasis:

إِذَا دُكَّتِ ٱلْأَرْضُ دَكًّا دَكًّا [89:21]

when the earth shall be pounded to bits

More commonly the verb is followed by an adjective, with the *maṣdar* and adjective usually translating most easily into English as an adverb:

يُرِيدُ ٱلَّذِينَ يَتَّبِعُونَ ٱلشَّهَوَاتِ أَنْ تَمِيلُوا مَيْلًا عَظِيمًا [4:27]

those who follow their own desires wish you to deviate greatly

But such translations are not always possible:

ضَلَّ ضَلَالًا بَعِيدًا	[4:116]	he wandered far astray
إِنَّكُمْ لَتَقُولُونَ قَوْلًا عَظِيمًا	[17:40]	you are saying something truly shocking

THE ACCUSATIVE OF SPECIFICATION

The main uses of the accusative of specification (Arabic اَلتَّمْيِيْز *tamyīz*) have already been dealt with: the accusative used with the cardinal numbers from eleven to ninety-nine (and with *kam*); and in the compound elative. It always takes the form of an indefinite noun placed immediately after the phrase it limits or defines. Typical of other, wide uses are:

اِشْتَعَلَ ٱلرَّأْسُ شَيْبًا	[19:4]	my head is aflame with hoariness
قَرِّي عَيْنًا	[19:26]	be consoled
إِنْ طِبْنَ نَفْسًا	[4:4]	if they are pleased

THE ACCUSATIVE OF CAUSE

The accusative is also used to indicate cause or motive, in Arabic اَلْمَفْعُول لَهُ *al-mafʿūl lahu*:

حَسَدًا مِنْ عِنْدِ أَنْفُسِهِمْ	[2:109]	through envy on their part
حَذَرَ ٱلْمَوْتِ	[2:19]	for fear of death
اِبْتِغَاءَ مَرْضَاةِ ٱللّٰهِ	[2:207]	in seeking God's approval

THE ACCUSATIVE OF CIRCUMSTANCE

This usage, known in Arabic as the اَلْحَال *ḥāl*, is common and used in a highly idiomatic way. The general rules devised by the Arab grammarians are complex and frequently broken. The framework that follows is slightly loose, but it should enable you to understand what is taking place.

1. The *ḥāl* must be additional to a complete sentence and must answer the question كَيْفَ *kayfa*, 'how?'
2. The *ḥāl* must refer back to something definite, a noun or a pronoun. It cannot normally refer to an indefinite word such as *rajulun*.
3. The *ḥāl* accusative must itself be indefinite, and normally either a participle or a noun/adjective equivalent to a participle.

Examples

أَصْبَحَ فِي ٱلْمَدِينَةِ خَائِفًا	[28:18]	in the morning he was in the city, fearing
دَعَانَا ... قَاعِدًا أَوْ قَائِمًا	[10:12]	he called to us... sitting or standing

This *ḥāl* also occurs in the plural, with broken plural forms:

[3:191] يَذْكُرُونَ ٱللّٰهَ قِيَامًا وَقُعُودًا

they remember God, standing or sitting

Other participial equivalents are:

تُتْلَى ... آيَاتُنَا بَيِّنَاتٍ	[45:25]	our signs are recited as clear proof
أَرْسَلْنَاكَ لِلنَّاسِ رَسُولًا	[4:79]	we sent you as a messenger for the people

It appears in exceptions, sometimes as a variation on a simple sentence:

[6:48] مَا نُرْسِلُ ٱلْمُرْسَلِينَ إِلَّا مُبَشِّرِينَ وَمُنْذِرِينَ

we only send the messengers as bearers of good tidings and warners

as a variation of

[2:213] بَعَثَ ٱللّٰهُ ٱلنَّبِيِّنَ مُبَشِّرِينَ وَمُنْذِرِينَ

God sent the prophets as bringers of good tidings and as warners

It will normally be linked to its object through *li-* and the genitive:

[3:3] نَزَّلَ عَلَيْكَ ٱلْكِتَابَ بِٱلْحَقِّ مُصَدِّقًا لِمَا بَيْنَ يَدَيْهِ

he has sent down to you the Scripture in truth, confirming what came before it

With a phrase attached it may be a compressed relative:

[4:14] يُدْخِلْهُ نَارًا خَالِدًا فِيهَا

he will cause him to enter a fire in which he will remain for ever

Note also such uses of the *ḥāl* as:

[3:95] اِتَّبِعْ مِلَّةَ إِبْرَاهِيمَ حَنِيفًا

follow the religion of Abraham, a man of pure faith

[5:48] إِلَى ٱللّٰهِ مَرْجِعُكُمْ جَمِيعًا

you will all return to God

Occasionally a *ḥāl* accusative is found with no previous phrase to which it can obviously be attached:

[56:16] مُتَّكِئِينَ عَلَيْهَا مُتَقَابِلِينَ

reclining on them, facing one another

In addition to *ḥāl* accusatives, there are *ḥāl* clauses. The simplest example is the continuation of 28:18, the first example above. In full the sentence runs:

أَصْبَحَ فِي ٱلْمَدِينَةِ خَائِفًا يَتَرَقَّبُ

in the morning he was in the city, fearing, watching

Vocabulary Thirty-Five

Perfect	Imperfect	Verbal noun	
تَلَا	يَتْلُو	تِلَاوَةٌ	to recite
خَرَّ	يَخِرُّ	خَرٌّ	to fall
رَهِبَ	يَرْهَبُ	رَهْبَةٌ	to fear, be in awe of
كَادَ	يَكِيدُ	كَيْدٌ	to strive, plot, outwit
مَالَ	يَمِيلُ	مَيْلٌ	to incline, lean, deviate
4 أَصْبَحَ	يُصْبِحُ	إِصْبَاحٌ	to become; be in the morning
4 أَنَابَ	يُنِيبُ	إِنَابَةٌ	to come back to; repent
6 تَرَاضَى	يَتَرَاضَى	تَرَاضٍ	to agree with one another
8 اِزْدَادَ	يَزْدَادُ	اِزْدِيَادٌ	to increase, grow
10 اِسْتَعَانَ	يَسْتَعِينُ	اِسْتِعَانَةٌ	to ask for help (+ acc.)

Singular	Plural	
حَنِيفٌ	حُنَفَاءُ	of pure faith
صَيْحَةٌ		cry
عِزَّةٌ		might, power
مَلْجَأٌ		refuge
مَكْرٌ		plot, trickery
مِلَّةٌ	مِلَلٌ	community
إِمْلَاقٌ		poverty
جَمِيعٌ		all
جَمٌّ		much
دَاخِرٌ		humble, lowly
سَاجِدٌ	سُجَّدٌ	prostrating oneself
مُغَاضِبٌ		angry
لَا جَرَمَ		undoubtedly, certainly

Idioms	طَابَ نَفْسًا	to be consoled
	قَرَّ عَيْنًا	to be pleased

Exercise Thirty-Five

1. [41:40] أَفَمَنْ يُلْقَى فِي آلنَّارِ خَيْرٌ أَمْ مَنْ يَأْتِي آمِنًا يَوْمَ آلْقِيَامَةِ
2. [15:83] أَخَذَتْهُمُ آلصَّيْحَةُ مُصْبِحِينَ
3. [27:87] أَتَوْهُ دَاخِرِينَ
4. [39:2] فَآعْبُدِ آللّٰهَ مُخْلِصًا لَهُ آلدِّينَ
5. [12:100] خَرُّوا لَهُ سُجَّدًا
6. [8:48] لَا غَالِبَ لَكُمُ آلْيَوْمَ
7. [9:118] لَا مَلْجَأَ مِنَ آللّٰهِ إِلَّا إِلَيْهِ
8. [2:32] لَا عِلْمَ لَنَا إِلَّا مَا عَلَّمْتَنَا
9. [4:24] لَا جُنَاحَ عَلَيْكُمْ فِيمَا تَرَاضَيْتُمْ بِهِ
10. [2:197] لَا جِدَالَ فِي آلْحَجِّ
11. [3:90] ثُمَّ آزْدَادُوا كُفْرًا
12. [10:21] قُلِ آللّٰهُ أَسْرَعُ مَكْرًا
13. [4:84] وَآللّٰهُ أَشَدُّ بَأْسًا
14. [18:7] أَيُّهُمْ أَحْسَنُ عَمَلًا
15. [86:15] إِنَّهُمْ يَكِيدُونَ كَيْدًا
16. [21:82] يَعْمَلُونَ عَمَلًا دُونَ ذٰلِكَ
17. [89:20] تُحِبُّونَ آلْمَالَ حُبًّا جَمًّا
18. [10:28] مَا كُنْتُمْ إِيَّانَا تَعْبُدُونَ
19. [17:31] نَرْزُقُهُمْ وَإِيَّاكُمْ
20. [17:31] لَا تَقْتُلُوا أَوْلَادَكُمْ خَشْيَةَ إِمْلَاقٍ

21. مَا تُنْفِقُونَ إِلَّا ٱبْتِغَآءَ وَجْهِ ٱللّٰهِ [2:272]

22. إِنَّ ٱلْعِزَّةَ لِلّٰهِ جَمِيعًا [4:139]

23. دَعَا رَبَّهُ مُنِيبًا إِلَيْهِ [39:8]

24. ذَهَبَ مُغَاضِبًا [21:87]

25. اِرْجِعِي إِلَى رَبِّكِ رَاضِيَةً مَرْضِيَّةً [89:28]

26. فَجَمَعْنَاهُمْ جَمْعًا [18:99]

27. لَا جَرَمَ أَنَّ لَهُمُ ٱلنَّارَ [16:62]

28. يُخْرِجُكُمْ إِخْرَاجًا [71:18]

Lesson Thirty-Six
Conditional Sentences

Conditional sentences consist of two halves: a clause containing a condition (Arabic اَلشَّرْط *al-sharṭ*, and a main clause, which is a response (Arabic اَلْجَوَاب *al-jawāb*) to the condition. In many grammars terminology going back to ancient Greek is used: the *sharṭ* is called the *protasis* and the *jawāb* the *apodosis*.

The general rules for conditionals worked out by the Arab grammarians apply by and large to the Qur'ān; but they do focus on a somewhat later period when the pattern of tense usage was slightly different. Also the words meaning 'if' are used in a slightly more distinctive way in the Qur'ān.

The explanations that follow are aimed at helping the reader to understand the numerous conditionals that occur in the Qur'ān. As should be expected from what has been said above, they do not cover some conditional expressions that occur in later Arabic, and thus these explanations do not provide the reader with the complete framework needed to cover medieval and modern Arabic.

As Arabic has a simple tense system, it cannot operate as many languages do and express shades of conditional meeting by using a wide range of tenses. However, this is not a problem, as many of the shades of meaning are expressed by the use of three words for 'if': *law*, *in* and *idhā*:

1. *law* indicates that the conditional proposition (whether positive or negative) has not happened or will not happen: an unreal or hypothetical condition. It can be translated into English as 'if [he] had [done]', 'if [he] were to [do]', or, 'had [he done]', 'were [he] to [do]'.
2. *in* indicates that the conditional proposition is expected to happen or has happened: a future or past real condition.

3. *idhā*, which has been partly dealt with in Lesson 21, indicates that the proposition has happened or is felt certain to happen. In the Qur'ān the original sense of 'when' applies, but conditional force is indicated both by the tense usage and by the use of *fa-* to introduce the *jawāb* [see B below].

The differentiation between *in* and *idhā* is a feature of early Arabic that has been steadily eroded with the passing of time. In modern Arabic it scarcely exists. However, the clear differentiation of all three particles is crucial to conditional expressions in the Qur'ān, as the Qur'ān does not make full use of the full range of tenses allowable under the general rules for conditional sentences.

These rules are that the Arabic perfect or jussive are the equivalent of the English present or future and the Arabic pluperfect represents the English past. This is not so in the Qur'ān, as the pluperfect occurs only a handful of times. It is also the case that tense usage varies somewhat with each of the three particles, and a separate explanation for each is required.

There are two other rules that should be known before the Qur'ānic conditionals are examined in detail:

1. If the *sharṭ* is a negative proposition, the negative is normally expressed by *lam* with the jussive [but see C 1b]. This is in contrast to the *jawāb*, in which a range of negatives appropriate to the accompanying tense is used.
2. With *in* and *idhā* the particle *fa-* is used to introduce the *jawāb* if a perfect or a jussive verb is not the first element in the *jawāb* [see B below]. This rule does not apply fully in the Qur'ān.

A. THE USE OF لَوْ *law*

1. a) The *sharṭ* is most frequently expressed by *law* with the perfect, though *law anna* (with an accusative) and *law* with the imperfect are also found. There is no example of *law* followed by the jussive.

b) Unlike its use in other Arabic, *law* is not used with a negative proposition, i.e. there is no example of *law lam*. Negative propositions are expressed by *law-lā an/anna*.[A]

2. If the *jawāb* to *law* begins with a verb, it will be a perfect, most frequently introduced by *la-*. However, *la-* is not used if the perfect is preceded by the negative *mā*.
3. It is uncommon for the *sharṭ* to follow the *jawāb*, unless the *sharṭ* is used to round off a verse with assonance in *-ūn*, as in:

إِنَّ أَوْهَنَ ٱلْبُيُوتِ لَبَيْتُ ٱلْعَنْكَبُوتِ لَوْ كَانُوا يَعْلَمُونَ [29:41]

the most fragile house is that of the spider, did they know [it]

4. The use of *wa-law* as the final clause of a sentence (normally coinciding with the end of a verse) needs special notice. It means 'if only' or 'even if' or 'although'. Note that *wa-law* is the only way in which 'although' is expressed in the Qur'ān—*wa-in* is not used in this way—and in this sense the clause may well not be hypothetical:

وَمَا أَنْتَ بِمُؤْمِنٍ لَنَا وَلَوْ كُنَّا صَادِقِينَ [12:17]

you will not believe us although we are telling the truth

Examples of the use of *law*

لَوْ شَاءَ رَبُّكَ لَجَعَلَ ٱلنَّاسَ أُمَّةً وَاحِدَةً [11:118]

had your Lord wished, He would have made men one community

لَوْ أَطَاعُونَا مَا قُتِلُوا [3:168]

had they obeyed us, they would not have been killed

لَوْ نَشَاءُ لَأَرَيْنَاكَهُمْ [47:30]

if we wished, we would show them to you

[A] For *law-lā* meaning either 'why not' or 'but for' see Lesson 37.

[39:57] لَوْ أَنَّ ٱللّٰهَ هَدَانِي لَكُنْتُ مِنَ ٱلْمُتَّقِينَ

if only God had guided me, I should have been one of those who protected themselves

[37:143-4] لَوْلَا أَنَّهُ كَانَ مِنَ ٱلْمُسَبِّحِينَ لَلَبِثَ فِي بَطْنِهِ

had he not been one of those who glorify God, he would have lingered in its belly

[4:39] مَا ذَا عَلَيْهِمْ لَوْ آمَنُوا بِٱللّٰهِ

what harm would it do them if they were to believe in God?

[5:100] لَا يَسْتَوِي ٱلْخَبِيثُ وَٱلطَّيِّبُ وَلَوْ أَعْجَبَكَ كَثْرَةُ ٱلْخَبِيثِ

evil and good are not equal, though the abundance of the evil may amaze you

[26:113] إِنْ حِسَابُهُمْ إِلَّا عَلَى رَبِّي لَوْ تَشْعُرُونَ

their account rests only with my Lord, if you did but know it

B. THE USE OF *fa-* IN REAL CONDITIONS

Before dealing with *in* and *idhā* in detail, it is necessary to look more fully at the way *fa-* is used in conditionals introduced by either of these words. As already mentioned, *fa-* is normally used to introduce the *jawāb* if a conditional verb (i.e. a perfect or a jussive) is not used to start the *jawāb*. Most grammars do not state this rule explicitly. They simply list the non-standard *jawāb*s [NSJs]: those beginning with an imperfect, an imperative, an indirect command, an interrogative, a negative or any other particle (*qad*, *inna*, etc.).

There are sentences in the Qur'ān that do not obey this rule and lack the *fa-*:

[6:25] إِنْ يَرَوْا كُلَّ آيَةٍ لَا يُؤْمِنُوا بِهَا

if they see a sign, they do not believe in it

[45:25] إِذَا تُتْلَى عَلَيْهِمْ آيَاتُنَا بَيِّنَاتٍ مَا كَانَ حُجَّتَهُمْ إِلَّا أَنْ قَالُوا

when Our signs are recited to them as clear proof their only argument is to say . . .

However, such sentences are rare and they do not follow any pattern. More rarely *fa-* appears at the beginning of the *jawāb* when one would not expect it:

[37:177] إِذَا نَزَلَ بِسَاحَتِهِمْ فَسَاءَ صَبَاحُ ٱلْمُنْذَرِينَ

when it descends into their courtyard, how terrible will be the morning of those who have been warned

There are a few examples where *fa-* is found, though the *jawāb* begins with a with a normal conditional perfect verb, to indicate that the perfect tense has a past meaning, despite the conditional structure. The clearest examples of this are in *sūra* 12:26 and 27.

C. THE USE OF إِنْ *in*

1. a) In the *sharṭ* the verb may be either a perfect or a jussive. There is also a handful of occurrences of the pluperfect.
   b) A negative condition is expressed by *in lam* or, very rarely, by *illā*. Both are followed by the jussive.
2. In the *jawāb* the jussive is much more commonly used than the perfect. In fact, the four most common types of NSJ (imperatives, nominal sentences, negatives and *inna*) are all more common than the perfect.
3. The only common negative in the *jawāb* is *lā*. Otherwise there are three occurrences of *mā* and two of *lan*. Note that with conditionals introduced by *in* there is no example of *lam* being used in the *jawāb*.
4. Reversed sentences, i.e. where the *sharṭ* forms the second half of the sentence, are relatively frequent with *in*.
5. Even more frequent are the reversed conditionals in which the *sharṭ* introduced by *in* rounds off a verse in assonance with *-īn, ūn*:

[36:48] مَتَى هٰذَا ٱلْوَعْدُ إِنْ كُنْتُمْ صَادِقِينَ

when is this promise, if you are telling the truth?

Examples of the use of *in*

[21:47] إِنْ كَانَ مِثْقَالَ حَبَّةٍ مِنْ خَرْدَلٍ أَتَيْنَا بِهَا

If it is the weight of a grain of mustard-seed, We will bring it.

[24:28] إِنْ قِيلَ لَكُمُ ٱرْجِعُوا فَٱرْجِعُوا

if you are told, 'return', return

[42:48] إِنْ أَعْرَضُوا فَمَا أَرْسَلْنَاكَ عَلَيْهِمْ حَفِيظًا

if they turn away, We have not sent you to be a guardian over them

[11:3] إِنْ تَوَلَّوْا فَإِنِّي أَخَافُ عَلَيْكُمْ عَذَابَ يَوْمٍ كَبِيرٍ

if you turn your backs, I fear for you the punishment of a great day

[26:4] إِنْ نَشَأْ نُنَزِّلْ عَلَيْهِمْ مِنَ ٱلسَّمَاءِ آيَةً

if We wish, We can send down a sign from the sky to them

[24:28] إِنْ لَمْ تَجِدُوا فِيهَا أَحَدًا فَلَا تَدْخُلُوهَا

if you find no one inside, still do not enter it

[22:42] إِنْ يُكَذِّبُوكَ فَقَدْ كَذَّبَتْ قَبْلَهُمْ قَوْمُ نُوحٍ

If they deny the truth of your message, so too did the people of Nūh before them

[3:160] إِنْ يَنْصُرْكُمُ ٱللّٰهُ فَلَا غَالِبَ لَكُمْ

if God helps you, none can overcome you

[22:73] إِنْ يَسْلُبْهُمُ ٱلذُّبَابُ شَيْئًا لَا يَسْتَنْقِذُوهُ مِنْهُ

if a fly robs them of anything, they will not rescue it from it

[12:33] إِلَّا تَصْرِفْ عَنِّي كَيْدَهُنَّ أَصْبُ إِلَيْهِنَّ

if you do not turn their wiles from me, I shall incline to them in youthful folly

D. THE USE OF إِذَا *idhā*

1. (a) In the *sharṭ* the perfect predominates, though there are a dozen or so occurrences of the imperfect.
   (b) There is a single occurrence of *idhā lam* and the jussive.
2. If the *jawāb* begins with a verb, the perfect predominates, though there are some examples of the imperfect.
3. Most of the examples of a negative *jawāb* involve *lā*, but two examples begin with the negative *in* (with no *fa-*) and one with *fa-laysa*. Unlike conditionals introduced by *in*, there is a handful of examples of *lam* (without *fa-*) in the *jawāb* of a sentence introduced by *idhā*.
4. Reversed sentences, i.e. where the *sharṭ* forms the second half of the sentence, are relatively frequent with *idhā*. However, *idhā* is not used in reversed conditionals to provide assonance at the end of a verse, in marked contrast to *in*. It should be noted that in the majority of occurrences *idhā* is almost always best translated as 'when'. However, the information given above and the fact that it conforms to conditional tense usage indicate that *idhā* is a genuine conditional particle.

Examples of the use of *idhā*

[22:35] إِذَا ذُكِرَ ٱللَّهُ وَجِلَتْ قُلُوبُهُمْ

their hearts are filled with awe when God is mentioned

[33:19] إِذَا جَاءَ ٱلْخَوْفُ رَأَيْتَهُمْ يَنْظُرُونَ إِلَيْكَ

when fear comes, you see them looking at you

[75:18] إِذَا قَرَأْنَاهُ فَٱتَّبِعْ قُرْآنَهُ

when we recite it, follow its recitation

[13:11] إِذَا أَرَادَ ٱللَّهُ بِقَوْمٍ سُوءًا فَلَا مَرَدَّ لَهُ

when God wills ill on a people, there is no turning it back

إِذَا جَاءَهُ لَمْ يَجِدْهُ شَيْئًا [24:39]

when he gets to it he finds it to be nothing

إِذَامَا غَضِبُوا هُمْ يَغْفِرُونَ [42:37]

they forgive when they are angry

E. لَئِنْ *la-in*

There are close on sixty examples in the Qur'ān where *in* is preceded by the particle *la-*, indicating that the *jawāb* will be an oath or a strong statement. Most of these have a *jawāb* beginning with *la-*, usually with the Energetic, but occasionally without it. In a few cases the *jawāb* begins with *inna... la-*, or with *idhan*, or with a negative. For examples see Lesson 39, which deals with the Energetic.

F. إِمَّا *immā*

Immā (but not *immā... wa-immā*, which means 'whether... or') appears always to mean 'if', though some of the commentators dispute this. It is always followed by the Energetic, and the *jawāb* then being introduced by *fa-* (without a conditional verb). For examples see Lesson 39.

G. IMPERATIVE *sharṭ*, JUSSIVE *jawāb*

A further form of conditional, in which the *sharṭ* is introduced by an imperative and the *jawāb* by a jussive, is reasonably prominent in the Qur'ān:

أَوْفُوا بِعَهْدِي أُوفِ بِعَهْدِكُمْ [2:40]

fulfil [your] covenant with me and I will fulfil [my] covenant with you

أَلْقُوهُ عَلَى وَجْهِ أَبِي يَأْتِ بَصِيرًا [12:93]

throw it over my father's face, and he will see again

ذَرُونَا نَتَّبِعْكُمْ [48:15]

let us follow you

This is normally the construction used with the imperative of *yadharu*.

H. QUASI-CONDITIONALS

There are a number of words that have the force of a conditional particle when they have a general sense, in which case they are followed by conditional sentence structures. You have already become familiar with the two most important words: مَنْ *man* (Lesson 17) and مَا *mā* (Lesson 10). When *man* and *mā* mean 'whoever' and 'whatever' respectively, and they appear at the beginning of a sentence, conditional tenses come into play.

Other words used in the Qur'ān in this way are أَنَّى *annā*, 'wherever', أَيْنَمَا *aynamā*, 'wherever', حَيْثُ *ḥaythu* and حَيْثُمَا *ḥaythumā*, 'wherever', مَهْمَا *mahmā* , 'whatever', كُلَّمَا *kullamā*, 'whenever', and أَيُّمَا *ayyumā* (which declines), 'whichever'. All are rare.

Examples of quasi-conditionals

[6:39] مَنْ يَشَإِ ٱللَّهُ يُضْلِلْهُ

God sends astray those whom He wishes

[5:64] كُلَّمَا أَوْقَدُوا نَارًا لِلْحَرْبِ أَطْفَأَهَا ٱللَّهُ

whenever they light a fire for war, God will extinguish it

[28:28] أَيَّمَا ٱلْأَجَلَيْنِ قَضَيْتُ فَلَا عُدْوَانَ عَلَيَّ

whichever of the two terms I fulfil, it will be no injustice to me

[7:132] مَهْمَا تَأْتِنَا بِهِ مِنْ آيَةٍ ... فَمَا نَحْنُ لَكَ بِمُؤْمِنِينَ

whatever sign you bring us... we will not put our faith in you

[7:161] كُلُوا مِنْهَا حَيْثُ شِئْتُمْ

eat of it wherever you will

[2:144] حَيْثُمَا كُنْتُمْ فَوَلُّوا وُجُوهَكُمْ شَطْرَهُ

wherever you may be, turn your faces towards it

[2:223] فَأْتُوا حَرْثَكُمْ أَنَّى شِئْتُمْ
go to your tillage however you wish

[4:78] أَيْنَمَا تَكُونُوا يُدْرِكُّمُ ٱلْمَوْتُ
wherever you are, death will overtake you

I. THE USE OF رَأَى *ra'ā* IN CONDITIONAL SENTENCES

The verb *ra'ā* is used in two completely different, highly idiomatic ways in conditional sentences. The first is its use in the imperfect after *law* to mean 'if only':

[6:30] لَوْ تَرَى إِذْ وُقِفُوا عَلَى رَبِّهِمْ
if you could see [them] when they are set before their Lord

The second is when the second person of the perfect follows the interrogative *a-* and precedes *in*:

[6:46] أَرَأَيْتُمْ إِنْ أَخَذَ ٱللّٰهُ سَمْعَكُمْ وَأَبْصَارَكُمْ
have you considered [what will happen] if God takes away your hearing and your sight?

In such sentences *a-ra'aytum in/a-ra'ayta in* translates most convincingly as 'have you considered the position if', or 'what will happen if'.

Vocabulary Thirty-Six

Perfect	Imperfect	Verbal noun	
رَتَعَ	يَرْتَعُ	رَتْعٌ	to enjoy oneself
سَعَى	يَسْعَى	سَعْيٌ	to strive, move, run
سَلَبَ	يَسْلُبُ	سَلْبٌ	to rob
لَعِبَ	يَلْعَبُ	لَعِبٌ	to play
نَهَى	يَنْهَى	نَهْيٌ	to forbid
هَزَّ	يَهِزُّ	هَزٌّ	to shake

Perfect	Imperfect	Verbal noun	
وَجِلَ	يُوجَلُ		to be in awe of
كَفَّرَ 2	يُكَفِّرُ	تَكْفِيرٌ	to forgive, redeem
سَاقَطَ 3	يُسَاقِطُ	مُسَاقَطَةٌ	to cause to fall, bring down
ضَاعَفَ 3	يُضَاعِفُ	مُضَاعَفَةٌ	to multiply
أَنْكَرَ 4	يُنْكِرُ	إِنْكَارٌ	to deny, disapprove; not to know
أَدْرَكَ 4	يُدْرِكُ	إِدْرَاكٌ	to overtake
أَعَادَ 4	يُعِيدُ	إِعَادَةٌ	to repeat, return (trans.)
أَسَاءَ 4	يُسِيءُ	إِسَاءَةٌ	to do wrong
تَزَكَّى 5	يَتَزَكَّى	تَزَكٍّ	to be purified
اِلْتَقَطَ 8	يَلْتَقِطُ	اِلْتِقَاطٌ	to pick up
اِسْتَأْخَرَ 10	يَسْتَأْخِرُ	اِسْتِئْخَارٌ	to postpone
اِسْتَقْدَمَ 10	يَسْتَقْدِمُ	اِسْتِقْدَامٌ	to bring forward
اِسْتَنْقَذَ 10	يَسْتَنْقِذُ	اِسْتِنْقَاذٌ	to rescue

Singular	Plural	
جُبٌّ		pit, well
جِذْعٌ		trunk of a palm-tree
مُدَّخَلٌ		place to enter
ذُبَابٌ		fly
	أَذْقَانٌ	chins

SINGULAR	PLURAL	
مَرَدٌّ		turning back
رُطَبٌ		fresh, ripe dates
صَرِيخٌ		help
مَغَارَةٌ		cave
غَيَابَةٌ	s.p.	bottom; recess
كَبِيرَةٌ	كَبَائِرُ	enormity
شَطْرَ		towards

EXERCISE THIRTY-SIX

1. [2:23] إِنْ كُنْتُمْ فِي رَيْبٍ مِمَّا نَزَّلْنَا عَلَى عَبْدِنَا فَأْتُوا بِسُورَةٍ مِنْ مِثْلِهِ
2. [3:75] إِنْ تَأْمَنْهُ بِدِينَارٍ لَا يُؤَدِّهِ إِلَيْكَ
3. [3:184] إِنْ كَذَّبُوكَ فَقَدْ كُذِّبَ رُسُلٌ مِنْ قَبْلِكَ
4. [4:31] إِنْ تَجْتَنِبُوا كَبَآئِرَ مَا تُنْهَوْنَ عَنْهُ نُكَفِّرْ عَنْكُمْ سَيِّئَاتِكُمْ
5. [5:42] وَإِنْ تُعْرِضْ عَنْهُمْ فَلَنْ يَضُرُّوكَ شَيْئًا
6. [22:68] إِنْ جَادَلُوكَ فَقُلِ ٱللّٰهُ أَعْلَمُ بِمَا تَعْمَلُونَ
7. [23:107] إِنْ عُدْنَا فَإِنَّا ظَالِمُونَ
8. [36:43] إِنْ نَشَأْ نُغْرِقْهُمْ
9. [12:10] أَلْقُوهُ فِي غَيَابَاتِ ٱلْجُبِّ يَلْتَقِطْهُ بَعْضُ ٱلسَّيَّارَةِ
10. [19:25] هُزِّي إِلَيْكِ بِجِذْعِ ٱلنَّخْلَةِ تُسَاقِطْ عَلَيْكِ رُطَبًا
11. [12:12] أَرْسِلْهُ مَعَنَا غَدًا يَرْتَعْ وَيَلْعَبْ

12. [7:73] ذَرُوهَا تَأْكُلْ فِي أَرْضِ ٱللَّٰهِ
13. [61:11] ذَٰلِكُمْ خَيْرٌ لَكُمْ إِنْ كُنْتُمْ تَعْلَمُونَ
14. [2:111] هَاتُوا بُرْهَانَكُمْ إِنْ كُنْتُمْ صَادِقِينَ
15. [2:205] إِذَا تَوَلَّى سَعَى فِي ٱلْأَرْضِ لِيُفْسِدَ فِيهَا
16. [4:103] إِذَا قَضَيْتُمُ ٱلصَّلَوٰةَ فَٱذْكُرُوا ٱللَّٰهَ قِيَامًا وَقُعُودًا
17. [16:61] إِذَا جَآءَ أَجَلُهُمْ لَا يَسْتَأْخِرُونَ سَاعَةً وَلَا يَسْتَقْدِمُونَ
18. [17:107] إِذَا يُتْلَى عَلَيْهِمْ يَخِرُّونَ لِلْأَذْقَانِ سُجَّدًا
19. [2:20] وَلَوْ شَآءَ ٱللَّٰهُ لَذَهَبَ بِسَمْعِهِمْ
20. [9:57] لَوْ يَجِدُونَ مَلْجَأً أَوْ مَغَارَاتٍ أَوْ مُدَّخَلًا لَوَلَّوَا إِلَيْهِ
21. [23:114] إِنْ لَبِثْتُمْ إِلَّا قَلِيلًا لَوْ أَنَّكُمْ كُنْتُمْ تَعْلَمُونَ
22. [3:156] لَوْ كَانُوا عِنْدَنَا مَا مَاتُوا وَمَا قُتِلُوا
23. [40:81] أَيَّ آيَاتِ ٱللَّٰهِ تُنْكِرُونَ
24. [58:7] هُوَ مَعَهُمْ أَيْنَمَا كَانُوا
25. [32:20] كُلَّمَا أَرَادُوا أَنْ يَخْرُجُوا مِنْهَا أُعِيدُوا فِيهَا
26. [41:46] مَنْ عَمِلَ صَالِحًا فَلِنَفْسِهِ وَمَنْ أَسَآءَ فَعَلَيْهَا
27. [6:93] لَوْ تَرَى إِذِ ٱلظَّالِمُونَ فِي غَمَرَاتِ ٱلْمَوْتِ
28. [46:10] أَرَأَيْتُمْ إِنْ كَانَ مِنْ عِنْدِ ٱللَّٰهِ وَكَفَرْتُمْ بِهِ
29. [87:14] قَدْ أَفْلَحَ مَنْ تَزَكَّى
30. [4:40] إِنْ تَكُ حَسَنَةً يُضَاعِفْهَا

Lesson Thirty-Seven
More about *an*; ʿ*asa* and *la*ʿ*alla*

أَنْ *an*

The most important use of *an*, as a conjunction meaning 'that', was dealt with in Lesson 18. However, there are half a dozen other uses of *an* in the Qur'ān that did not survive as important features in later Arabic, although occasional examples are to be found. It is usually possible to see how they developed from the central use of *an*. Three of these further uses are important enough to need explanation here.

1. The most common of these uses is known by the Arab grammarians as *an il-mufassira*, the *an* that introduces direct speech. There are over fifty examples of it in the Qur'ān. The function of *an il-mufassira* is to introduce direct speech after a verb other than *qāla* (though in 5:117 it is used after *qāla* itself). A dozen verbs, all with the general sense of 'conveying a message' are involved, the most common being أَوْحَى *awḥā* 'to inspire' and نَادَى *nādā* 'to call out.' The *an* is normally followed by an imperative or the equivalent of an imperative (a prohibition, wish, salutation or a vocative). Other constructions are unusual.

نَادَيْنَاهُ أَنْ يَا إِبْرَاهِيمُ [37:104]

We called out to him, 'O Ibrāhīm'

أَوْحَيْنَا إِلَى مُوسَى أَنْ أَلْقِ عَصَاكَ [7:117]

We inspired Mūsā, saying, 'Throw your staff.'

أَرْسَلْنَا نُوحًا إِلَى قَوْمِهِ أَنْ أَنْذِرْ قَوْمَكَ [71:1]

We sent Nūḥ to his people, saying 'Warn your people.'

2. Secondly, *an* may mean 'because'. This is the least common of the three usages explained here. It would appear that it is used where *bi-an* (or *bi-anna* and the accusative) might normally have been expected; though in at least one verse [49:17] the difference between 'that' and 'because' is small and might indicate another way in which the usage developed. Clear examples are the second *an* in 26:51:

نَطْمَعُ أَنْ يَغْفِرَ لَنَا رَبُّنَا خَطَايَانَا أَنْ كُنَّا أَوَّلَ ٱلْمُؤْمِنِينَ

we earnestly hope that our Lord will forgive us our sins because we were the first of the believers

and the second *an* in 29:2:

أَحَسِبَ ٱلنَّاسُ أَنْ يُتْرَكُوا أَنْ يَقُولُوا آمَنَّا

do the people think that they will be left alone because they say, 'We believe'?

See also 40:28:

أَتَقْتُلُونَ رَجُلًا أَنْ يَقُولَ رَبِّيَ ٱللّٰهُ

would you kill a man because he says, 'My Lord is God'?

3. Thirdly, there are over thirty examples when *an* is best understood as أَلَّا *allā* or لِئَلَّا *li-allā* 'that not'. There is some uncertainty about the basis of this usage, and some grammarians look to the ellipse of *makhāfata*, with *an* standing for *makhāfata an* 'for fear that' i.e. 'lest'. This is quite clearly so in 4:6, where there cannot be any other meaning:

لَا تَأْكُلُوهَا إِسْرَافًا وَبِدَارًا أَنْ يَكْبَرُوا

do not devour it in squandering and in haste lest they grow up (for fear that they will grow up)

With a number of other examples, e.g. after the verb *amina*, one can understand the verse by assuming that a preposition (in this case *min*) has been omitted. However there is a basic core of examples that can only be understood by taking *an* in the sense of *allā* or *li-allā*:

[6:25] جَعَلْنَا عَلَى قُلُوبِهِمْ أَكِنَّةً أَنْ يَفْقَهُوهُ

we have placed veils on their hearts so that they do not understand it

[24:22] لَا يَأْتَلِ أُولُو ٱلْفَضْلِ مِنْكُمْ وَٱلسَّعَةِ أَنْ يُؤْتُوا أُولِي ٱلْقُرْبَى

let not those of you who possess bounty and abundance swear that they will not give to relations

My own explanation is that from time to time negatives that one would expect to appear in the text simply do not do so, possibly due to some Ḥijāzī influence. There are also examples of this construction in seventh century poetry, but it soon dropped out of use.

عَسَى *ʿasā*

The most common way of expressing 'perhaps', 'it may be that' in the Qur'ān is by use of *ʿasā*, a verb that occurs only in the perfect, with a following *an* clause. *ʿAsā* can be used either personally or impersonally. Eventually Arabic came to prefer the impersonal verb, but in the Qur'ān, as elsewhere in early Arabic, the personal form is more common. In only two examples does it conjugate (*ʿasaytum*, 2:246 and 47:22), but in most cases the verb is followed by a subject:

[4:99] عَسَى ٱللَّهُ أَنْ يَعْفُوَ عَنْهُمْ

it may be that God will pardon them

[7:129] عَسَى رَبُّكُمْ أَنْ يُهْلِكَ عَدُوَّكُمْ

perhaps your Lord will destroy your enemy

[68:32] عَسَى رَبُّنَا أَنْ يُبْدِلَنَا خَيْرًا مِنْهَا

perhaps our Lord will give us better than this in its place

[4:19] عَسَى أَنْ تَكْرَهُو شَيْئًا

perhaps you dislike a thing

لَعَلَّ *la*ʿ*alla*

In later Arabic *la*ʿ*alla*, which is a fossilized verb with the construction of *inna*, means 'perhaps'. However, in early Arabic *la*ʿ*alla* had two meanings: 'perhaps' and 'so that'. If it occurs near the end of the verse you can expect it to mean 'so that'. This covers over ninety percent of the instances where it appears. If it occurs elsewhere in the sentence, particularly at the beginning, it is likely to mean 'perhaps'.

The translation 'that haply', often used in translations of the Qur'ān, goes back to ingenious efforts by some Arab grammarians and commentators to combine the meaning 'perhaps', with which they were perfectly familiar, with 'so that', which was obsolete by the time they wrote. From time to time they would grasp the nettle and acknowledge that *la*ʿ*alla* means 'so that', but more often they were reluctant to abandon the meaning they knew best.

The frequent usage of *la*ʿ*alla* in the sense of 'so that' is because *la*ʿ*alla* + a 3 m.p. or 2 m.p. suffix allows a verb ending in *-ūn(a)* to complete the verse and thus maintain the appropriate assonance. This is most clearly shown in verses where *li-* plus the subjunctive is followed by *wa-la*ʿ*alla* + a suffix + an imperfect verb.

Examples of 'so that'

[5:90] فَٱجْتَنِبُوهُ لَعَلَّكُمْ تُفْلِحُونَ

avoid it, so that you may prosper

[43:10] جَعَلَ لَكُمْ فِيهَا سُبُلًا لَعَلَّكُمْ تَهْتَدُونَ

He has put roads in it for you, that you may find the right way

[7:63] لِيُنْذِرَكُمْ وَلِتَتَّقُوا وَلَعَلَّكُمْ تُرْحَمُونَ

that he may warn you and that you may protect yourselves and that you may be given mercy

Examples of 'perhaps'

لَعَلَّهُ فِتْنَةٌ لَكُمْ وَمَتَاعٌ إِلَى حِينٍ [21:111]

perhaps it is a trial for you, with enjoyment for a time

لَعَلَّ آلسَّاعَةَ تَكُونُ قَرِيبًا [33:63]

perhaps the hour is something near

When the 1 s. pronominal suffix is attached to *laᶜalla*, the resulting form is *laᶜall-ī*:

لَعَلِّي أَرْجِعُ إِلَى آلنَّاسِ [12:46] so that I may return to the people

Vocabulary Thirty-Seven

Perfect	Imperfect	Verbal noun	
عَبَسَ	يَعْبُسُ		to frown
عَفَا	يَعْفُو	عَفْوٌ	to pardon (+ᶜ*an*)
عَادَ	يَعُودُ	مَعَادٌ	to return; do again
عَاذَ	يَعُوذُ		to seek refuge with
غَدَا	يَغْدُو	غُدُوٌّ	to be/do in the morning
كَبِرَ	يَكْبَرُ	كِبَرٌ	to grow up
كَرِهَ	يَكْرَهُ	كَرْهٌ	to be reluctant, hate
مَادَ	يَمِيدُ		to shake
بَيَّنَ 2	يُبَيِّنُ	تِبْيَانٌ	to make clear
أَسْرَفَ 4	يُسْرِفُ	إِسْرَافٌ	to be prodigal
أَمْسَكَ 4	يُمْسِكُ	إِمْسَاكٌ	to hold fast, withold
تَفَكَّرَ 5	يَتَفَكَّرُ	تَفَكُّرٌ	to think, reflect

PERFECT	IMPERFECT	VERBAL NOUN	
تَنَادَى 6	يَتَنَادَى	تَنَادٍ	to call to one another
اِيتَلَى 8	يَأْتَلِي	اِيتِلَاءٌ	to swear
اِجْتَنَبَ 8	يَجْتَنِبُ	اِجْتِنَابٌ	to avoid

SINGULAR	PLURAL	
حَلَّافٌ		accustomed to swear
بِدَارٌ		haste, anticipation
حَرْثٌ		tillage
رُؤْيَا (f.)		dream
	رَوَاسٍ	firm mountains
كِنَانٌ	أَكِنَّةٌ	coverings
نَحْلٌ		bees
هَدٌّ		crash, destruction
أَعْمَى	عُمْيٌ	blind
شَقِيٌّ	أَشْقِيَاءُ	unfortunate, wretched
مَهِينٌ		contemptible

Idioms

أُولُو ٱلْقُرْبَى	relations
ضَرَبَ ٱلذِّكْرَ صَفْحًا عَنْ	to neglect

EXERCISE THIRTY-SEVEN

1. وَٱحْذَرْهُمْ أَنْ يَفْتِنُوكَ عَنْ بَعْضِ مَا أَنْزَلَ ٱللهُ إِلَيْكَ [5:49]
2. يَعِظُكُمُ ٱللهُ أَنْ تَعُودُوا لِمِثْلِهِ أَبَدًا [24:17]
3. أَعُوذُ بِٱللهِ أَنْ أَكُونَ مِنَ ٱلْجَاهِلِينَ [2:67]
4. أَلْقَى فِي ٱلْأَرْضِ رَوَاسِيَ أَنْ تَمِيدَ بِكُمْ [16:15]
5. يُمْسِكُ ٱلسَّمَآءَ أَنْ تَقَعَ عَلَى ٱلْأَرْضِ [22:65]
6. أَفَأَمِنَ أَهْلُ ٱلْقُرَى أَنْ يَأْتِيَهُمْ بَأْسُنَا [7:97]
7. إِنَّا أَرْسَلْنَا نُوحًا إِلَى قَوْمِهِ أَنْ أَنْذِرْ قَوْمَكَ مِنْ قَبْلِ [71:1]
   أَنْ يَأْتِيَهُمْ عَذَابٌ أَلِيمٌ
8. أَوْحَيْنَا إِلَى مُوسَى أَنِ ٱضْرِبْ بِعَصَاكَ ٱلْبَحْرَ [26:63]
9. أَوْحَى رَبُّكَ إِلَى ٱلنَّحْلِ أَنِ ٱتَّخِذِي مِنَ ٱلْجِبَالِ بُيُوتًا [16:68]
10. نَادَيْنَاهُ أَنْ يَا إِبْرَاهِيمُ قَدْ صَدَّقْتَ ٱلرُّؤْيَا [37:104-5]
11. تَنَادَوْا مُصْبِحِينَ أَنِ ٱغْدُوا عَلَى حَرْثِكُمْ [68:21-2]
12. أُنْزِلَتْ سُورَةٌ أَنْ آمِنُوا بِٱللهِ وَجَاهِدُوا مَعَ رَسُولِهِ [9:86]
13. آخِرُ دَعْوَاهُمْ أَنِ ٱلْحَمْدُ لِلهِ رَبِّ ٱلْعَالَمِينَ [10:10]
14. عَبَسَ وَتَوَلَّى أَنْ جَآءَهُ ٱلْأَعْمَى [80:1-2]
15. أَفَنَضْرِبُ عَنْكُمُ ٱلذِّكْرَ صَفْحًا أَنْ كُنْتُمْ قَوْمًا مُسْرِفِينَ [43:5]
16. لَا تُطِعْ كُلَّ حَلَّافٍ مَهِينٍ ... أَنْ كَانَ ذَا مَالٍ وَبَنِينَ [68:10, 14]
17. تَخِرُّ ٱلْجِبَالُ هَدًّا أَنْ دَعَوْا لِلرَّحْمَانِ وَلَدًا [19:90-1]
18. ذٰلِكَ أَنْ لَمْ يَكُ رَبُّكَ مُهْلِكَ ٱلْقُرَى بِظُلْمٍ [6:131]

19. فَلَعَلَّكَ تَارِكٌ بَعْضَ مَا يُوحَى إِلَيْكَ ... أَنْ يَقُولُوا [11:12]

20. يُرِيكُمْ آيَاتِهِ لَعَلَّكُمْ تَعْقِلُونَ [2:73]

21. جَاهِدُوا فِي سَبِيلِهِ لَعَلَّكُمْ تُفْلِحُونَ [5:35]

22. أَنْزَلْنَا إِلَيْكَ آلذِّكْرَ لِتُبَيِّنَ لِلنَّاسِ مَا نُزِّلَ إِلَيْهِمْ وَلَعَلَّهُمْ يَتَفَكَّرُونَ [16:44]

23. إِنَّا جَعَلْنَاهُ قُرْآنًا عَرَبِيًّا لَعَلَّكُمْ تَعْقِلُونَ [43:3]

24. عَسَى أَنْ تُحِبُّوا شَيْئًا وَهُوَ شَرٌّ لَكُمْ [2:216]

25. عَسَى رَبُّكُمْ أَنْ يُهْلِكَ عَدُوَّكُمْ [7:129]

26. عَسَى آللّٰهُ أَنْ يَأْتِيَنِي بِهِمْ جَمِيعًا [12:83]

27. عَسَى أَلَّا أَكُونَ بِدُعَاءِ رَبِّي شَقِيًّا [19:48]

Lesson Thirty-Eight
Special verbs; *law-lā*

Special Verbs

THE 'SISTERS OF *kāna*'

Arabic has over twenty verbs that behave similarly to *kāna*. They are known as 'the sisters of *kāna*'. Over half of them occur in the Qur'ān, but only five: لَيْسَ *laysa*, مَا زَالَ *mā zāla*, ظَلَّ *ẓalla*, مَا دَامَ *mā dāma*, and أَصْبَحَ *aṣbaḥa* are important.

The verb that is closest to *kāna* in meaning is *laysa*; but, as was set out in Lesson 21, the two verbs are not particularly close in construction, because of the common use of *bi-* to introduce the predicate after *laysa*.

The characteristic of the other four verbs is that they take the same construction as *kāna*, i.e. an accusative predicate or an imperfect verb, though they differ markedly in meaning.

مَا زَالَ *mā zāla*

مَا زَالَ *mā zāla*, imperfect لَا يَزَالُ *lā yazālu* or مَا يَزَالُ *mā yazālu*, means 'not to cease', i.e. 'to continue':

مَا زِلْتُمْ فِي شَكٍّ [40:34]
you continued to be in doubt

لَا يَزَالُونَ يُقَاتِلُونَكُمْ [2:217]
they will continue to fight you

لَا يَزَالُونَ مُخْتَلِفِينَ [11:118]
they continue to differ

ظَلَّ *ẓalla*

Uniquely, ظَلَّ *ẓalla*, 'to continue', contracted from *ẓalila*, is found from time to time with only one *lām*. Two of these shorter forms occur in the Qur'ān: ظَلْتَ *ẓalta*[20:97] and ظَلْتُمْ *ẓaltum*[56:65].

نَظَلُّ لَهَا عَاكِفِينَ	[26:71]	we remain devoted to them
ظَلْتُمْ تَفَكَّهُونَ [A]	[56:65]	you would continue to jest

مَا دَامَ *mā dāma*

With مَا دَامَ *mā dāma* the *mā* is not the negative that we find in *mā zāla* but a special use of *mā* that has not yet been introduced. It requires a perfect verb and means 'as long as'. *mā dāma* basically means 'as long as x remains' or 'as long as x is', and these are the meanings you will find in the Qur'ān. Elsewhere, *mā dāma* may mean nothing more than 'as long as'.

مَا دُمْتُ حَيًّا	[19:31]	as long as I remain alive
مَا دُمْتَ عَلَيْهِ قَائِمًا	[3:75]	as long as you stand over him

أَصْبَحَ *aṣbaḥa*

Aṣbaḥa means 'to do in the morning' or 'to be in the morning', as mentioned in Lesson 34. To translate the verb and the following phrase into English, one normally has to say 'In the morning he. . . .' etc. The verb may also mean, simply, 'to become'.

[7:91] أَصْبَحُوا فِي دَارِهِمْ جَاثِمِينَ
in the morning they were crouching in their dwellings

[5:53] أَصْبَحُوا خَاسِرِينَ
they became losers

[A] On this form of the verb with *ta-* for *tata-* see Lesson 15.

Remember too the example quoted in the section on the *ḥāl* accusative:

[28:18] أَصْبَحَ فِي ٱلْمَدِينَةِ خَائِفًا يَتَرَقَّبُ

In the morning he was in the city, afraid and vigilant

كَادَ *kāda*

The verb *kāda*, imperfect *yakādu*, is closely allied to 'the sisters of *kānā*'. In the positive it means 'almost', with the tense of *kāda* determining the tense of the following verb in English:

كَادُوا يَقْتُلُونَنِي	[7:150]	they almost killed me
تَكَادُ ٱلسَّمَاوَاتُ يَتَفَطَّرْنَ	[42:5]	the heavens are almost torn asunder

With a negative preceding it *kāda* means 'scarcely':

لَا يَكَادُونَ يَفْقَهُونَ قَوْلًا	[18:93]	they scarcely understand any speech
لَمْ يَكَدْ يَرَاهَا	[24:40]	he scarcely saw it

'Verbs of Beginning'

A further set of verbs connected with those mentioned above is that known as 'the verbs of beginning'. These verbs are used in the perfect, followed by another verb in the imperfect. With this construction the verbs mean 'he began to…'. They fall into two groups:

a) those, such as بَدَأَ *bada'a*, شَرَعَ *sharaʿa* and طَفِقَ *ṭafiqa*, whose basic meaning is 'to begin'. Only one of these verbs occurs in the Qur'ān. It is *ṭafiqa*, which in general is not very common:

[7:22] طَفِقَا يَخْصِفَانِ عَلَيْهِمَا مِنْ وَرَقِ ٱلْجَنَّةِ

the two of them began to cover themselves with the leaves of paradise

b) verbs, such as أَخَذَ *akhadha* and جَعَلَ *jaʿala*, whose basic meaning is not 'to begin' but something quite different. Again, there is only one of these verbs that occurs in the Qur'ān. It is *aṣbaḥa*, which has just been treated above:

[18:42] أَصْبَحَ يُقَلِّبُ كَفَّيْهِ

in the morning he began wringing his hands

لَوْلَا *law-lā*

law-lā, mentioned briefly in Lesson 36, functions in two ways:

1. it means 'why not?'. This is the more common usage in the Qur'ān, with *law-lā* being followed by a verb, sometimes with an intervening subordinate clause:

   [13:7] لَوْلَا أُنْزِلَ عَلَيْهِ آيَةٌ مِنْ رَبِّهِ

   why has not a sign from his Lord been sent down to him?

   [24:13] لَوْلَا جَاؤُا عَلَيْهِ بِأَرْبَعَةِ شُهَدَاءَ

   why did they not produce four witnesses against it?

   [56:62] لَوْلَا تَذَكَّرُونَ [A]

   why are you not reminded?

2. *law-lā* also means 'but for'. In the Qur'ān this usage requires a nominative [whereas in later Arabic nouns are put in the nominative, but the suffixed forms of pronouns are used]:

   [37:57] لَوْلَا نِعْمَةُ رَبِّي

   but for the blessing of my Lord

   [48:25] لَوْلَا رِجَالٌ مُؤْمِنُونَ

   but for believing men

[A] On this form of the verb with *ta-* for *tata-* see Lesson 15.

لَوْلَا أَنْتُمْ [34:31]

but for you

لَوْلَا كَلِمَةٌ سَبَقَتْ مِنْ رَبِّكَ لَقُضِيَ بَيْنَهُمْ [41:45]

but for a word that had gone before from your Lord, there would have been judgement between them

VOCABULARY THIRTY-EIGHT

PERFECT	IMPERFECT	VERBAL NOUN	
فَقِهَ	يَفْقَهُ	فِقْهٌ	to understand
5 تَفَكَّهَ	يَتَفَكَّهُ	تَفَكُّهٌ	to jest
خَصَفَ	يَخْصِفُ		to cover oneself
خَطِفَ	يَخْطَفُ	خَطْفٌ	to snatch
عَرَجَ	يَعْرُجُ		to mount
2 قَلَّبَ	يُقَلِّبُ	تَقْلِيبٌ	to turn over, wring
4 أَبَانَ	يُبِينُ	إِبَانَةٌ	to make clear
4 أَضَاءَ	يُضِيءُ	إِضَاءَةٌ	to give light
5 تَرَقَّبَ	يَتَرَقَّبُ	تَرَقُّبٌ	to be vigilant
8 اِطَّلَعَ	يَطَّلِعُ	اِطِّلَاعٌ	to study

SINGULAR	PLURAL	
بَرْقٌ		lightning
زَيْتٌ		oil
شَكٌّ	شُكُوكٌ	doubt
(f.) كَفٌّ	أَكُفٌّ	palm of the hand, hand

SINGULAR	PLURAL	
مِرْيَةٌ		doubt
حَيٌّ	أَحْيَاءٌ	alive
جَاثِمٌ		crouching
عَاكِفٌ		devoted
نَادِمٌ		repentant
مُحْضَرٌ		brought forward
مُسْوَدٌّ		black

EXERCISE THIRTY-EIGHT

1. لَا يَزَالُ ٱلَّذِينَ كَفَرُوا فِي مِرْيَةٍ [22:55]
2. مَا زَالَتْ تِلْكَ دَعْوَاهُمْ [21:15]
3. لَا تَزَالُ تَطَّلِعُ [5:13]
4. ظَلَّ وَجْهُهُ مُسْوَدًّا [16:58]
5. فَظَلْتُمْ تَفَكَّهُونَ [56:65]
6. ظَلُّوا فِيهِ يَعْرُجُونَ [15:14]
7. مَا دَامُوا فِيهَا [5:24]
8. مَا دُمْتُمْ حُرُمًا [5:96]
9. وَكُنْتُ عَلَيْهِمْ شَهِيدًا مَا دُمْتُ فِيهِمْ [5:117]
10. أَصْبَحُوا نَادِمِينَ [26:157]
11. أَصْبَحْتُمْ بِنِعْمَتِهِ إِخْوَانًا [3:103]
12. أَصْبَحْتُمْ مِنَ ٱلْخَاسِرِينَ [41:23]

13. يَكَادُ ٱلْبَرْقُ يَخْطَفُ أَبْصَارَهُمْ [2:20]

14. يَكَادُ زَيْتُهَا يُضِيءُ وَلَوْ لَمْ تَمْسَسْهُ نَارٌ [24:35]

15. لَا يَكَادُ يُبِينُ [43:52]

16. لَا يَكَادُونَ يَفْقَهُونَ حَدِيثًا [4:78]

17. لَوْلَا يُكَلِّمُنَا ٱللَّهُ [2:118]

18. لَوْلَا أُنْزِلَ عَلَيْهِ مَلَكٌ [6:8]

19. رَبَّنَا لَوْلَا أَرْسَلْتَ إِلَيْنَا رَسُولًا [20:134]

20. لَوْلَا تَشْكُرُونَ [56:70]

21. لَوْلَا تَسْتَغْفِرُونَ ٱللَّهَ [27:46]

22. لَوْلَا فَضْلُ ٱللَّهِ عَلَيْكُمْ وَرَحْمَتُهُ لَكُنْتُمْ مِنَ ٱلْخَاسِرِينَ [2:64]

23. لَوْلَا كِتَابٌ مِنَ ٱللَّهِ سَبَقَ لَمَسَّكُمْ فِيمَا أَخَذْتُمْ [8:68]
عَذَابٌ عَظِيمٌ

24. وَلَوْلَا أَجَلٌ مُسَمًّى لَجَاءَهُمُ ٱلْعَذَابُ [29:53]

25. لَوْلَا نِعْمَةُ رَبِّي لَكُنْتُ مِنَ ٱلْمُحْضَرِينَ [37:57]

Lesson Thirty-Nine
The Energetic; Oaths and Exclamations

The Energetic

The Energetic is used in special circumstances to signify the future. Energetic forms are not common, but they occur often enough for it to be necessary to recognise them at sight. They are formed by adding the ending *-anna* or *-an* to the Jussive.[A] In addition, a final *-ū/ī* before the suffix will be shortened to *u/i* with the suffix losing the initial *a*. Thus the jussive 3 m.p. يَقُولُوا *yaqūlū* has an energetic form of يَقُولُنَّ *yaqūlunna* (as opposed to the 3 m.s. يَقُولَنَّ *yaqūlanna*). Similarly, *-ay* + the energetic ending becomes *-ayinna*: hence تَرَيِنَّ *tarayinna*, 2 f.s. energetic of رَأَى *ra'ā* . A third point is that final *u/i* followed by the energetic ending becomes *uw/iy* hence يُنْسِيَنَّ *yunsiyanna* , 3 m.s. Energetic of أَنْسَى *ansā*; تَرَوُنَّ *tarawunna* , 2 m.p. of *ra'ā* [102:7].

Forms of the Energetic in *-an* are rare, and somewhat confusingly they are normally written with the *-an* accusative ending.

The use of the Energetic is normally triggered in four ways. These are, in descending order of frequency:

1. after لَ *la-*:

[23:40] لَتُصْبِحُنَّ نَادِمِينَ

you will be repentant

[12:15] لَتُنَبِّئَنَّهُمْ بِأَمْرِهِمْ هٰذَا

you will tell them about this affair of theirs

[A] There are also Energetic forms of the Imperative, but these are very rare, and not found in the Qur'ān. For a fuller treatment of the Energetic see Wright, *Arabic Grammar*, I, p. 61 and the tables in I, pp. 298–316.

[22:40] لَيَنْصُرَنَّهُ ٱللَّهُ
God will help him

2. in the *jawāb* to a *sharṭ* introduced by لَئِنْ *la-in*:

[29:10] لَئِنْ جَاءَ نَصْرٌ مِنْ رَبِّكَ لَيَقُولُنَّ إِنَّا كُنَّا مَعَكُمْ
if a victory comes to you from your Lord, they will say, 'We were with you.'

[96:15] لَئِنْ لَمْ يَنْتَهِ لَنَسْفَعًا بِٱلنَّاصِيَةِ
if he does not desist, We shall seize [him] by the forelock

[12:32] لَئِنْ لَمْ يَفْعَلْ مَا آمُرُهُ لَيُسْجَنَنَّ وَلَيَكُونًا مِنَ ٱلصَّاغِرِينَ
if he does not do what I tell him to do, he will be imprisoned and be one of those brought low

3. in the *sharṭ* after إِمَّا *immā*:

[19:26] إِمَّا تَرَيِنَّ مِنَ ٱلْبَشَرِ أَحَدًا فَقُولِي إِنِّي نَذَرْتُ لِلرَّحْمٰنِ صَوْمًا
if you see any man, say, 'I have vowed a fast to the Merciful.'

[43:41] إِمَّا نَذْهَبَنَّ بِكَ فَإِنَّا مِنْهُمْ مُنْتَقِمُونَ
if We take you away, We shall take vengeance on them

4. after the negative لَا *lā*:

[2:132] لَا تَمُوتُنَّ إِلَّا وَأَنْتُمْ مُسْلِمُونَ
die only as Muslims

[6:14] لَا تَكُونَنَّ مِنَ ٱلْمُشْرِكِينَ
do not be among the polytheists

Other categories may also trigger the use of the Energetic, but of these the only one found in the Qur'ān is the interrogative:

[22:15] هَلْ يُذْهِبَنَّ كَيْدُهُ مَا يَغِيظُ
will his trick remove what is enraging [him]?

OATHS

In general, oaths are most commonly introduced by the prepositions *wa-*, *bi-* or the rare *ta-*, all with the sense of 'by' and all taking the genitive. Thus وَٱللّٰهِ *wa-llāhi*, بِٱللّٰهِ *bi-llāhi* and تَٱللّٰهِ *ta-llāhi* all mean 'by God'. However, in the Qur'ān *bi-llāhi* never stands on its own in an oath. Also, though the *wāw al-qasam* (*wa-* plus the genitive 'by') is quite common, particularly in early Meccan material, *wa-llāhi* occurs only once [6:23].

The general rules for the introduction of the complement to a prepositional oath apply in the Qur'ān, though the range of examples in it does not cover all possibilities that Arabic provides.

1. In a nominal sentence using *la-* or *inna*... *la-*:

   وَٱلْقُرْآنِ ٱلْحَكِيمِ إِنَّكَ لَمِنَ ٱلْمُرْسَلِينَ [36:2-3]

   by the decisive recitation, you are one of those who have been sent!

2. In a positive verbal sentence using *la-* and the energetic (present and future) or *laqad* (sometimes just *qad*) and the perfect (past), or by *inna*:

   تَٱللّٰهِ لَتُسْأَلُنَّ عَمَّا كُنْتُمْ تَفْتَرُونَ [16:56]

   by God you will be asked about what you concocted!

   وَهٰذَا ٱلْبَلَدِ ٱلْأَمِينِ لَقَدْ خَلَقْنَا ٱلْإِنْسَانَ [95:3-4]

   by this secure territory, We have created man!

   وَنَفْسٍ ... قَدْ أَفْلَحَ مَنْ زَكَّاهَا [91:7-9]

   by a soul... the one who keeps it pure will prosper!

   وَٱلْكِتَابِ ٱلْمُبِينِ إِنَّا جَعَلْنَاهُ قُرْآنًا عَرَبِيًّا [43:2-3]

   by the clear Scripture, We have made it an Arabic recitation!

   3. In a negative sentence:
      a) with *mā* + the perfect or *lā* + the imperfect or *mā*[A] with a nominal sentence:

[A] The negative *in* is found in 86:4.

[6:23] وَٱللَّهِ ... مَا كُنَّا مُشْرِكِينَ

by God we were not polytheists!

[93:1, 3] وَٱلضُّحَىٰ ... مَا وَدَّعَكَ رَبُّكَ

by the forenoon. . . your Lord has not said farewell to you!

[68:1-2] وَٱلْقَلَمِ ... مَا أَنْتَ بِمَجْنُونٍ

by the pen. . . you are not possessed!

b) With the absence of any particle, either positive or negative, as in:

[12:85] تَٱللَّهِ تَفْتَأُ تَذْكُرُ يُوسُفَ

by God, you do **not** cease remembering Yūsuf!

As oaths are prominent in rhetorical pieces, sometimes the rhetoric causes an interruption in the flow of the sentence, with words like *bal* and *hal* starting the main sentence, e.g.:

[50:1-2] وَٱلْقُرْآنِ ٱلْمَجِيدِ بَلْ عَجِبُوا

by the glorious Qur'ān, no, they wondered!

Other rhetorical modifications occasionally appear:

[85:3-4] وَشَاهِدٍ وَمَشْهُودٍ قُتِلَ أَصْحَابُ ٱلْأُخْدُودِ

by that which witnesses and that which is witnessed, slain were the men of the pit

The commentators are agreed that this is not an example of 3(b), but of the oath being followed by a strongly positive statement.

As indicated above, oaths may also be introduced by verbs such as حَلَفَ *ḥalafa* and أَقْسَمَ *aqsama* 'to swear'. Even شَهِدَ *shahida*, 'to witness' can operate in the same way:

[9:56] يَحْلِفُونَ بِٱللَّهِ إِنَّهُمْ لَمِنْكُمْ

they swear by God that they are of you

يُقْسِمَانِ بِٱللّٰهِ لَشَهَادَتُنَا أَحَقُّ مِنْ شَهَادَتِهِمَا [5:107]

let the two of them swear by God, 'Our testimony is truer than theirs.'

نَشْهَدُ إِنَّكَ لَرَسُولُ ٱللّٰهِ [63:1]

we bear witness that you are God's messenger

There is one very problematical usage: the phrase لَا أُقْسِمُ *lā uqsimu* that occurs in 56:75; 69:38; 70:40; 75:1; 75:2; 81:15; 84:16; and 90:1. The commentators are split on whether the phrase means 'No! I swear' or simply 'I swear', the second possibility being the converse of oaths where no particle is involved. On the basis of the other examples of *ḥalafa* and *aqsama*, I am inclined to think that the phrase means 'No! I swear'.

لَيْتَ *layta*

Layta, 'would that', acts like *inna*, *anna*, *laʿalla*: it takes a noun in the accusative or a pronominal suffix. In the case of the 1st person singular this is *-nī*. In the Qur'ān all the examples of *layta* but one are preceded by *yā*. The exception is 25:28, where وَيْلَتَا *waylatā* (see below) is interposed.

يَا لَيْتَ قَوْمِي يَعْلَمُونَ	[36:26]	would that my people knew!
يَا لَيْتَنَا أَطَعْنَا ٱللّٰهَ	[33:66]	would that we had obeyed God!
يَا لَيْتَنِي مِتُّ قَبْلَ هٰذَا	[19:23]	would that I had died before this!

وَيْلٌ *waylun*, وَيْلَةٌ *waylatun*

Waylun, 'woe', is most commonly found in the Qur'ān in the indefinite nominative, with *li-* to indicate those on whom the woe falls and *min* to indicate the cause of the woe:

[41:6] وَيْلٌ لِلْمُشْرِكِينَ

woe to the polytheists!

[14:2] وَيْلٌ لِلْكَافِرِينَ مِنْ عَذَابٍ شَدِيدٍ

woe to those who do not believe, because of a severe torment!

There is a rare example of the definite:

[21:18] لَكُمُ ٱلْوَيْلُ مِمَّا تَصِفُونَ

woe to you for what you describe!

The accusative and a suffix is also found: وَيْلَكَ *wayla-ka*, وَيْلَكُمْ *wayla-kum*, وَيْلَنَا *wayla-nā*.

There are also four examples of the feminine وَيْلَةٌ *waylatun*. Three have the pausal form وَيْلَتَى *waylatā* after the *yā* of lamentation (see below) [5:31; 11:72; 25:28], and one is in the accusative followed by a suffix, وَيْلَتَنَا *waylata-nā* [18:49].

REGRET

The particle most used to express regret, *wā*, does not occur in the Qur'ān. However, its alternative, *yā*, does. At first sight it looks indistinguishable from the vocative *yā*, and in some cases, as in the examples with *layta* and *wayl* above, one might perhaps view the *yā* either way. However, only the *yā* of regret is followed by the pausal form in *-ā* mentioned under *waylatun* above. It is also found in such phrases as:

يَا أَسَفَى عَلَى يُوسُفَ	[12:84]	Oh, how I grieve for Joseph
يَا حَسْرَتَا	[39:56]	Oh, woe is me!

It is also found with the accusative in such phrases as *yā ḥasratan* [36:30] and *yā ḥasrata-nā* [6:31].

Vocabulary Thirty-Nine

Perfect	Imperfect	Verbal noun	
حَلَفَ	يَحْلِفُ	حِلْفٌ	to swear
رَجَمَ	يَرْجُمُ	رَجْمٌ	to stone
سَجَنَ	يَسْجُنُ	سَجْنٌ	to imprison
سَفَعَ	يَسْفَعُ	سَفْعٌ	to drag
شَهِدَ	يَشْهَدُ	شَهَادَةٌ	to witness
عَجِبَ	يَعْجَبُ	عَجَبٌ	to wonder
غَلَبَ	يَغْلِبُ	غَلَبٌ	to overcome
قَعَدَ	يَقْعُدُ	قُعُودٌ	to sit, lurk
نَذَرَ	يَنْذُرُ	نَذْرٌ	to vow
غَاظَ	يَغِيظُ	غَيْظٌ	to enrage
زَكَّى 2	يُزَكِّي	تَزْكِيَةٌ	to purify, keep pure
وَدَّعَ 2	يُوَدِّعُ	يَوْدِيعٌ	to bid farewell to
أَقْسَمَ 4	يُقْسِمُ	إِقْسَامٌ	to swear
أَنْجَى 4	يُنْجِي	إِنْجَاءٌ	to save
أَنْسَى 4	يُنْسِي	إِنْسَاءٌ	to cause to forget
اِنْتَقَمَ 8	يَنْتَقِمُ	اِنْتِقَامٌ	to take revenge on (+ *min*)
اِنْتَهَى 8	يَنْتَهِي	اِنْتِهَاءٌ	to cease, desist
اِسْتَخَفَّ 10	يَسْتَخِفُّ	اِسْتِخْفَافٌ	to make unstable

Singular	Plural	
أَسَفٌ		grief
حَسْرَةٌ		sorrow, anguish
صَوْمٌ		fast
ضُحًى		forenoon
نَاصِيَةٌ	نَوَاصٍ	forelock
أَجْمَعُ		all
صَاغِرٌ		humbled
قَدِيمٌ	قُدَمَاءُ	old, ancient
يَوْمَئِذٍ		on that day

Exercise Thirty-Nine

1. [38:27] وَيْلٌ لِلَّذِينَ كَفَرُوا مِنَ ٱلنَّارِ
2. [52:11] وَيْلٌ يَوْمَئِذٍ لِلْمُكَذِّبِينَ
3. [2:79] وَيْلٌ لِلَّذِينَ يَكْتُبُونَ ٱلْكِتَابَ بِأَيْدِيهِمْ ثُمَّ يَقُولُونَ هٰذَا مِنْ عِنْدَ ٱللّٰهِ
4. [41:6] وَيْلٌ لِلْمُشْرِكِينَ
5. [21:97] يَا وَيْلَنَا قَدْ كُنَّا فِي غَفْلَةٍ مِنْ هٰذَا
6. [18:42] يَا لَيْتَنِي لَمْ أُشْرِكْ بِرَبِّي أَحَدًا
7. [33:66] يَا لَيْتَنَا أَطَعْنَا ٱللّٰهَ
8. [36:26] يَا لَيْتَ قَوْمِي يَعْلَمُونَ
9. [78:40] يَقُولُ ٱلْكَافِرُ يَا لَيْتَنِي كُنْتُ تُرَابًا

10. [90:1] لَا أُقْسِمُ بِهَٰذَا ٱلْبَلَدِ

11. [9:107] وَٱللَّهُ يَشْهَدُ إِنَّهُمْ لَكَاذِبُونَ

12. [12:95] قَالُوا تَٱللَّهِ إِنَّكَ لَفِي ضَلَالِكَ ٱلْقَدِيمِ

13. [6:23] وَٱللَّهِ رَبِّنَا مَا كُنَّا مُشْرِكِينَ

14. [15:92] فَوَرَبِّكَ لَنَسْأَلَنَّهُمْ أَجْمَعِينَ

15. [19:68] فَوَرَبِّكَ لَنَحْشُرَنَّهُمْ

16. [34:3] وَرَبِّي لَتَأْتِيَنَّكُمْ

17. [43:87] لَئِنْ سَأَلْتَهُمْ مَنْ خَلَقَهُمْ لَيَقُولُنَّ ٱللَّهُ

18. [58:21] كَتَبَ ٱللَّهُ لَأَغْلِبَنَّ أَنَا وَرُسُلِي

19. [14:13] لَنُخْرِجَنَّكُمْ مِنْ أَرْضِنَا

20. [4:87] لَيَجْمَعَنَّكُمْ إِلَىٰ يَوْمِ ٱلْقِيَامَةِ

21. [43:62] لَا يَصُدَّنَّكُمُ ٱلشَّيْطَانُ

22. [14:42] لَا تَحْسَبَنَّ ٱللَّهَ غَافِلًا عَمَّا يَعْمَلُ ٱلظَّالِمُونَ

23. [19:46] لَئِنْ لَمْ تَنْتَهِ لَأَرْجُمَنَّكَ

24. [6:63] لَئِنْ أَنْجَانَا مِنْ هَٰذِهِ لَنَكُونَنَّ مِنَ ٱلشَّاكِرِينَ

25. [6:68] إِمَّا يُنْسِيَنَّكَ ٱلشَّيْطَانُ فَلَا تَقْعُدْ بَعْدَ ٱلذِّكْرَىٰ مَعَ ٱلْقَوْمِ ٱلظَّالِمِينَ

26. [7:27] يَا بَنِي آدَمَ لَا يَفْتِنَنَّكُمُ ٱلشَّيْطَانُ

27. [6:77] لَئِنْ لَمْ يَهْدِنِي رَبِّي لَأَكُونَنَّ مِنَ ٱلْقَوْمِ ٱلضَّالِّينَ

28. [30:60] لَا يَسْتَخِفَّنَّكَ ٱلَّذِينَ لَا يُوقِنُونَ

Lesson Forty
Special Uses of *mā kāna*; Verbs of Wonder, Praise and Blame

Special uses of *mā kāna*

There are two idiomatic uses of *mā kāna* that are common enough to need explanation.

1. *Mā kāna* followed by a subject and then by *li-*. In this construction the subordinate clause introduced by *li-* is the equivalent of the predicate of *kāna*. The literal meaning is 'x [the nominative] is/was not one to', but it is often more satisfactory to translate the phrase as 'x would not', 'x should not' or even as 'x cannot' or 'x could not'.

[2:143] مَا كَانَ ٱللَّهُ لِيُضِيعَ إِيمَانَكُمْ

God is not one to see your faith wasted

[11:117] مَا كَانَ رَبُّكَ لِيُهْلِكَ ٱلْقُرَى بِظُلْمٍ

your Lord was not one to destroy the settlements unjustly

[9:122] مَا كَانَ ٱلْمُؤْمِنُونَ لِيَنْفِرُوا كَافَّةً

the believers should not go out to fight all in one body

The only example without an explicit subject is:

[12:76] مَا كَانَ لِيَأْخُذَ أَخَاهُ

'He was not one to take his brother'

Here the subject Yūsuf is implicit from the previous verses.

2. *Mā kāna li-* [+ genitive] *an*: This is the more common construction. In meaning it is similar to 1, and again it is satisfactory to translate the phrase as 'x should not', etc.

مَا كَانَ لَنَا أَنْ نُشْرِكَ بِٱللَّهِ [12:38]

it was not for us to associate anything with God

مَا كَانَ لِنَبِيٍّ أَنْ يَغُلَّ [3:161]

it is not for any prophet to deceive [the people]

مَا كَانَ لِلَّهِ أَنْ يَتَّخِذَ مِنْ وَلَدٍ [19:35]

God is not one to take to Himself any son

Verbs of wonder, praise and blame

The verbs classified by the Arab grammarians as 'verbs of wonder' are rare in the Qur'ān and barely deserve a mention. There are two forms.

1. The 3 m.s. of the perfect of the 4th form immediately after *mā*:

   مَا أَكْفَرَهُ [80:17] how ungrateful he is

2. The 2 m.s. imperative of the 4th form, with the object attached by *bi-*:

   أَبْصِرْ بِهِ وَأَسْمِعْ [18:26] how well He sees and hears

بِئْسَ *bi'sa*and نِعْمَ *niʿma* are termed by the Arab grammarians 'the verbs of praise and blame', but they are fossilized verbs that do not conjugate. Both are relatively common in the Qur'ān, with 'the verb of blame' [*bi'sa* 'how bad'] being more than twice as frequent as 'the verb of praise' [*niʿma* 'how good']. *bi'sa* and *niʿma* are normally followed by a clause beginning with *mā* or a single noun in the nominative:

بِئْسَ مَا ٱشْتَرَوْا بِهِ أَنْفُسَهُمْ [2:93]

evil is what they have sold themselves/ their souls for

بِئْسَ ٱلْمَصِيرُ [2:126]

evil is the journeying [to Hell]

[37:75] لَنِعْمَ ٱلْمُجِيبُونَ
how excellent are those who answer

[16:30] نِعْمَ دَارُ ٱلْمُتَّقِينَ
how excellent is the dwelling of the God-fearing

Two verses, however, show different constructions.

[18:50] بِئْسَ لِلظَّالِمِينَ بَدَلًا
that is an evil exchange for the wrongdoers

Here an accusative takes the place of the nominative.

[49:11] بِئْسَ ٱلِاسْمُ ٱلْفُسُوقُ بَعْدَ ٱلْإِيمَانِ
evil is the term 'dissoluteness', after belief

Here we have the full construction with two nominatives, analogous to the example quoted in Wright (2, 290):

نِعْمَ ٱلْمَرْأَةُ زَيْنَبُ how excellent a woman Zaynab is

The perfect of the verb سَاءَ *sā'a*, 'to be bad' has more or less the same force and constructions as *bi'sa*, with a similar predominance of the nominative over the accusative. However, *sā'a* does conjugate:

[4:97] مَأْوَاهُمْ جَهَنَّمُ وَسَاءَتْ مَصِيرًا
their abode in Jahannam, and it is an evil journey's end

[37:177] سَاءَ صَبَاحُ ٱلْمُنْذَرِينَ
terrible will be the morning of those who have been warned

Vocabulary Forty

Perfect	Imperfect	Verbal noun	
صَنَعَ	يَصْنَعُ	صُنْعٌ	to make, work
نَفَرَ	يَنْفِرُ	نَفْرٌ	to go forth
غَلَّ	يَغُلُّ	غُلُولٌ	to deceive
عَمَرَ	يَعْمُرُ	عُمْرَةٌ	to visit
أَطْلَعَ 4	يُطْلِعُ	إِطْلَاعٌ	to acquaint
أَضَاعَ 4	يُضِيعُ	إِضَاعَةٌ	to cause to be wasted
آذَى 4	يُوذِي	إِيذَاءٌ	to hurt, vex
اِشْتَرَى	يَشْتَرِي	شِرَاءٌ	to buy

Singular	Plural	
مَأْوًى		shelter
بَدَلٌ		exchange
ثَمَنٌ	أَثْمَانٌ	price, gain
خِيَرَةٌ		choice
مُرْتَفَقٌ		resting-place
مَسْجِدٌ	مَسَاجِدُ	mosque, place of prayer
سُلْطَانٌ		authority, power
شَرَابٌ		drink
مَصِيرٌ		course, journey's end
فُسُوقٌ		dissoluteness
وَحْيٌ		inspiration

Exercise Forty

1. مَا كَانَ ٱللهُ لِيَظْلِمَهُمْ [29:40]
2. مَا كَانَ ٱللهُ لِيَذَرَ ٱلْمُؤْمِنِينَ عَلَى مَا أَنْتُمْ عَلَيْهِ [3:179]
3. مَا كَانَ ٱللهُ لِيُضِلَّ قَوْمًا بَعْدَ إِذْ هَدَاهُمْ [9:115]
4. مَا كَانَ ٱللهُ لِيُطْلِعَكُمْ عَلَى ٱلْغَيْبِ [3:179]
5. مَا كَانَ لَهُمْ أَنْ يَدْخُلُوهَا [2:114]
6. مَا كَانَ لِنَفْسٍ أَنْ تَمُوتَ إِلَّا بِإِذْنِ ٱللهِ [3:145]
7. مَا كَانَ لِرَسُولٍ أَنْ يَأْتِيَ بِآيَةٍ إِلَّا بِإِذْنِ ٱللهِ [13:38]
8. مَا كَانَ لِمُؤْمِنٍ أَنْ يَقْتُلَ مُؤْمِنًا [4:92]
9. مَا كَانَ لِلْمُشْرِكِينَ أَنْ يَعْمُرُوا مَسَاجِدَ ٱللهِ [9:17]
10. مَا كَانَ لَنَا أَنْ نَأْتِيَكُمْ بِسُلْطَانٍ [14:11]
11. مَا كَانَ لِبَشَرٍ أَنْ يُكَلِّمَهُ ٱللهُ إِلَّا وَحْيًا [42:51]
12. مَا كَانَ لِمُؤْمِنٍ وَلَا مُؤْمِنَةٍ أَنْ يَكُونَ لَهُمُ ٱلْخِيَرَةُ [33:36]
13. مَا كَانَ لَكُمْ أَنْ تُؤْذُوا رَسُولَ ٱللهِ [33:53]
14. نِعْمَ ٱلنَّصِيرُ [8:40]
15. نِعْمَ أَجْرُ ٱلْعَامِلِينَ [29:58]
16. نِعِمَّا يَعِظُكُمْ بِهِ [4:58]
17. سَآءَ مَا كَانُوا يَعْمَلُونَ [58:15]
18. سَآءَ سَبِيلًا [4:22]
19. بِئْسَ ٱلشَّرَابُ وَسَآءَتْ مُرْتَفَقًا [18:29]
20. اِشْتَرَوْا بِهِ ثَمَنًا قَلِيلًا فَبِئْسَ مَا يَشْتَرُونَ [3:187]

21. [5:63] بِئْسَ مَا كَانُوا يَصْنَعُونَ

22. [62:5] بِئْسَ مَثَلُ ٱلْقَوْمِ ٱلَّذِينَ كَذَّبُوا بِآيَاتِ ٱللّٰهِ

23. [3:151] مَأْوَاهُمُ ٱلنَّارُ وَبِئْسَ مَثْوَى ٱلظَّالِمِينَ

24. [3:162] مَأْوَاهُ جَهَنَّمُ وَبِئْسَ ٱلْمَصِيرُ

25. [38:30] نِعْمَ ٱلْعَبْدُ

Key to the Exercises

Exercise One

1. The clear book. 2. A clear book. 3. A noble book. 4. A clear recitation. 5. The glorious recitation. 6. A noble recitation. 7. A glorious recitation. 8. The mighty recitation. 9. An ample mercy. 10. Another sign. 11. The last day. 12. A great day. 13. The severe punishment. 14. A mighty day. 15. A severe punishment. 16. A great reward. 17. A noble reward. 18. A mighty punishment. 19. A great reward. 20. A faithful messenger. 21. A noble messenger. 22. The secure town. 23. Another god. 24. A clear messenger. 25. The first and the last. 26. The first and the last. 27. God is mighty. 28. God is strong. 29. God is strong and mighty. 30. The strong and faithful one.

Exercise Two

1. Other gods. 2. Many benefits. 3. Many fruits. 4. The first (previous) generations. 5. The settlements are doing wrong. 6. A wrongdoing settlement. 7. The Jews and the Christians. 8. The heavens and the earth. 9. Non-Arab and Arab. 10. The people who do wrong. 11. Unbelieving people. 12. A believer and an unbeliever. 13. Believing men. 14. The believing men and the believing women. 15. Believing men and believing women. 16. The first and the last. 17. God is relenting. 18. Honoured servants. 19. A believing man. 20. Other days. 21. Heaven and earth (the heaven and the earth). 22. The Muslim men and the Muslim women.

Exercise Three A

1. You are Muslims. 2. They are Muslims. 3. We are a temptation. 4. I am a warner. 5. A lofty garden. 6. You are the Relenting One. 7. You are wrongdoers. 8. You are the poor. 9. She is a wrongdoer. 10. He is a believer. 11. He is the gentle one. 12. You are believers. 13. I am God, the Mighty (the mighty God). 14. It is white. 15. He/it is strong. 16. You are the Mighty One. 17. It is a trial. 18. You are a warner. 19. You are ignorant ones. 20. I am the Relenting One.

Exercise Four

1. In the alms. 2. In manifest error. 3. Over the fire. 4. Between heaven and earth. 5. Among the believers. 6. Among the people. 7. With the people who do wrong. 8. With the believers. 9. With the messenger. 10. On a guidance. 11. On the messenger. 12. Against the unbelievers. 13. From a way. 14. To a town. 15. To a great punishment. 16. From the messengers. 17. From other days. 18. From a god. 19. By God. 20. In the next world. 21. In a valley. 22. Good news for the believers. 23. For the people who do wrong. 24. For the believing women. 25. To God belongs this world (the first world) and the next.

Exercise Five

1. My punishment is severe. 2. My Lord is merciful. 3. My Lord is near. 4. My protector is God. 5. God is my Lord. 6. My son is [one] of my family. 7. My punishment is the severe one. 8. My Lord is with me. 9. Between me and my brothers. 10. God is my reckoning. 11. God is guidance. 12. God is truth. 13. My Lord is gentle. 14. He is God, my Lord. 15. It is my stick. 16. God is the one who hears. 17. God is my Lord. 18. My messengers and I. 19. It is from the Book. 20. He is in manifest error. 21. My punishment is severe. 22. He remains for ever in the Fire. 23. He is the First and thc Last. 24. I am [one] of the Muslims. 25. My reward is with God.

Exercise Six

1. That is the great bounty. 2. This is permissible and this is forbidden. 3. This (man) is a warner from the warners of old (first). 4. This is an Arabic tongue. 5. This is a mercy from my Lord. 6. That bounty is from God. 7. This is a straight path. 8. This life. 9. That is the next abode (world). 10. This is a strange thing. 11. Those have a guidance. 12. That is far-reaching error. 13. This is my way. 14. That is a difficult day. 15. Those men are the believers. 16. This is my Lord. 17. This is manifest magic. 18. That is easy for God. 19. Those men are of the righteous. 20. These are a sinful people. 21. Those men are honoured in gardens. 22. These are few. 23. That is in a book. 24. That is my path. 25. Those are God's signs. 26. My Lord is on a straight path. 27. The unbelievers will have a humiliating punishment.

Exercise Seven

1. In God's way. 2. The nieces (the daughters of the brother). 3. A few from the rest. 4. The way of the sinners. 5. Bounty is in God's hand. 6. The hands of the people. 7. The signs of the Merciful. 8. God's land is wide. 9. This is God's she-camel. 10. Before the day of reckoning. 11. Those are the party of the Devil. 12. God is possessed of great bounty. 13. Many of the people. 14. Those are the inhabitants (companions) of the Fire. 15. God is an enemy for the unbelievers. 16. The effect of God's mercy. 17. I am the first of the believers. 18. Lord of the heavens and the earth. 19. A party of the People of the Book. 20. A party of the Children of Israel. 21. God is the protector of the faithful. 22. The outcome of affairs is with God. 23. Mischief and great corruption on earth. 24. On the edge of a pit of the Fire. 25. Praise belongs to God, the Lord of all created beings.

Exercise Eight

1. He entered the city. 2. They entered a settlement. 3. He made the sun an illumination and the moon a light. 4. God has sent a messenger. 5. She carried a light load. 6. He created the heavens and the earth. 7. God created that. 8. We created man. 9. They remembered/mentioned God. 10. We returned to the city. 11. You returned. 12. God has coined a likeness. 13. You have journeyed in the way of God. 14. They lingered in humiliating punishment. 15. You have lingered in God's book until the Day of Resurrection. 16. We have written in the Psalms after the Reminder. 17. He found a people. 18. I found a woman. 19. They found God relenting. 20. God promised the believing men and women gardens. 21. He reached the place where the sun rises. 22. God's command was made manifest (appeared). 23. Corruption has appeared on land and sea. 24. We have sent a messenger to (into) each community.

Exercise Nine

1. From God and His Prophet. 2. They are their mothers. 3. You did your deed. 4. He put rivers between them. 5. They left their homes. 6. We went out with you. 7. The matter is between me and you. 8. My curse is on you. 9. We made the son of Mary and his mother a sign. 10. God helped you at Badr. 11. They returned to them. 12. The matter rests with you. 13. They lied against themselves. 14. He followed my guidance. 15. You asked them (f.p.). 16. By the permission of their Lord.

17. My blessing is on you. 18. You entered it. 19. By permission of their family/folk. 20. A people before you asked her. 21. My servants asked you about me. 22. He followed you. 23. He followed me. 24. God raised it to him. 25. Peace be upon you. Your Lord has prescribed mercy for Himself. 26. He entered his garden. 27. God seized them for their sins.

Exercise Ten

1. God did not wrong them. 2. God has not made any way for you against them. 3. That is not a great matter for God. 4. There is not a witness among us. 5. They have no helpers. 6. They did not do it. 7. They did not linger in the humiliating punishment. 8. Whatever reward I have asked you for. 9. There is no way against them. 10. I am merely a clear warner. 11. They have no knowledge of it. 12. We did not prescribe it for them. 13. We are not dead. 14. We found what he promised us. 15. Whatever proper thing (what of that which is recognised/regarded as proper) they did (f.p.) concerning themselves. 16. Concerning what you have taken. 17. This is what you hoarded for yourselves. 18. What God has ordered. 19. What is in front of us and what is behind us. 20. We know what we have ordained for them. 21. What their right hands have laboured [on]. 22. To God belongs the sovereignty of the heavens and the earth and what is in them. 23. The Saying has fallen on them for the wrong that they have done. 24. They found all that they had done. 25. Whatever is on land and in the sea. 26. Half of what you have settled on. 27. Corruption has appeared on land and sea because of what the hands of the people have gained.

Exercise Eleven

1. We have made some of you a test for others. 2. Each of you is an enemy of the other. 3. We have raised some of them above others. 4. Some suspicion is a sin. 5. Those are friends of one another. 6. We have left some of them. 7. They looked at one another. 8. The believers, male and female, are friends to one another. 9. God has power over everything. 10. You are witness over everything. 11. We opened for them the gates of everything. 12. We have appointed an enemy from among the sinners for every prophet. 13. Every community has [its] term. 14. Death [comes on] him from every side. 15. Each god took what it had created. 16. We have raised a messenger in every community. 17. Your Lord is guardian over everything. 18. Every soul is a hostage for what it has earned. 19. Everything little and great is recorded. 20. In it they will have some

of every kind of fruit and forgiveness from their Lord. 21. All you asked for. 22. We have tarried a day or part of a day. 23. They entered it the first time.

Exercise Twelve

1. They (f.p.) have children. 2. They were a sinful people. 3. They were like stubble. 4. We were Muslims. 5. You were in neglect of this. 6. God's command is done. 7. He was an enemy to God and His angels and His messengers. 8. It was with him. 9. He was aware of and saw His servants. 10. Your Lord was observant. 11. They were witnesses against him. 12. The people were a community. 13. You were the watcher over them. 14. We were not thieves. 15. You were sinners. 16. You were on the lip of a pit of the Fire. 17. He was from the generations before you. 18. They were an evil people. 19. That was easy for God. 20. She was from an unbelieving people. 21. There was no difficulty for the Prophet. 22. In the Messenger of God you have a good example. 23. He was in manifest error. 24. When the anger abated in Moses, he took the tablets. 25. When they opened their belongings they discovered their goods. 26. We were unaware of this.

Exercise Thirteen

1. From that which parents have left. 2. Two men said. 3. His hands are spread out. 4. Two other people. 5. Two young men entered the prison with him. 6. These two men are sorcerers. 7. He found two men in it. 8. These are two proofs from your Lord. 9. Two parties of the believers. 10. In the two of them are two springs. 11. These two daughters of mine (gen.). 12. He found, apart from them, two women. 13. They reached their confluence. 14. There is much sin in the two of them. 15. Between the two groups is a veil. 16. They assigned associates to Him. 17. We do not believe the two of you. 18. He created the heavens and the earth and what is between them. 19. He set cultivated land between them. 20. We only created them in truth. 21. In the two of them are fruits and palms and pomegranates. 22. We have appointed the night and the day as two signs.

Exercise Fifteen

1. He taught the recitation. 2. I taught you the book. 3. That is because of what your hands have forwarded. 4. What he has sent forward and left behind. 5. They denied the truth of Our signs. 6. He denied the

truth of the Hour. 7. They have striven in God's way. 8. The two have striven with you. 9. You have disputed with us. 10. God confound them! 11. They have fought you over religion. 12. We have sent it down as a recitation in Arabic. 13. God has sent down water from the sky. 14. God has not sent down anything to any mortal. 15. We destroyed them for their sins. 16. We have not destroyed any settlement without it having a known decree. 17. He has sent His Messenger with the guidance. 18. We sent Noah to his people. 19. You sent a messenger to us. 20. I have put my trust in God, my Lord and your Lord. 21. He has turned on his face. 22. They went back to their own people. 23. They have helped him and followed the light. 24. They have followed the truth from their Lord. 25. They have differed about the scripture. 26. The parties among them differed. 27. The Messenger sought forgiveness for them. 28. They have sought forgiveness for their sins. 29. You were haughty and were one of the unbelievers. 30. They were haughty and were a sinful people.

Exercise Sixteen

1. We shall raise up in every community a witness. 2. I will reach the confluence of the two seas. 3. We will place the two beneath our feet. 4. He eats what you eat and drinks what you drink. 5. She carries him. 6. They will not return. 7. They will go in through every gate to see them. 8. You will remember them. 9. God coins comparisons for men. 10. They write the document with their hands. 11. A punishment that is near will seize you. 12. He used to tell his people to pray and give alms. 13. They are not going out with them. 14. They ask you about the sacred month. 15. He hears the words of God. 16. He knows what each soul earns. 17. God will not speak to them nor look at them. 18. They will help you. 19. God witnesses what you do. 20. They put their trust in their Lord. 21. They will seek His forgiveness. God is forgiving and merciful. 22. He will teach you the Scripture and the Wisdom. 23. They are not proud. 24. We do not deny the truth of the signs of our Lord. 25. You strive in God's way with your possessions and your persons. 26. Those possessed of understanding are reminded. 27. I will send down the like of what God has sent down. 28. They destroy themselves. 29. They will not fight you. 30. They will see/observe.

Exercise Seventeen

1. Will you not be reminded? 2. We shall see whether you have spoken the truth or are one of the liars. 3. Shall We treat those who submit like

those who sin? 4. When will this promise [happen]? 5. How will they have the reminder? 6. What are the companions of the right? 7. What will give you knowledge of what the Day of Judgement is? 8. Have you found that which your Lord promised you? 9. Have you any knowledge? 10. Do they not know? 11. Has God sent a mortal as His messenger? 12. Truly, His is the judgement. 13. We see how you act. 14. Do you not understand? 15. Have you brought me good tidings? 16. Did you deny the truth of My signs? 17. Do they divide out your Lord's mercy? 18. Did you know what you had done? 19. Have you hastened the command of your Lord? 20. Do they seek to hasten Our punishment? 21. Do they hear you? 22. It was made clear to you how We dealt with them. 23. Do we not die? 24. Are you Muslims? 25. Truly that will be the clear loss. 26. What will give you knowledge of what the calamity is? 27. Can you make the deaf hear? 28. How can you take it? 29. Is it a wonder for mankind? 30. Do they not consider (look at) camels?

Exercise Eighteen

1. The People of the Scripture ask you to bring down a scripture for them from heaven. 2. We have made you a moderate community that you may be witnesses to the people. 3. They were averse to striving with their possessions and their persons in God's way. 4. Their recompense is that the curse of God will be upon them. 5. They offer allegiance to you on the basis that they will not associate anything with God. 6. Am I unable to be like this crow? 7. That will be because they have followed that which angers God. 8. Your sign will be that you cannot speak to people for three nights. 9. He has brought it down upon your heart, that you may be one of the warners. 10. We desire our Lord to cause us to enter with the people who are righteous. 11. God will not grant deferment to any soul. 12. God commands you to sacrifice a cow. 13. It is the truth from your Lord, that you may warn a people. 14. It gives good tidings to the believers that they shall have a great reward. 15. We made the night for them to rest in. 16. He is able to send a punishment against you. 17. It has become clear to them that they are companions of the Fire. 18. It has become clear to him that he was an enemy of God. 19. We prescribed in it: a soul for a soul. and an eye for an eye. 20. He has subjected the sea, so that you may eat [fresh fish] flesh from it. 21. That is their recompense because they did not believe in our signs. 22. We are eager for our Lord to forgive us our sins. 23. Does man not remember that We created him? 24. He sent down with them the Scripture with

the truth, that He might decide between the people. 25. May I follow you on condition that you teach me?

Exercise Nineteen

1. We shall return to him. 2. You are the gatherer of the people. 3. Thus we deal with the sinners. 4. They said, 'We are moving to our Lord.' 5. God enjoins justice and doing good. 6. We have made you a viceroy in the earth. 7. Hell will be your recompense. 8. You are possessed. 9. God is forgiving and merciful. 10. The unbelievers say, 'This man is a clear sorcerer.' 11. We will not enter it. 12. God is an enemy to the unbelievers. 13. We have sent down to you the Scripture with the truth. 14. He has a father who is a very old man indeed. 15. He was one of Our devoted servants. 16. This is a very strange thing. 17. Satan is a very clear enemy to man. 18. He is one of the righteous. 19. He sees what you do. 20. The earthquake of the Hour is a tremendous thing. 21. She is a yellow cow. 22. God has power over everything. 23. I have put my trust in God. 24. Many of the people are heedless of Our signs. 25. In the livestock there is a lesson for you. 26. Truly, to God belongs whatever is in the heavens and the earth. 27. The hypocrites try to deceive God. 28. We have sent you with the truth, as a bearer of good tidings and a warner. 29. They said, 'We bear witness against ourselves.' 30. They said, 'We found our fathers serving them.'

Exercise Twenty

1. You did not warn them. 2. He will teach you what you did not know. 3. I did not associate anyone with my Lord. 4. He has no protector. 5. Did you not know that God knows all that is in heaven and earth? 6. He has no partner in sovereignty. 7. They have not reached puberty. 8. God has not made a light for him. 9. Did I not say to you...? 10. Do not seek to hasten. 11. He knew what you did not know. 12. Have they not looked at the heaven above them? 13. He has taught man that which he did not know. 14. They found no helpers apart from God. 15. Did We not assign to him two eyes? 16. Did We not destroy the ancients? 17. You were not believers. 18. He did not hear it. 19. Did your Lord not make you a fair promise? 20. Do not approach (dual) this tree. 21. There is no equal to Him. 22. Do not be sad. 23. Do not serve Satan. 24. Do not ask me about anything. 25. Do not be with the unbelievers. 26. Do not kill your children. 27. Do not break your oaths. 28. Do not enter by one gate.

Exercise Twenty-One

1. Is not this the truth? 2. There is nothing like Him. 3. They say with their tongues what is not in their hearts. 4. They shall not have any food. 5. He is not one of your family. 6. Is there not a lodging for the unbelievers in Hell? 7. There is no sin for you in any mistakes you have made. 8. He cannot emerge from it. 9. Do I not possess the kingdom of Egypt? 10. Lo, they sit on it. 11. Those who surrender their faces to God will have their reward with their Lord. 12. Amongst them were those whom We drowned. 13. Is there any of those you associate [with God] who can do any of that? 14. From the *jinn* there were those who worked before him by permission of his Lord. 15. You cannot make those in the graves hear. 16. Among them there are those who made a covenant with God. 17. Among the parties there are those who deny some of it. 18. Among the people are those who dispute about God without knowledge. 19. See them running from it! 20. Lo, they are two parties. 21. Behold, you are mortals. 22. Lo, a party of them associate others with their Lord. 23. [Recall] when Satan made their actions seem fair to them. 24. [Recall] when We appointed for Moses forty nights.

Exercise Twenty-Two

1. They drew near to one another, asking each other questions. 2. Those recite their Scripture. 3. He recited it to them. 4. The Merciful has given permission to him. 5. I shall not leave the land until my father gives me permission. 6. My servants asked you about Me. 7. They ask, 'When is the Day of Resurrection?' 8. The people ask you about the Hour. 9. He has produced you from a single soul. 10. Are you the ones who made its tree grow, or are We the One who causes [it] to grow? 11. After them We produced other generations. 12. He used to tell his people to pray and give alms. 13. He has believed in God and His angels and His scriptures and His messengers. 14. Shall we believe in two mortals like us? 15. Do they then believe in vanity and disbelieve in the blessing of God? 16. They prefer the life of this world. 17. God has preferred you over us. 18. He told them their names. 19. He will tell them what they have been doing. 20. Will you tell God what He does not know. 21. Who told you this? 22. They sought your permission to go out. 23. I have perceived a fire. 24. I will tell you what you should eat.

Exercise Twenty-Three

1. My blessing which I bestowed on you. 2. This is the fire which you used to deny. 3. The Fire, whose fuel is men and stones. 4. Do not kill the soul that God has made sacred [forbidden]. 5. My protector is God who has sent down the Scripture. 6. [It is] He who has subjected the sea, so that you may eat from it. 7. Is this the one whom God has sent as a messenger? 8. And whom I desire to forgive me my sins on the Day of Judgement. 9. Who is it that will lend God a fair loan? 10. Blessed is He in whose hand is sovereignty. 11. [It is] He who has driven out those who disbelieved. 12. He has made well everything that He has created. 13. Those whose works have failed in this world and the next. 14. Do not be like those who have split up and disagreed. 15. It gives good tidings to the believers who do righteous deeds that they will have a great reward. 16. He puts abomination on those who do not understand. 17. Those who do not believe say, 'You have not been sent as a messenger.' 18. It is a tree that comes out of the root of Hell. 19. We give you very good tidings of a son whose name shall be John. 20. Seven fat cows which were devoured by seven thin ones. 21. In that are signs for a people who understand. 22. They [were] youths who believed in their Lord. 23. A *sūra* which We have sent down. 24. We have brought forth green shoots from which We bring forth grain. 25. On the heights are men who recognize each by their marks. 26. He is from a people with whom you have a covenant. 27. We sent down iron, in which there is great strength and [many] benefits for the people. 28. Communities to whom We shall give enjoyment.

Exercise Twenty-Four

1. We shall inherit the earth and all who are on it. 2. It shall be inherited by My righteous servants. 3. Will you leave Moses and his people to make mischief in the land? 4. Do not leave me alone. 5. No laden soul bears the burden of another. 6. My Lord embraces everything in His knowledge. 7. Their tongues describe the lie. 8. From that which you describe. 9. They will not reach the two of you. 10. They will not reach you. 11. He has set the balance. 12. We shall set up the balances for the Day of Resurrection. 13. God has promised you a promise of truth. 14. Did your Lord not make you a fair promise? 15. I exhort you to one thing. 16. God admonishes you. 17. The truth came to pass, and what they were doing was in vain. 18. We gave them some of Our mercy.

19. My Lord gave me judgement. 20. Those despaired of My mercy. 21. They have despaired of the World to Come. 22. They are sure about the World to Come. 23. They were convinced by Our signs. 24. Do you take idols as gods? 25. He takes witnesses from among you. 26. They choose the unbelievers as their friends.

Exercise Twenty-Five

1. They asked Moses for something greater than that. 2. We have more wealth and children [than you]. 3. Do you know better, or God? 4. The wage of the world to come is greater. 5. They are like stones or harder. 6. The word of those who disbelieve is the lowest and the word of God is the highest. 7. The noblest of you in the sight of God are the most god-fearing. 8. The vilest men have followed you. 9. Which of you is fairer in conduct? 10. Is that better or the Garden of Eternity? 11. God is better and more enduring. 12. Who is further astray than the one who is in distant schism? 13. God is closer to the two of them. 14. Most of them do not understand. 15. The most hostile people. 16. You were on the nearest bank, and they were in the furthest part of the bank. 17. Who does greater wrong than those who deny the truth of God's signs? 18. Shall I tell you of [someone] worse than that? 19. He has the fairest names. 20. God knows best what is in their hearts. 21. On that day the companions of the Garden will be better in the place they stay and the place they rest at midday. 22. What is with God is better for the pious. 23. He is the best of providers. 24. Your Lord knows best how long you have tarried. 25. That is purer for them. 26. The creation of the heavens and the earth is greater than the creation of mankind, but most people do not know [that]. 27. They listen to the declaration and follow the best of it. 28. We are nearer to him than you.

Exercise Twenty-Six

1. God has made trading lawful, and He has forbidden usury. 2. They allow it one year and forbid it another year. 3. They will fight you until they turn you away from your religion. 4. We returned him to his mother. 5. Evil has touched him. 6. Adversity has touched man. 7. We will tell you their tidings in truth. 8. We have told you about them before. 9. We were a people who strayed. 10. They stray from the way of God. 11. God leads astray the wrongdoers. 12. They lead you astray without any knowledge. 13. Pharaoh said to him, 'I think that you are bewitched, O Moses.' 14. You thought that God would not know much of what you were

doing. 15. That which neither profits us nor harms us. 16. You cannot injure Him in any way. 17. Then I shall compel him to the torment of the Fire. 18. He has prepared a painful torment for the unbelievers. 19. God has prepared for them gardens. 20. We counted them amongst the wicked. 21. A day with your Lord is like a thousand years of your counting. 22. God does not love those who work mischief. 23. Why do you argue with us about that of which you have no knowledge? 24. Do you argue with us about God? 25. They will indeed turn them aside from the way. 26. How many a sign is there in the heavens and the earth that they pass by!

Exercise Twenty-Seven

1. Who but God can forgive sins? 2. They remember God only a little. 3. He is simply a clear warner. 4. Most of them follow only conjecture. 5. None of your people will believe unless they are already believers. 6. We shall postpone it only to a term that will be counted. 7. We testify only to that which we know. 8. We never sent any messenger except with the tongue of his people. 9. We did not create the heavens and the earth and all that is between them save with the truth. 10. We are only mortals like you. 11. They have followed him, save for a group of believers. 12. Most of them do not believe in God unless they associate others with Him. 13. They serve only [what they serve] as did their fathers before. 14. We send it down only in a known measure. 15. We have sent before you as messengers only men. 16. The unbelievers say, 'You are only following a man who is bewitched.' 17. We come down only by command of your Lord. 18. They are only like animals. 19. He tarried amongst them for a thousand years all but fifty years. 20. Only those with knowledge will understand them. 21. No female becomes pregnant or gives birth except with His knowledge. 22. There is no settlement but We shall destroy it before the Day of Resurrection. 23. None but the sinners eat it. 24. This is simply a lie. 25. Muḥammad is only a messenger. 26. There is no beast on the earth but that its sustenance depends on God.

Exercise Twenty-Eight

1. Do not fear nor grieve. 2. Have they not travelled in the land? 3. It is evil as a resting place. 4. What they have been doing is evil. 5. You will wish [so] only if God wishes. 6. We make Our mercy reach those whom We wish. 7. A painful torment will befall those of them who disbelieve. 8. They came to them with the clear proofs. 9. Have you come to us that

we should serve God alone? 10. Do you want to kill me as you killed a soul yesterday? 11. He has desired only the present life. 12. We wanted their Lord to give the two of them [one] better than him in exchange. 13. They could not hear a sound. 14. They said, 'We hear and obey.' 15. We will obey you in some of the affair. 16. [One] of His signs is that heaven stands. 17. Let a party of them stand with you. 18. We shall not assign any weight to them on the Day of Resurrection. 19. They shall taste neither cool nor drink in it. 20. It tasted the mischief of its affair. 21. He answers those who believe and do righteous deeds. 22. So his Lord answered him and turned their wiles from him. 23. He will say, 'What answer did you give to the messengers?' 24. I have comprehended what you have not comprehended.

Exercise Twenty-Nine

1. Moses said to his people, 'O my people, you have done wrong.' 2. 'O Mary, God gives you good news of a word from Him. 3. O Moses, we will never enter it. 4. Children of Adam! We have sent down to you clothing. 5. 'O Noah, he is not one of your family.' 6. O people of the Scripture, why do you not believe in God's signs? 7. 'O David, We have made you a viceroy in the earth. 8. O My servants who believe, My land is wide. 9. 'O people of the book, you have no base.' 10. O Jesus, son of Mary, is your Lord able to send a table down to us? 11. O my people, there is no error in me. 12. He said, 'O my people, I conveyed to you a message of my Lord.' 13. O people of the Scripture, why do you turn those who believe from God's way? 14. My people, I am not asking you for any payment for this. 15. O my father, why do you worship something that cannot hear. 16. O my people, is my clan stronger against you than God? 17. O my people, these are my daughters. 18. Moses said, 'O Pharaoh, I am a messenger from the Lord of created beings.' 19. They said, 'O Noah, you have disputed with us, and disputed much with us.' 20. O people, a proof has come to you from your Lord. 21. O Messenger, let not those who vie with one another in unbelief grieve you. 22. O men, you are the ones who are in need of God. 23. O you who believe why do you say what you do not do? 24. O you who have disbelieved, make no excuses for yourselves today.

Exercise Thirty

1. She brought him to her own folk. 2. The hour will come upon them suddenly when they are unaware. 3. How many clear signs we gave them!

4. They perform prayer and pay the *zakāt*. 5. I see you and your people in manifest error. 6. Have you considered the water that you drink? 7. Those [can] hope for God's mercy. 8. I have summoned my people night and day. 9. God will reward the thankful. 10. He created you from clay and then fixed a term. 11. They walk on the earth. 12. He eats food and walks round the markets. 13. Today We forget them as they forgot that they would meet this day of theirs. 14. They fear no one else apart from God. 15. He has named you 'those who surrender'. 16. The angels called out to him whilst he was standing praying. 17. We guided them to a straight path. 18. God does not guide those who are lying and ungrateful. 19. He flung down his staff. 20. We will cast terror into the hearts of those who disbelieve. 21. We saved those who believed and were god-fearing. 22. He has fulfilled his covenant and feared God. 23. Have you considered the person who turns his back and gives little? 24. He turned from them and said, 'O my people, I conveyed to you the messages of my Lord.' 25. Then a group of them turns away and moves aside.

Exercise Thirty-One

1. To each one of them a sixth. 2. There is no private meeting of three men but He is the fourth of them. 3. The fourth of them [was] their dog. 4. You [receive] a quarter of what they leave. 5. A third [goes] to his mother. 6. Theirs is two-thirds of what he leaves. 7. Unbelievers are those who say, 'God is the third of three.' 8. I am first among the servants. 9. Do not be the first to disbelieve it. 10. This is in the ancient (first) scrolls. 11. Did not We destroy the first generations? 12. The promise of the first of the two came to pass. 13. They will say, 'Seven, and their dog the eighth of them.' 14. They receive one eighth of what you leave. 15. They have not attained a tenth of what we bestowed on them. 16. Your Lord knows that you stay up close to two-thirds of the night or a half or a third of it. 17. To you is half of what your wives leave. 18. God is pleased with them, and they with Him. 19. He showed him the greatest sign. 20. Thus God will show them their works. 21. Is it not sufficient for them that We have sent down to you the Book? 22. God is sufficient as a friend/protector. 23. God is a sufficient witness between you and us. 24. It is no sin for you to seek a bounty from your Lord.

Exercise Thirty-Two

1. Turn away from them and put your trust in God. 2. Take firm hold of what We have given you, and remember what is in it. 3. Dwell in

the Garden with your wife, and the two of you eat from it. 4. Order your people to pray and be steadfast in it. 5. Believe in God and His messenger. 6. Give the hypocrites the good tidings that they will have a painful doom. 7. Seek (f. s.) forgiveness for your sin. 8. Make your houses places to turn to, and perform prayer. 9. Satan is an enemy for you, so treat him as an enemy. 10. Warn your people before a painful punishment comes upon them. 11. Fear (pl.) God and be with the truthful. 12. O my Lord, make this a secure land and provide some of its fruits as sustenance for its people. 13. Refer it to God and the messenger. 14. Show me what part of the earth they have created. 15. Arise and warn. 16. Say, 'Enjoy your ingratitude for a little. You are one of the companions of the Fire.' 17. He said, 'My Lord, help me against the people who wreak mischief.' 18. Give us full measure and be charitable to us. 19. Do what you will. He is the Observer of what you do. 20. Expel the family of Lot from your settlement. 21. Bring a *sūra* like it, and call your witnesses. 22. They say, 'Peace be upon you. Enter the garden as a recompense for what you used to do.' 23. Say, 'Obey God and the Messenger.' 24. Endure patiently what they say, and withdraw from them politely. 25. Say, 'Journey in the land and see how He originated creation.'

Exercise Thirty-Three

1. They have been expelled from their homes. 2. They were seized from a nearby place. 3. You have been given only little knowledge. 4. We will not believe till we are given the same as God's messengers are given. 5. The prophets and witnesses are brought, and judgement will be decided between them. 6. You will be summoned against a people of great might. 7. Their faces were covered with pieces of night. 8. Then every soul will be paid in full what it has earned, and they will not be wronged. 9. We and our forefathers were promised this previously. 10. They see what they are promised. 11. It has been revealed to us that torment will be for those who deny the truth and turn their backs. 12. There was mockery of messengers before you. 13. Will any be destroyed apart from the people who do wrong? 14. Say, 'We believe in that which has been revealed to us.' 15. They will not be helped. 16. You do not do wrong, and you are not wronged. 17. They will be given sustenance without reckoning in it. 18. These are our goods returned to us. 19. Do not eat of that over which God's name has not been mentioned. 20. Are you being recompensed except for what you used to earn? 21. This is a message for men, that they may be warned by

it. 22. Those are called to from afar. 23. Messengers before you were said to lie, who came with the clear signs. 24. I convey to you that with which I have been sent. 25. There will be a blast on the trumpet. 26. Protect yourselves from the Fire that has been prepared for the unbelievers. 27. They thought that they are engulfed. 28. That is a thing to be desired.

Exercise Thirty-Four

1. On the day when their tongues testify against them. 2. On the day when We round them all up. 3. On the day that He created the heavens and the earth. 4. The day when they hear the Shout. 5. On a day when they are tormented over the fire. 6. On the day when there is a blast on the trumpet. 7. On the day when a man shall flee from his brother. 8. Our father is a very old man. 9. The hands of Abū Lahab will perish. 10. Return to your father and say, 'O our father, your son stole.' 11. He said to his father and his people, 'What are you worshipping?' 12. Your father was not a wicked man. 13. His parents were believers. 14. He caused your parents to leave the Garden. 15. Their brother Noah said to them, 'Will you not protect yourselves?' 16. We sent Moses and his brother Aaron with Our signs. 17. Shall I entrust him to you in any other way than I entrusted his brother to you? 18. Set things right between your two brothers. 19. Your Lord is wide in His forgiveness. 20. God is strong and severe in punishment. 21. The night does not outstrip the day. 22. The angels are stretching out their hands. 23. Today We seal their mouths. 24. O you who believe, do not enter houses other than your own. 25. Shall I seek any judge other than God? 26. You shall have an unbroken reward. 27. Peace be upon me the day I was born and the day that I die.

Exercise Thirty-Five

1. Are those who are hurled into the Fire better or those who come in security on the Day of Resurrection? 2. The Shout took them in the morning. 3. They came to Him abject. 4. So serve God, devoting [your] religion solely to him 5. They fell down before him, prostrating themselves. 6. No one will overcome you today. 7. The only refuge from God is to turn to him. 8. The only knowledge we have is what You have taught us. 9. It is not a sin for you in what you may agree to with one another. 10. Let there be no wrangling during the Pilgrimage. 11. They have increased in their unbelief. 12. Say, 'God is swifter in plotting.' 13. God is stronger in might. 14. Which of them is best (better)

in deed. 15. They devise trickery. 16. They did other work. 17. You love wealth greatly. 18. It was not us you served. 19. We shall make provision for you and them. 20. Do not slay your children through fear of poverty. 21. You spend only to seek God's face. 22. [All] glory belongs to God. 23. He called on his Lord, turning to Him in penitence. 24. He departed in anger. 25. Return to your Lord, pleased and pleasing. 26. We gathered them together. 27. There is no doubt that theirs will be the Fire. 28. He will bring you forth [again].

Exercise Thirty-Six

1. If you are in doubt about what We have sent down to Our servant, then bring a *sūra* like it. 2. If you entrust him with a dinar, he will not pay it back to you. 3. If they say that you lie, messengers before you were said to lie. 4. If you avoid the serious things that you are forbidden, We will remit your evil deeds from you. 5. If you turn from them, they will do you no harm. 6. If they argue with you, say, 'God is well aware of what you are doing.' 7. If we revert, we shall be wrongdoers. 8. If We wish, We drown them. 9. Throw him into the recesses of the pit, and some caravan will pick him out. 10. Shake the trunk of the palm-tree towards you, and it will cause ripe dates to fall down to you. 11. Send him with us tomorrow, and he can enjoy himself and play. 12. Let her eat in God's land. 13. That is better for you, did you but know it. 14. Bring your proof, if you tell the truth. 15. When he turns away, he strives to make mischief in the land. 16. When you have performed prayer, remember God, standing or sitting. 17. When their term comes, they shall not delay it an hour or advance it an hour. 18. They fall down on their chins in prostration when it is recited to them. 19. Had God wished, He could have taken their hearing. 20. If they could find a place to flee to, or caves or a hiding place, they would turn straight for it. 21. You remained but a little, if you only knew. 22. Had they been with us, they would not have died [or] been slain. 23. Which of God's signs will you deny? 24. He is with them, wherever they may be. 25. Whenever they desire to leave it, they will be returned into it. 26. He who does a righteous deed does so for himself and he who does wrong does so against himself. 27. If you could see when the wrongdoers are in the floods of death. 28. Have you considered if it is from God and you do not believe in it? 29. He who purifies himself will prosper. 30. If there is a good deed He will double it.

Exercise Thirty-Seven

1. Beware of them lest they tempt you away from some of what God has sent down to you. 2. God admonishes you never to repeat the like of that. 3. I take refuge with God from being among the ignorant. 4. He has cast on to the earth firm mountains, lest it sway with you. 5. He holds back the heaven from falling on to the earth. 6. Do the people of the settlements feel secure that Our might will not come upon them? 7. We sent Noah to his people, saying 'Warn your people before a painful punishment comes upon them.' 8. We suggested to Moses, 'Strike the sea with your staff.' 9. Your Lord gave a message to the bees, 'Take for yourselves houses in the mountains.' 10. We called out to him, 'O Abraham, you have made [your] vision come true. 11. They cried out to one another in the morning, 'Go early to your field.' 12. A *sūra* has been sent down, saying, 'Believe in God and strive with His Messenger.' 13. The conclusion of their call will be, 'Praise belongs to God, Lord of created beings.' 14. He frowned and turned away, because the blind man came to him. 15. Shall We ignore you because you have been a profligate people? 16. Do not obey every contempible swearer... because he has wealth and sons. 17. The mountains fall in ruins, because they have ascribed a son to the Merciful. 18. This is because your Lord would not destroy the settlements wrongfully. 19. Perhaps you are forsaking part of what is revealed to you... because they say. 20. He shows you His signs, so that you may understand. 21. Strive in His way so that you may prosper. 22. We have sent down to you the reminder that you may make clear to men what has been sent down to them and that they may reflect. 23. We have made it an Arabic recitation, so that you may understand. 24. It may be that you love a thing which is bad for you. 25. Perhaps your Lord will destroy your enemy. 26. It may be that God will bring them all to me. 27. Perhaps I shall not be unfortunate in my prayer to my Lord.

Exercise Thirty-Eight

1. Those who do not believe will continue to be in doubt. 2. Their calls continued. 3. You will continue to observe. 4. His face stayed black. 5. You will still jest. 6. They kept on mounting into it. 7. As long as they remained in them. 8. As long as you are in the sacred state. 9. I was a witness over them as long as I was among them. 10. They became repentant. 11. By His blessing you became brothers. 12. You are now among the losers. 13. The lightning almost snatches away their sight.

14. Its oil almost glows, even though no fire has touched it. 15. He scarcely makes [things] clear. 16. They scarcely understand any tiding. 17. Why does God not speak to us? 18. Why has an angel been not sent down to him? 19. O our Lord, why did You not send us a messenger? 20. Why do you not give thanks? 21. Why do you not seek forgiveness from God? 22. But for the bounty of your Lord to you and His mercy, you would have been among the losers. 23. Had it not been for an ordinance from God that has gone before, a mighty torment would have touched you on account of what you took. 24. But for a stated term the torment would have come to them. 25. But for the blessing of my Lord I would have been one of those haled [into Hell].

Exercise Thirty-Nine

1. Woe to the ungrateful because of the fire. 2. Woe on that day to those who deny the truth. 3. Woe to those who write the book with their own hands and then say, 'This is from God'. 4. Woe to those who associate partners with God. 5. Woe on us. We have been heedless of this. 6. Would that I had not associated anyone with my Lord. 7. Would that we had obeyed God! 8. Would that my people knew! 9. The unbeliever will say, 'Would that I were dust.' 10. No! I swear by this settlement. 11. God bears witness that they are liars. 12. They said, 'By God, you are in your ancient error.' 13. By God, our Lord, we did not associate others with God.' 14. By your Lord, We shall question them all. 15. By your Lord, We shall round them up. 16. By my Lord, it will certainly come to you. 17. If you ask them who created them, they will say, 'God'. 18. God has written, 'I shall conquer, along with My messengers.' 19. We will expel you from our land. 20. He will indeed gather you to the Day of Resurrection. 21. Let not Satan turn you aside. 22. Do not reckon that God is heedless of what the wrongdoers do. 23. If you do not desist, I shall surely stone you. 24. If He delivers us from this, we shall indeed be among the thankful. 25. If Satan causes you to forget, do not sit, after the reminder, with the people who do wrong. 26. Children of Adam! Let not Satan tempt you. 27. If my Lord does not guide me, I shall be one of the people who go astray. 28. Let not those who have no certainty make you unsteady.

Exercise Forty

1. God would not wrong them. 2. God is not one to leave the believers in the state in which you are. 3. God would never lead a people astray after

He had guided them. 4. God is not one to inform you of the unseen. 5. They should not enter them. 6. No soul may die except by God's permission. 7. It is not for a messenger to bring a sign save with God's leave. 8. A believer should not kill a believer. 9. It is not for the polytheists to visit God's places of worship. 10. It is not for us to bring you any authority. 11. It [has not been granted] to any mortal to be spoken to by God except by revelation. 12. It is not for any believing man or woman to have any choice in the affair. 13. It is not for you to annoy God's Messenger. 14. How excellent a helper! 15. Excellent is the reward of those who labour. 16. Excellent is the admonition which He gives you. 17. What they have been doing is truly evil. 18. It is an evil way. 19. How evil a drink; how evil a resting-place. 20. They bought a small gain with it. Evil is what they purchase. 21. What they have been doing is truly evil. 22. Evil is the likeness of the people who deny the truth of God's signs. 23. Their lodging will be the Fire. How evil is the lodging of the wrongdoers. 24. His abode is Hell—evil is [his] journey's end. 25. How excellent a servant!

Technical Terms

It is assumed that the reader will know the names of the letters of the Arabic alphabet.

ENGLISH

ACCUSATIVE: the Arabic case that indicates the direct object (and has many other uses).

ACTIVE: voice of the verb in which the subject performs the action of or is in the state of the verb.

ADJECTIVE: a word that gives information about a noun.

ADVERB: a word that gives information about a verb or adjective.

ANTECEDENT: the noun to which a pronoun refers back—an important feature in RELATIVE SENTENCES.

ASSONANCE: similarity of vowel and/or consonant at the end of a phrase.

CASE: the ending which indicates the role of a noun or its equivalent.

CLAUSE: a significant section of a sentence.

COLLECTIVE: a noun that is singular in form but refers to a group.

CONDITIONAL SENTENCES: sentences containing a clause introduced by 'if' or its equivalent.

CONJUGATION: the way in which verb forms change to show person, number and tense.

CONJUNCTION: a particle that joins sentences or clauses.

- CO-ORDINATING CONJUNCTION: a particle, such as 'and', that joins two sentences.
- SUBORDINATING CONJUNCTION: a particle, such as 'because' or 'when', that introduces a clause that would not normally be able to stand on its own.

CONTRACTION: in a DOUBLED VERB the dropping of a short vowel to enable the final two radicals to be pronounced together.

DECLENSION: the way in which nouns change to show number and case.

DEFINITE: an Arabic word is made definite by the prefixing of the definite article or by the attachment of a following genitive.

DEMONSTRATIVE: pronoun or adjective such as 'this' and 'that'.

DERIVED FORMS: forms of the verb other than the basic first form.

DUAL: see NUMBER.

ELATIVE: the form used in Arabic to express the English comparative and superlative.

ELLIPSE: the omission of a word or phrase.

ENERGETIC: special emphatic form of the verb, formed from the JUSSIVE.

EXCEPTIVE: a sentence in which a phrase or clause is introduced by 'except'.

FEMININE: one of the two GENDERS in Arabic.

GENDER: in this book GENDER refers to grammatical gender, which may or may not correspond to natural gender.

GENITIVE: the case used in Arabic to denote possession or to follow a preposition.

IDIOM: expression that is peculiar to a language and cannot be translated literally.

IMPERATIVE: the form of the verb used to give commands.

IMPERFECT: the Arabic tense that has the role of the English present or future.

IMPERFECT INDICATIVE: the imperfect mood indicating fact.

INDECLINABLE: a noun or pronoun that does not change for case.

INDEFINITE: a noun or adjective that is not definite.

INDIRECT QUESTION: a question that occurs after a verb, e.g. 'he asked where the book was'.

INFLECTED: having case endings, as opposed to INDECLINABLE.

INFIX: a syllable that is inserted into a root, in particular the *tā'* of the 8th form.

INTERROGATIVE: a particle or sentence of enquiry.

INTRANSITIVE: a verb that cannot take a DIRECT OBJECT.

JUSSIVE: the imperfect mood indicating indirect commands etc.

MASCULINE: one of the two GENDERS in Arabic.

NEGATION: making a word, phrase or clause negative.
NOMINAL SENTENCE: an Arabic sentence that does not have a verb.
NOMINATIVE: the Arabic case that indicates the subject/predicate of a sentence.
NOUN: words that name persons and things etc.
NUMBER: indication of whether a noun etc. represents 'one' (singular), 'two' (dual), or 'more than two' (plural).
NUMERALS, NUMBERS: the counting system of a language.
CARDINAL NUMBERS: numbers used for quantity.
ORDINAL NUMBERS: numbers used for order.
OBJECT: the noun or pronoun affected by the operation of the verb.
DIRECT OBJECT: an object put in the Arabic ACCUSATIVE.
OTIOSE: redundant, not having any obvious function.
PARTICLE: an uninflected function word.
PARTICIPLE: a verbal adjective.
PASSIVE: voice of the verb in which the subject is the recipient of the action of the verb.
PERFECT: verb tense that refers to a completed action or state in the past. The Arabic perfect covers various English tenses, e.g. 'she wrote', 'she did write', 'she has written'.
PLUPERFECT: the past of the past tense, e.g. 'she had written'.
PLURAL: see NUMBER.
PREDICATE: in Arabic the second half of a non-verbal sentence.
PREFIX: a syllable or syllables placed at the beginning of a word.
PREPOSITION: particle placed before a noun or pronoun to indicate position, time, direction etc.
PRONOUN: word that stands in place of a noun, such as 'me', 'this', 'who'.
PROSTHETIC: term used to describe a temporary vowel placed at the beginning of a word.
RADICALS: the root letters of Arabic words, other than particles, normally three or four in number.
RELATIVE SENTENCE: sentence or clause giving information about the ANTECEDENT.
SINGULAR: see NUMBER.

SUBJECT: the noun or pronoun that performs the action of the verb or is described by its state, or is followed by a non-verbal predicate.

SUBJUNCTIVE: the imperfect mood suggesting possibility.

SUFFIX: a syllable or syllables placed at the end of a word.

TENSE: the time of action represented in a verb form.

TRANSITIVE: a verb that takes a DIRECT OBJECT.

VERB: word expressing the action performed or state experienced by the subject of a sentence.

- TRILITERAL VERB: a verb with three radicals.
- QUADRILITERAL VERB: a verb with four radicals.
- ASSIMILATED VERB: a verb with *wāw* or *yā'* as its first radical.
- DOUBLED VERB: a verb with the same letter as second and third radicals.
- HOLLOW VERB: a verb with *wāw* or *yā'* as its second radical.
- DEFECTIVE VERB: a verb with *wāw* or *yā'* as its second radical.
- AUXILIARY VERB: in Arabic an auxiliary verb combines with another verb to help form its TENSE or state. The basic auxiliary in Arabic is *kāna*.

VOCATIVE: the form used to introduce direct address.

ARABIC

أَخَوَات كَانَ [*akhawāt kāna*]: 'the sisters of *kāna*', verbs related to *kāna*.

أَلِف مَقْصُورَة [*alif maqsūra*]: *alif* written in the form of a *yā'* at the end of a word.

أَن آلْمُفَسِّرَة [*an il-mufassira*]: the particle *an* when it introduces direct speech.

بَسْمَلَة [*basmala*]: the formula *bi-smi llāhi l-raḥmāni l-raḥīmi.*

تَاء مَرْبُوطَة [*tā' marbūṭa*]: the form of *tā'* used at the end of a noun or adjective to show the feminine ending, written as a *hā'* with two dots.

تَاء مَفْتُوحَة [*tā' maftūḥa*]: *tā'* written normally.

اَلتَّمييز [*tamyīz*]: the ACCUSATIVE of specification.

تَنْوِين [*tanwīn*]: the adding of an *n* sound to indicate that a noun or adjective is indefinite.

اَلْجَوَاب [*al-jawāb*]: the main clause in a conditional sentence.

اَلْحُرُوف آلشَّمْسِيَّة [*al-ḥurūf al-shamsiyya*]: 'the sun letters', letters of the alphabet to which the definite article is assimilated.

اَلْحُرُوف آلْقَمَرِيَّة [*al-ḥurūf al-qamariyya*]: 'the moon letters', letters of the alphabet to which the definite article is not assimilated.

اَلْحَال [*al-ḥāl*]: the ACCUSATIVE of circumstance.

سُكُون [*sukūn*]: the sign indicating that a consonant does not have a vowel.

شَدَّة [*shadda*]: the sign for a doubled consonant.

اَلشَّرْط [*al-sharṭ*]: the conditional clause in a conditional sentence.

ضَمِيرُ آلْفَصْل [*ḍamīr al-faṣl*]: the pronoun used to separate phrases.

ضَمَّة [*ḍamma*]: the vowel sign for *u*.

إِضَافَة [*iḍāfa*]: annexation, the construct state, the attachment of a GENITIVE of possession.

فَتْحَة [*fatḥa*]: the vowel sign for *a*.

كَسْرَة [*kasra*]: the vowel sign for *i*.

لَا لِنَفْيِ ٱلْجِنْسِ [*lā li-nafyi l-jinsi*]: the use of *lā* to negate a category.

مَا ٱلْحِجَازِيَّة [*mā l-ḥijāziyya*]: Ḥijāzī *mā*, the negative *mā* that is followed by *bi-* and the GENITIVE or by the ACCUSATIVE.

اَلْمَاضِي [*al-māḍī*]: the basic Arabic past TENSE.

مَصْدَر [*maṣdar*]: the Arabic equivalent of the verbal noun.

مَصْدَر مِيمِي [*maṣdar mīmī*]: a *maṣdar* that begins with a prefixed *mīm*.

اَلْمُضَارِع [*al-muḍāri*ᶜ]: the imperfect TENSE.

اَلْمُضَارِع الْمَرْفُوع [*al-muḍāri*ᶜ *al-marfū*ᶜ]: the indicative mood of the imperfect TENSE.

مَفْعُول مُطْلَق [*mafᶜūl muṭlaq*]: the cognate or absolute ACCUSATIVE.

اَلْمَفْعُول لَهُ [*mafᶜūl lahu*]: the ACCUSATIVE of cause.

هَمْزَة [*hamza*]: the glottal stop sound.

- هَمْزَة الوَصْل [*hamzat al-waṣl*]: the temporary vowel prefixed to words beginning with a consonant without a vowel, always displaced by the final consonant of a previous word.
- هَمْزَة ٱلْقَطْع [*hamzat al-qaṭ*ᶜ]: the true glottal stop.

وَاو الْقَسَم [*wāw al-qasam*]: the particle *wa-* followed by the GENITIVE to introduce an oath.

وَصْلَة [*waṣla*]: the sign showing that a *hamzat al-waṣl* vowel has been removed.

General Vocabulary

ء

ever			أَبَدًا
she-camels	إِبِلٌ		[نَاقَةٌ]
son	بَنُونَ / أَبْنَاءٌ		اِبْنٌ
daughter	بَنَاتٌ		اِبْنَةٌ
father	آبَاءٌ		أَبٌ
to come	إِتْيَانٌ	يَأْتِي	أَتَى
to give	إِيتَاءٌ	يُؤْتِي	آتَى
to prefer	إِيثَارٌ	يُؤْثِرُ	آثَرَ
track; effect	آثَارٌ		أَثَرٌ
sin	آثَامٌ		إِثْمٌ
reward	أُجُورٌ		أَجْرٌ
term	آجَالٌ		أَجَلٌ
to take, seize	أَخْذٌ	يَأْخُذُ	أَخَذَ
to take, adopt	اِتِّخَاذٌ	يَتَّخِذُ	اِتَّخَذَ
to defer	تَأْخِيرٌ	يُؤَخِّرُ	أَخَّرَ
to postpone	اِسْتِئْخَارٌ	يَسْتَأْخِرُ	اِسْتَأْخَرَ
last, [next]	آخِرُونَ		آخِرٌ
other	آخَرُونَ		آخَرُ

أُخْرَى f.		أُخَرُ	other
أَخٌ		إِخْوَانٌ / إِخْوَةٌ	brother
أَذِنَ	يَأْذَنُ	إِذْنٌ	to permit, allow
اِسْتَأْذَنَ	يَسْتَأْذِنُ	اِسْتِئْذَانٌ	to seek permission
إِذْنٌ			permission
آذَى	يُوذِي	إِيذَاءٌ	to hurt, vex
أَرْضٌ		أَرَاضٍ	earth
أَسَفٌ			grief
أُسْوَةٌ			example
أَصْلٌ		أُصُولٌ	root
أُفُقٌ		آفَاقٌ	horizon
إِفْكٌ			lie
أَلِيمٌ			painful
إِلَاهٌ		آلِهَةٌ	a god
اَللّٰهُ			God
[ذُو]		أُولُو	possessors of
اِيتَلَى	يَأْتَلِي	اِيتِلَاءٌ	to swear
إِلَى			to (motion)
أُمٌّ		أُمَّهَاتٌ	mother
أُمَّةٌ		أُمَمٌ	community
أَمَرَ	يَأْمُرُ	أَمْرٌ	to order
أَمْرٌ		أُمُورٌ	affair, command

أَمِنَ	يَأْمَنُ	أَمْنٌ	to be secure; to trust in
آمَنَ	يُؤْمِنُ	إِيمَانٌ	to believe
أَمِينٌ			faithful, secure
مُؤْمِنٌ		s.p.	believer
f. أُنْثَى		إِنَاثٌ	female
آنَسَ	يُؤْنِسُ	إِينَاسٌ	to see
إِنْسَانٌ		اَلنَّاسُ	man; (p.) people
أَهْلٌ		أَهْلُونَ / أَهَالٍ	people, family
أَوَّلُ	f. أُولَى	أَوَّلُونَ	first, the ancient
آلٌ			family
[ذُو]		أُولُو	possessors of
مَأْوًى			shelter, refuge
آيَةٌ		آيَاتٌ	sign, verse

ب

بِـ			in, at, by
بَأْسٌ			might
بَحْرٌ		بِحَارٌ	sea
بَدَأَ	يَبْدَأُ	بَدْءٌ	to begin
بِدَارٌ			haste, anticipation
أَبْدَلَ	يُبْدِلُ	إِبْدَالٌ	to give in exchange
بَدَلٌ			exchange
بَرٌّ			land
بَرٌّ		أَبْرَارٌ	pious, god-fearing

بَرِحَ	يَبْرَحُ	بَرَحٌ	to leave
بَرْدٌ			cold (noun)
بَرْقٌ			lightning
تَبَارَكَ	يَتَبَارَكُ	تَبَارُكٌ	to be blessed
بُرْهَانٌ		بَرَاهِينُ	proof
بَسَطَ	يَبْسُطُ	بَسْطٌ	to spread, extend
مَبْسُوطٌ			spread, extended
بَشَّرَ	يُبَشِّرُ	تَبْشِيرٌ	to bring good news
بَشَرٌ			(s.) human being; (pl.) men, human beings
بَشِيرٌ			bringer of good news
أَبْصَرَ	يُبْصِرُ	إِبْصَارٌ	(+*bi*-) to see, observe
بَصَرٌ		أَبْصَارٌ	sight; eye
بَصِيرٌ			observant, seeing
بِضَاعَةٌ		بَضَائِعُ	merchandise
بَطْشٌ			might
بَطَلَ	يَبْطُلُ	بَطْلٌ	to be worthless
بَاطِلٌ			false, worthless
بَعَثَ	يَبْعَثُ	بَعْثٌ	to send, raise
بَعِيدٌ			distant
بَعْدَ			after (preposition)
بَعْدَ إِذْ			after (conjunction)
بَغْتَةً			suddenly
بَغَى	يَبْغِي	بَغْيٌ	to outrage; to seek
اِبْتَغَى	يَبْتَغِي	اِبْتِغَاءٌ	to seek
بَقَرَةٌ		s.p.	cow

أَبْقَى		[بَاقٍ]	more lasting
بَلَدٌ		بِلاَدٌ	town, settlement
بَلَغَ	يَبْلُغُ	بُلُوغٌ	to reach
بَلَّغَ	يُبَلِّغُ	تَبْلِيغٌ	to convey
أَبْلَغَ	يُبْلِغُ	إِبْلاَغٌ	to convey
بَلاَغٌ			message, conveyance
اِبْنٌ		بَنُونَ / أَبْنَاءٌ	son
بَابٌ		أَبْوَابٌ	door
بَيْتٌ		بُيُوتٌ	house
أَبْيَضُ	f. بَيْضَاءُ	بِيضٌ	white
بَاعَ	يَبِيعُ	بَيْعٌ	to sell
بَايَعَ	يُبَايِعُ	مُبَايَعَةٌ	to do allegiance to
بَيَّنَ	يُبَيِّنُ	تِبْيَانٌ	to make clear
أَبَانَ	يُبِينُ	إِبَانَةٌ	to make clear
تَبَيَّنَ	يَتَبَيَّنُ	تَبَيُّنٌ	to become clear
بَيِّنَةٌ		s.p.	clear proof
بَيْنَ			between, among
مُبِينٌ			clear

ت

تَبَّ			to wither, perish
تَابُوتٌ			ark, casket
تَبِعَ	يَتْبَعُ	تَبَعٌ	to follow
اِتَّبَعَ	يَتَّبِعُ	اِتِّبَاعٌ	to follow
تَحْتَ			beneath

تُرَابٌ			earth, dust
تَرَكَ	يَتْرُكُ	تَرْكٌ	to leave
تَلَا	يَتْلُو	تِلَاوَةٌ	to recite
تَوَّابٌ		s.p.	s. relenting, p. repenting

ث

ثُمَّ			then
ثَمَرَةٌ		s.p.	fruit
ثَمَنٌ			price, gain
مَثْوًى			lodging

ج

جُبٌّ			pit
جَاثِمٌ		s.p.	crouching
جَادَلَ	يُجَادِلُ	مُجَادَلَةٌ	to dispute, contend with
جَدَلٌ			contention
جِذْعٌ			trunk of a palm-tree
لَا جَرَمَ			undoubtedly, certainly
مُجْرِمٌ		s.p.	sinner
جَارِيَةٌ		جَوَارٍ	ship (young woman)
جَزَى	يَجْزِي	جَزَاءٌ	to requite
جَزَاءٌ			recompense, reward
جَعَلَ	يَجْعَلُ	جَعْلٌ	to make, assign, appoint
جَلْدَةٌ			lash, stripe

جَمٌّ			much
جَمَعَ	يَجْمَعُ	جَمْعٌ	to gather, collect
جَمِيعٌ			all
أَجْمَعُ		s.p.	all
مَجْمَعٌ			meeting, meeting-place
جِنٌّ			*Jinn*
جَنَّةٌ		s.p.	garden
مَجْنُونٌ		s.p.	possessed (by *Jinn*)
اِجْتَنَبَ	يَجْتَنِبُ	اِجْتِنَابٌ	to avoid
جُنَاحٌ			sin
جَاهَدَ	يُجَاهِدُ	جِهَادٌ	to strive
جَاهِلٌ		s.p.	ignorant
أَجَابَ	يُجِيبُ	جَوَابٌ	to answer
اِسْتَجَابَ	يَسْتَجِيبُ	جَوَابٌ	to answer
جَاءَ	يَجِيءُ		to come

ح

أَحَبَّ	يُحِبُّ	حُبٌّ	to love
حَبٌّ		حُبُوبٌ	grain
حَبِطَ	يَحْبَطُ	حُبُوطٌ	to be useless
حَاجَّ	يُحَاجُّ	حِجَاجٌ	to argue about (*fī*)
حُجَّةٌ		s.p.	proof
حِجَّةٌ		حِجَجٌ	year
حِجَابٌ			obstacle, partition
حِجَارَةٌ		حَجَرٌ	stone
حَدِيدٌ			iron

حَرْثٌ			tillage
حَرَجٌ			trouble, difficulty
حَرَّمَ	يُحَرِّمُ	تَحْرِيمٌ	to forbid, prohibit
حَرَامٌ		حُرُمٌ	forbidden, sacred, in the sacred state
حِزْبٌ		أَحْزَابٌ	party
حَزِنَ	يَحْزَنُ	حُزْنٌ	to be sad
حَسِبَ	يَحْسِبُ	مَحْسِبَةٌ	to think, reckon
حَسْبٌ			reckoning
حِسَابٌ			reckoning
حَسْرَةٌ			sorrow, anguish
أَحْسَنَ	يُحْسِنُ	إِحْسَانٌ	to do good
حَسَنٌ			fine, good
حَشَرَ	يَحْشُرُ	حَشْرٌ	to round up
مُحْضَرٌ		s.p.	brought forward
حُفْرَةٌ			pit
حَفِظَ	يَحْفَظُ	حِفْظٌ	to guard, preserve, keep
حَفِيظٌ			guardian
حَقٌّ			truth; true
حَكَمَ	يَحْكُمُ	حُكْمٌ	to judge
حَكَمٌ			arbiter
حِكْمَةٌ			wisdom
حُكْمٌ			judgement
أَحَلَّ	يُحِلُّ	إِحْلَالٌ	to make lawful, permit
حَلَفَ	يَحْلِفُ	حِلْفٌ	to swear

حَلَّافٌ			wont to swear
حُلُمٌ			puberty
حَمْدٌ			praise
حِمَارٌ		حَمِيرٌ	donkey
حَمَلَ	يَحْمِلُ	حَمْلٌ	to carry
حَنِيذٌ			roast
حَنِيفٌ		حُنَفَاءُ	of pure faith
أَحَاطَ	يُحِيطُ	إِحَاطَةٌ	to surround (+ *bi*)
حَيَاةٌ / حَيَوٰةٌ		حَيَوَاتٌ	life
حَيٌّ		أَحْيَاءٌ	alive

خ

خَبِيثٌ			bad
خَبِيرٌ			aware
خَتَمَ	يَخْتِمُ	خَتْمٌ	to seal
خَادَعَ	يُخَادِعُ	خِدَاعٌ	to try to deceive
		أَخْدَانٌ	companions
خَرَّ	يَخِرُّ	خَرٌّ	to fall
خَرَجَ	يَخْرُجُ	خُرُوجٌ	to go out
خُسْرَانٌ			loss, ruin
خَشِيَ	يَخْشَى	خَشْيَةٌ	to fear
خَصَفَ	يَخْصِفُ		to cover oneself
خَضِرٌ			green crop
خَطِيئَةٌ		خَطَايَا / s.p.	sin
خَاطِئٌ		s.p.	sinner

أَخْطَأَ	يُخْطِئُ	إِخْطَاءٌ	to make a mistake
خَطِفَ	يَخْطَفُ	خَطْفٌ	to snatch
إِسْتَخَفَّ	يَسْتَخِفُّ	إِسْتِخْفَافٌ	to make unstable
خَفِيفٌ			light (adj.)
خِلَالَ			through
خُلْدٌ			eternity
خَالِدٌ		s.p.	remaining in, everlasting
أَخْلَصَ	يُخْلِصُ	إِخْلَاصٌ	to be sincere
خَالِصٌ			pure
إِخْتَلَفَ	يَخْتَلِفُ	إِخْتِلَافٌ	to vary, differ
خَلِيفَةٌ		خُلَفَاءُ	successor
خَلْفَ			behind
خَلَقَ	يَخْلُقُ	خَلْقٌ	to create
خَافَ	يَخَافُ	خَوْفٌ	to fear
خَيْرٌ			good, better, best
خِيَرَةٌ			choice

د

دَابَّةٌ		دَوَابُّ	beast
دَبَّرَ	يُدَبِّرُ	تَدْبِيرٌ	to manage, arrange
دَاخِرٌ			humble, lowly
دَخَلَ	يَدْخُلُ	دُخُولٌ	to enter
أَدْخَلَ	يُدْخِلُ	إِدْخَالٌ	to cause to enter
مُدَّخَلٌ			place to enter
أَدْرَكَ	يُدْرِكُ	إِدْرَاكٌ	to overtake

دَعَى	يَدْعُو	دُعَاءٌ	to call, pray
دَارٌ f.		دُورٌ	abode
مَا دَامَ			as long as
دِينٌ		أَدْيَانٌ	religion

ذ

ذُبَابٌ			fly
ذَبَحَ	يَذْبَحُ	ذَبْحٌ	to sacrifice
ذُرِّيَّةٌ			seed, offspring, descendants
ذَقَنٌ		أَذْقَانٌ	chin
ذَكَرَ	يَذْكُرُ	ذِكْرٌ	to mention
ذِكْرَى			remembrance, reminder
تَذَكَّرَ	يَتَذَكَّرُ	تَذَكُّرٌ	to remember, bear in mind
ذَنْبٌ		ذُنُوبٌ	sin
ذَهَبَ	يَذْهَبُ	ذَهَابٌ	to go away
ذُو		[أُولُو]	possessor of
ذَاقَ	يَذُوقُ	ذَوْقٌ	to taste

ر

رَأَى	يَرَى	رَأْيٌ	to see
أَرَى	يُرِي		to show
رُؤْيَا f.			dream
رَبٌّ		أَرْبَابٌ	lord

رِبًا، اَلرِّبَوٰا			usury
رَتَعَ	يَرْتَعُ	رَتْعٌ	to enjoy oneself
رَجَعَ	يَرْجِعُ	رُجُوعٌ	to return
رِجْسٌ			abomination
رَجُلٌ		رِجَالٌ	man
رِجْلٌ f.		أَرْجُلٌ	foot
رَجَمَ	يَرْجُمُ	رَجْمٌ	to stone
رَجِيمٌ			accursed
رَجَا	يَرْجُو	رَجَاءٌ	to hope
رَحْمَةٌ			mercy
اَلرَّحْمٰنُ			the Merciful
رَحِيمٌ			compassionate
رَدَّ	يَرُدُّ	رَدٌّ	to return, restore
مَرَدٌّ			turning back
رَزَقَ	يَرْزُقُ	رِزْقٌ	to give sustenance to
رِزْقٌ			sustenance
رَازِقٌ			provider of sustenance
أَرْسَلَ	يُرْسِلُ	إِرْسَالٌ	to send
رَسُولٌ		رُسُلٌ	messenger
رِسَالَةٌ		s.p.	message
		رَوَاسٍ	firm mountains
رَضِيَ	يَرْضَى	رِضْوَانٌ / مَرْضَاةٌ	to be pleased with (ʿan)
رُطَبٌ			fresh, ripe dates
رُعْبٌ			terror
رَفَعَ	يَرْفَعُ	رَفْعٌ	to raise

resting-place			مُرْتَفَقٌ
to be vigilant	تَرَقُّبٌ	يَتَرَقَّبُ	تَرَقَّبَ
watcher			رَقِيبٌ
to run	رَكْضٌ	يَرْكُضُ	رَكَضَ
pomegranates			رُمَّانٌ
to fear	رَهْبَةٌ	يَرْهَبُ	رَهِبَ
kin; person			رَهْطٌ
hostage			رَهِينٌ
to want	إِرَادَةٌ	يُرِيدُ	أَرَادَ
doubt			رَيْبٌ

ز

the psalms			اَلزَّبُورُ
cultivation; green crops			زَرْعٌ
to purify, keep pure	تَزْكِيَةٌ	يُزَكِّي	زَكَّى
to be purified	تَزَكٍّ	يَتَزَكَّى	تَزَكَّى
purer	[زَكِيٌّ]		أَزْكَى
alms			زَكَاةٌ / زَكَوٰةٌ
earthquake			زَلْزَلَةٌ
spouse	أَزْوَاجٌ		زَوْجٌ
oil			زَيْتٌ
to increase	زِيَادَةٌ	يَزِيدُ	زَادَ
to increase, grow	اِزْدِيَادٌ	يَزْدَادُ	اِزْدَادَ
to continue		لَا يَزَالُ	مَا زَالَ
to cause to seem good	تَزْيِينٌ	يُزَيِّنُ	زَيَّنَ

س

سَأَلَ	يَسْأَلُ	سُؤَالٌ	to ask
تَسَاءَلَ	يَتَسَاءَلُ	تَسَاؤُلٌ	to ask one another
سَبَقَ	يَسْبِقُ	سَبْقٌ	to precede
f. سَبِيلٌ		سُبُلٌ	way
سَجَدَ	يَسْجُدُ	سُجُودٌ	to prostrate oneself
سَاجِدٌ		سُجَّدٌ	prostrating oneself
مَسْجِدٌ		مَسَاجِدُ	mosque, place of prayer
سَجَنَ	يَسْجُنُ	سَجْنٌ	to imprison
سَحَرَ	يَسْحِرُ	سِحْرٌ	to bewitch
سِحْرٌ			magic
سَاحِرٌ			magician
سَخَّرَ	يُسَخِّرُ	تَسْخِيرٌ	to subject
أَسْخَطَ	يُسْخِطُ	إِسْخَاطٌ	to vex
سِرٌّ		أَسْرَارٌ	secret
سَارَعَ	يُسَارِعُ	سِرَاعٌ	to vie in; race
سَرِيعٌ			quick, swift
أَسْرَفَ	يُسْرِفُ	إِسْرَافٌ	to be prodigal
سَرَقَ	يَسْرِقُ		to steal
سَارِقٌ		s.p.	thief
مُسْتَطَرٌ			inscribed
سَعَى	يَسْعَى	سَعْيٌ	to strive, move, run
سَفَرٌ			journey
		أَسْفَارٌ	books
سَفَعَ	يَسْفَعُ	سَفْعٌ	to drag

أَسْفَلُ			lower, lowest
سَقَطَ	يَسْقُطُ	سُقُوطٌ	to fall
سَاقَطَ	يُسَاقِطُ	سِقَاطٌ	to cause to fall, bring down
سَقِيمٌ			sick, ill
سَكَتَ	يَسْكُتُ	سُكُوتٌ	to abate; (+ ʿ*an*) to leave
سَكَنَ	يَسْكُنُ	سُكُونٌ	to dwell, be at rest
سَكِينَةٌ			tranquility, reassurance
مِسْكِينٌ			poor, destitute
سَلَبَ	يَسْلُبُ	سَلْبٌ	to rob
سُلْطَانٌ			authority, power
أَسْلَمَ	يُسْلِمُ	إِسْلَامٌ	to submit
سَلَامٌ			peace
مُسْلِمٌ		s.p.	Muslim
سَمِعَ	يَسْمَعُ	سَمْعٌ	to hear
أَسْمَعَ	يُسْمِعُ	إِسْمَاعٌ	to make hear
اِسْتَمَعَ	يَسْتَمِعُ	اِسْتِمَاعٌ	to listen to
سَمِيعٌ			hearing (adj.)
سَمِينٌ		سِمَانٌ	fat
سَمَّى	يُسَمِّي	تَسْمِيَةٌ	to name
سَمَاءٌ		سَمَاوَاتٌ	heaven, sky
اِسْمٌ		أَسْمَاءٌ	name
سَاءَ	يَسُوءُ	سُوءٌ	to be bad, wrong
أَسَاءَ	يُسِيءُ	إِسَاءَةٌ	to do wrong
سُوءٌ			evil, wrong
سَوْءٌ			evil, corpse

سَيِّئَةٌ		s.p.	evil, ill
أَسْوَدُ	f. سَوْدَاءُ	سُودٌ	black
مُسْوَدٌّ		s.p.	black
سُورَةٌ		سُوَرٌ	*sūra*
سَاعَةٌ		s.p.	hour
f. سُوقٌ		أَسْوَاقٌ	market
f. سَاقٌ		سُوقٌ	leg
سَارَ	يَسِيرُ	سَيْرٌ	to journey

ش

شَجَرَةٌ		شَجَرٌ	tree
شَدِيدٌ			strong, severe
شَرٌّ			bad, worse, worst
		أَشْرَارٌ	evil men
شَرِبَ	يَشْرَبُ	شُرْبٌ	to drink
شَرَابٌ			drink
أَشْرَكَ	يُشْرِكُ	إِشْرَاكٌ	to ascribe partners to
شَرِيكٌ		شُرَكَاءُ	partner
اِشْتَرَى	يَشْتَرِي	شِرَاءٌ	to buy
شَطْرَ			towards
شَيْطَانٌ		شَيَاطِينُ	devil
شَعَرَ	يَشْعُرُ	شُعُورٌ	to feel, perceive
شَفًا			lip, rim, edge
شِقَاقٌ			dissension
شَقِيٌّ		أَشْقِيَاءُ	unfortunate, wretched

شَكٌّ		شُكُوكٌ	doubt
شَكَرَ	يَشْكُرُ	شُكْرٌ	to thank, be thankful
شَمْسٌ			sun
شِمَالٌ			left, left hand
شَهِدَ	يَشْهَدُ	شَهَادَةٌ	to witness
شَهِيدٌ		شُهَدَاءُ	witness
شَهْرٌ		أَشْهُرٌ	month
شَاءَ	يَشَاءُ		to wish
شَيْءٌ		أَشْيَاءُ	thing
شَيْخٌ		شُيُوخٌ / مَشَايِخُ	old man

ص

أَصْبَحَ	يُصْبِحُ	إِصْبَاحٌ	to become; to be in the morning
صَبَرَ	يَصْبِرُ	صَبْرٌ	to be patient
صَابِرٌ		s.p.	steadfast
صَاحِبٌ		أَصْحَابٌ	companion
		صُحُفٌ	sheets
صَدَّ	يَصُدُّ	صَدٌّ	to block, divert
صَدَقَ	يَصْدُقُ	صِدْقٌ	to tell the truth
تَصَدَّقَ	يَتَصَدَّقُ	تَصَدُّقٌ	to give alms
صَدَقَةٌ		صَدَقَاتٌ	alms
صِدِّيقٌ			truthful
صَرِيخٌ			help
صِرَاطٌ			way, path

صَرَفَ	يَصْرِفُ	صَرْفٌ	to turn, turn away (trans.)
أَصْعَدَ	يُصْعِدُ	صُعُودٌ	to ascend
صَغِيرٌ			small
صَاغِرٌ			humbled
أَصْفَرُ	f. صَفْرَاءُ	صُفْرٌ	yellow
أَصْلَحَ	يُصْلِحُ	إِصْلَاحٌ	to put right
صَالِحٌ		s.p.	righteous
صَلَّى	يُصَلِّي	صَلَوٰةٌ	to pray
صَلَاةٌ / صَلَوٰةٌ		صَلَوَاتٌ	prayer
أَصَمُّ		صُمٌّ	deaf
صَنَعَ	يَصْنَعُ	صُنْعٌ	to make, work
صَنَمٌ		أَصْنَامٌ	idol
أَصَابَ	يُصِيبُ	إِصَابَةٌ	to smite, befall
صُورٌ			trumpet
صُورَةٌ		صُوَرٌ	form, picture
صَوْمٌ			fast
صَيْحَةٌ			cry
مَصِيرٌ			course, journeying

ض

ضُحًى			forenoon
ضَرَّ	يَضُرُّ	ضُرٌّ	to harm
اِضْطَرَّ	يَضْطَرُّ	اِضْطِرَارٌ	to force, compel
ضَرَبَ	يَضْرِبُ	ضَرْبٌ	to strike, coin
		ضَرَبَ ٱلذِّكْرَى صَفْحًا عَنْ	to neglect

ضَاعَفَ	يُضَاعِفُ	مُضَاعَفَةٌ	to multiply
ضَلَّ	يَضِلُّ	ضَلَالٌ	to stray, err
أَضَلَّ	يُضِلُّ	إِضْلَالٌ	to cause to stray
ضَلَالٌ			error
أَضَاءَ	يُضِيءُ	إِضَاءَةٌ	to give light
ضِيَاءٌ			light
أَضَاعَ	يُضِيعُ	إِضَاعَةٌ	to cause to be wasted
ضَيْفٌ			guest; guests

ط

طَعَامٌ		أَطْعِمَةٌ	food
أَطْلَعَ	يُطْلِعُ	إِطْلَاعٌ	to acquaint
تَطَلَّعَ	يَتَطَلَّعُ	تَطَلُّعٌ	to study
مَطْلِعٌ		مَطَالِعُ	rising-place
طَمِعَ	يَطْمَعُ	طَمَعٌ	to desire
أَطَاعَ	يُطِيعُ	إِطَاعَةٌ	to obey
اِسْتَطَاعَ	يَسْتَطِيعُ	اِسْتِطَاعَةٌ	to be able
طَائِفَةٌ			group, number
طِينٌ			clay

ظ

ظَلَّ	يَظَلُّ		to continue
ظَلَمَ	يَظْلِمُ	ظُلْمٌ	to do wrong
ظَالِمٌ		s.p.	wrong-doer
ظَنَّ	يَظُنُّ	ظَنٌّ	to think

ظَنٌّ		ظُنُونٌ	thought, supposition
ظَهَرَ	يَظْهَرُ	ظُهُورٌ	to appear

ع

عَبَدَ	يَعْبُدُ	عِبَادَةٌ	to serve, worship
عَبْدٌ		عِبَادٌ	servant, slave
عَبَسَ	يَعْبِسُ		to frown
عِبْرَةٌ			lesson
عَجِبَ	يَعْجَبُ	عَجَبٌ	to wonder
عَجَبٌ			wonder
عَجِيبٌ			amazing, wonderful
عَجِزَ	يَعْجَزُ	عَجْزٌ	to be unable
أَعْجَزَ	يُعْجِزُ	إِعْجَازٌ	to frustrate
عَجِيفٌ		عِجَافٌ	thin
عَجِلَ	يَعْجَلُ	عَجَلٌ	to hasten to
اِسْتَعْجَلَ	يَسْتَعْجِلُ	اِسْتِعْجَالٌ	to hasten
عِجْلٌ			calf
أَعْجَمِيٌّ		s.p.	foreign
عَدَّ	يَعُدُّ	عَدٌّ	to count
أَعَدَّ	يُعِدُّ	إِعْدَادٌ	to prepare, make ready
عَدَدٌ			number
عَدْلٌ			justice
عَدَا	يَعْدُو	عَدْوٌ	to transgress, turn away, run
عَدُوٌّ		أَعْدَاءٌ	enemy
عَدَاوَةٌ			enmity

عَذَابٌ			punishment
اِعْتَذَرَ	يَعْتَذِرُ	اِعْتِذَارٌ	to make excuses
عَرَبِيٌّ		s.p.	Arabic, Arab
عَرَجَ	يَعْرُجُ	مِعْرَجٌ	to mount
عَرْشٌ			throne
مَعْرُوشٌ			in trellises
أَعْرَضَ	يُعْرِضُ	إِعْرَاضٌ	to turn away
عَرَفَ	يَعْرِفُ	مَعْرِفَةٌ	to know, recognize
عُرْفٌ		أَعْرَافٌ	crest, ridge, height
مَعْرُوفٌ			kindness
عُرْوَةٌ			handle
عِزَّةٌ			might, power
عَزِيزٌ			mighty
عُسْرٌ			difficulty
عَسِيرٌ			difficult
عَصًا f.		عِصِيٌّ	stick
أَعْطَى	يُعْطِي	إِعْطَاءٌ	to give
عَظِيمٌ			great
عَفَا	يَعْفُو	عَفْوٌ	to pardon (+ ʿ*an*)
عِقَابٌ			punishment, requital
عَاقِبَةٌ			end, consequence
عَقَلَ	يَعْقِلُ	عَقْلٌ	to understand
عَاكِفٌ		s.p.	devoted
	(gen. only)	اَلْعَالَمِينَ	created beings
عَلِمَ	يَعْلَمُ	عِلْمٌ	to know
مَعْلُومٌ			known

عَلَّمَ	يُعَلِّمُ	تَعْلِيمٌ	to teach
عَلَى			on, against
عَالٍ	f. عَالِيَةٌ		high, lofty
عِمَادٌ		عَمَدٌ	columns, supports
عَمَرَ	يَعْمُرُ	عَمْرٌ	to build, build up, visit
عَمَّرَ	يُعَمِّرُ	تَعْمِيرٌ	to build
عَمِلَ	يَعْمَلُ	عَمَلٌ	to do, work
أَعْمَى			blind
عَنْ			away from; concerning
عِنْدَ			with, in the possession of
عَاهَدَ	يُعَاهِدُ	مُعَاهَدَةٌ	to make a covenant with
عَادَ	يَعُودُ	مَعَادٌ	to return; do again
أَعَادَ	يُعِيدُ	إِعَادَةٌ	to repeat, return (trans.)
عَاذَ	يَعُوذُ		to seek refuge with
عَامٌ		أَعْوَامٌ	year
تَعَاوَنَ	يَتَعَاوَنُ	تَعَاوُنٌ	to co-operate, help one another
اِسْتَعَانَ	يَسْتَعِينُ	اِسْتِعَانَةٌ	to ask for help
f. عَيْنٌ		عُيُونٌ / أَعْيُنٌ	spring; eye

غ

غَدَا	يَغْدُو	غُدُوٌّ	to be/do in the morning
مَغْرِبٌ		مَغَارِبُ	settling-place
أَغْرَقَ	يُغْرِقُ	إِغْرَاقٌ	to drown

غَضِبَ	يَغْضَبُ	غَضَبٌ	to be angry with (+ ʿ*alā*)
غَضَبٌ			anger
مُغَاضِبٌ			angry
غَفَرَ	يَغْفِرُ	مَغْفِرَةٌ	to forgive
اِسْتَغْفَرَ	يَسْتَغْفِرُ	اِسْتِغْفَارٌ	to seek forgiveness
غَفُورٌ			forgiving
مَغْفِرَةٌ			forgiveness
غَفَلَ	يَغْفُلُ	غَفْلَةٌ	to be heedless, forget
غَفْلَةٌ			heedlessness
غَلَّ	يَغُلُّ	غُلُولٌ	to deceive
غَلَبَ	يَغْلِبُ	غَلَبٌ	to overcome
غَلِيظٌ			thick, rough, hard
غُلَامٌ		غِلْمَانٌ	boy
غَمْرَةٌ		غَمَرَاتٌ	pang
مَغَارَةٌ		s.p.	cave
اَلْغَيْبُ			the unseen, the invisible
غَيَابَةٌ		s.p.	bottom; recess
غَيْرٌ			other than
غَيْرَ، بِغَيْرِ، مِنْ غَيْرِ			without

ف

فَتَحَ	يَفْتَحُ	فَتْحٌ	to open
فَتَنَ	يَفْتِنُ	فِتْنَةٌ	to tempt, afflict, stir up
فِتْنَةٌ		فِتَنٌ	affliction
فَتًى		فِتْيَةٌ	youth

فَرَّ	يَفِرُّ	فِرَارٌ	to flee
مَفَرٌّ			refuge
فَرِحَ	يَفْرَحُ	فَرَحٌ	to rejoice in
فَرْدٌ		أَفْرَادٌ	individual
فُرَادَى			singly
فَرَضَ	يَفْرُضُ	فَرْضٌ	to assign, prescribe
تَفَرَّقَ	يَتَفَرَّقُ	تَفَرُّقٌ	to be divided
فَرِيقٌ			party, company
أَفْسَدَ	يُفْسِدُ	إِفْسَادٌ	to cause mischief
فَسَادٌ			corruption
فُسُوقٌ			dissoluteness
فَضْلٌ			bounty
فَطَرَ	يَفْطُرُ	فَطْرٌ	to create
اِنْفَطَرَ	يَنْفَطِرُ	اِنْفِطَارٌ	to be split
فَعَلَ	يَفْعَلُ	فَعْلَةٌ	to do
مَفْعُولٌ			done
فَقِيرٌ		فُقَرَاءُ	poor
فَقِهَ	يَفْقَهُ	فِقْهٌ	to understand
تَفَكَّرَ	يَتَفَكَّرُ	تَفَكُّرٌ	to think, reflect
فَكِهَ	يَفْكَهُ	فَكَاهَةٌ	to jest
تَفَكَّهَ	يَتَفَكَّهُ	تَفَكُّهٌ	to jest
أَفْلَحَ	يُفْلِحُ	إِفْلَاحٌ	to prosper
فَمٌ		أَفْوَاهٌ	mouth
فَوْقَ			above, over
فِي			in, concerning

ق

قَبْرٌ		قُبُورٌ	grave
أَقْبَلَ	يُقْبِلُ	إِقْبَالٌ	to advance
قِبْلَةٌ			direction, *qibla*
قَبْلَ			before
قَاتَلَ	يُقَاتِلُ	قِتَالٌ	to fight
قَدَرَ	يَقْدِرُ	قَدَرٌ	to measure carefully
قَدِيرٌ			having power over
قَدِمَ	يَقْدَمَ	قُدُومٌ	to come, advance on
قَدَّمَ	يُقَدِّمُ	تَقْدِيمٌ	to send forward, to bring forward
اِسْتَقْدَمَ	يَسْتَقْدِمُ	اِسْتِقْدَامٌ	to bring forward
قَدَمٌ f.		أَقْدَامٌ	foot
قَدِيمٌ			old, ancient
مُسْتَقَرٌّ			abode
قَرَأَ	يَقْرَأُ	قُرْآنٌ	to recite
قُرْآنٌ			Qur'ān, recitation
قَرِبَ	يَقْرَبُ	قُرْبٌ	to come near, approach
قَرِيبٌ			near
قَارِعَةٌ			calamity
أَقْرَضَ	يُقْرِضُ	قَرْضٌ	to lend, make a loan
قَرْنٌ		قُرُونٌ	generation [horn]
قَرْيَةٌ		قُرًى	village
قَسَمَ	يَقْسِمُ	قِسْمٌ	to divide

أَقْسَمَ	يُقْسِمُ	إِقْسَامٌ	to swear
قَسْوَةٌ			hardness
قَصَّ	يَقُصُّ	قَصَصٌ	to tell
قَصَصٌ			story
قَضَى	يَقْضِي	قَضَاءٌ	to determine
قَعَدَ	يَقْعُدُ	قُعُودٌ	to sit, lurk
قَاعِدٌ		قُعُودٌ	seated
قَلِيلٌ		s.p.	few
قَلَّبَ	يُقَلِّبُ	تَقْلِيبٌ	to turn over, wring
اِنْقَلَبَ	يَنْقَلِبُ	اِنْقِلَابٌ	to turn back, return, be overturned
قَلْبٌ		قُلُوبٌ	heart
قَمَرٌ			moon
قَمِيصٌ			shirt
قَوْلٌ	p. أَقْوَالٌ	p.p. أَقَاوِيلُ	saying, words
قَامَ	يَقُومُ	قِيَامٌ	to stand, rise
أَقَامَ	يُقِيمُ	إِقَامٌ	to perform, uphold
قَوْمٌ		أَقْوَامٌ	people
مَقَامٌ			station
مُسْتَقِيمٌ			straight
تَقْوِيمٌ			form
قُوَّةٌ		قُوًى	power, force
مَقِيلٌ			noon resting-place

ك

كَ			like (preposition)
كَمَا			like (conjunction)
كَبِرَ	يَكْبَرُ	كِبَرٌ	to grow up
اِسْتَكْبَرَ	يَسْتَكْبِرُ	اِسْتِكْبَارٌ	to be haughty, insolent
كَبِيرٌ		كِبَارٌ / s.p.	big
كَبِيرَةٌ		كَبَائِرُ	enormity
كَتَبَ	يَكْتُبُ	كِتَابَةٌ	to write
كِتَابٌ		كُتُبٌ	scripture, document
أَكْثَرَ	يُكْثِرُ	إِكْثَارٌ	to multiply, make much of
كَثِيرٌ		كِثَارٌ / s.p.	many
كَذَبَ	يَكْذِبُ	كِذْبٌ	to tell lies
كَذَّبَ	يُكَذِّبُ	تَكْذِيبٌ	to deny, give the lie to
أَكْرَمُ		[كَرِيمٌ]	nobler
مُكْرَمٌ		s.p.	honoured
كَرِهَ	يَكْرَهُ	كُرْهٌ	to be reluctant, hate
كَسَبَ	يَكْسِبُ	كَسْبٌ	to acquire, earn
كَشَفَ	يَكْشِفُ	كَشْفٌ	to uncover, remove, relieve
f. كَفٌّ		أَكُفٌّ	palm of the hand, hand
كَفَرَ	يَكْفُرُ	كُفْرٌ	to deny, not to believe in
كَفَّرَ	يُكَفِّرُ	تَكْفِيرٌ	to forgive, redeem
كُفُوٌّ			equal
كَفَى	يَكْفِي	كِفَايَةٌ	to be sufficient

كَافِرٌ		s.p.	unbeliever, ungrateful
كَلْبٌ		كِلَابٌ	dog
كَلَّمَ	يُكَلِّمُ	تَكْلِيمٌ	to speak to, address
كَلَامٌ			speech, words
كَلِمَةٌ		s.p.	word
كِنٌّ / كِنَانٌ		أَكِنَّةٌ	coverings
كَنَزَ	يَكْنُزُ	كَنْزٌ	to store
كَادَ	يَكَادُ		'almost'; with negative 'scarcely'
كَوَّرَ	يُكَوِّرُ	تَكْوِيرٌ	to envelop
كَادَ	يَكِيدُ	كَيْدٌ	to strive, plot, outwit
كَيْدٌ			plotting, wiles
كَيْلٌ			measure

ل

لِ			to, for
لُبٌّ		أَلْبَابٌ	heart, intellect
لَبِثَ	يَلْبَثُ	لُبْثٌ	to tarry, linger
لَبَسَ	يَلْبِسُ	لَبْسٌ	to confound
لِبَاسٌ		أَلْبِسَةٌ	clothing; garment
مَلْجَأٌ		مَلَاجِئُ	refuge
لَحْمٌ		لُحُومٌ	flesh
لِسَانٌ		أَلْسِنَةٌ	tongue
لَطِيفٌ			gentle, subtle
لَعِبَ	يَلْعَبُ		to play

لَعْنَةٌ		s.p.	curse
اِلْتَقَطَ	يَلْتَقِطُ	اِلْتِقَاطٌ	to pick up
لَقِيَ	يَلْقَى	لِقَاءٌ	to meet
أَلْقَى	يُلْقِي	إِلْقَاءٌ	to throw
لَوْحٌ		أَلْوَاحٌ	tablet
مَلُومٌ			blamed, blameworthy
لَيْلٌ		لَيَالٍ	night, night time

م

مَتَّعَ	يُمَتِّعُ	تَمْتِيعٌ	to let enjoy; make provision for
تَمَتَّعَ	يَتَمَتَّعُ	تَمَتُّعٌ	to enjoy, enjoy oneself
مَتَاعٌ		أَمْتِعَةٌ	goods, baggage
مَثَلٌ		أَمْثَالٌ	likeness, parallel
مِثْلَ			like (preposition)
مَجِيدٌ			glorious
مِحَالٌ			might
مَدِينَةٌ		مُدُنٌ	city
مَرَّ	يَمُرُّ	مَرٌّ	to pass
مَرَّةٌ		s.p.	time, occasion
اِمْرُؤٌ			man
اِمْرَأَةٌ		[نِسَاءٌ / نِسْوَةٌ]	woman
مَرَضٌ		أَمْرَاضٌ	illness, sickness
مَرِيضٌ		مَرْضَى	ill, sick
مِرْيَةٌ			doubt

مَسَّ	يَمَسُّ	مَسٌّ	to touch
اَلْمَسِيحُ			the Anointed One
مِصْرُ			Egypt
أَمْسَكَ	يُمْسِكُ	إِمْسَاكٌ	to hold fast; withhold
بِالْأَمْسِ			yesterday
مَشَى	يَمْشِي	مَشْيٌ	to walk
مَعَ			with
مَكَّةُ			Mecca
مَكْرٌ			plot
مَكَانٌ		أَمْكِنَةٌ	place
مِلَّةٌ		مِلَلٌ	community, religion
إِمْلَاقٌ			poverty
مَلَكٌ		مَلَائِكَةٌ	angel
مُلْكٌ			possession, dominion
مِنْ			from, of
مَمْنُونٌ			broken, cut
مَنَعَ	يَمْنَعُ	مَنْعٌ	to prevent
مَاءٌ		مِيَاهٌ	water
مَاتَ	يَمُوتُ	مَوْتٌ	to die
مَوْتٌ			death
مَيِّتٌ		مَوْتَى / s.p.	dead
مَالٌ		أَمْوَالٌ	property
مَادَ	يَمِيدُ		to shake
مَائِدَةٌ		مَوَائِدُ	table

ن

نَبَّأَ	يُنَبِّئُ	تَنْبِئَةٌ	to inform
أَنْبَأَ	يُنْبِئُ	إِنْبَاءٌ	to inform
نَبَأٌ		أَنْبَاءٌ	news
نَبِيٌّ		أَنْبِيَاءُ	prophet
أَنْجَى	يُنْجِي	إِنْجَاءٌ	to save
نَجْوَى			secret conference
نَحْلٌ			bees
نَخْلٌ			date-palms
نَادِمٌ		s.p.	repentant
نَادَى	يُنَادِي	نِدَاءٌ	to call out to
تَنَادَى	يَتَنَادَى	تَنَادٍ	to call out to one another
نَذَرَ	يَنْذُرُ	نَذْرٌ	to vow
أَنْذَرَ	يُنْذِرُ	إِنْذَارٌ	to warn
نَذِيرٌ		نُذُرٌ	warner
نَزَغَ	يَنْزَغُ	نَزْغٌ	to cause strife
نَزَّلَ	يُنَزِّلُ	تَنْزِيلٌ	to send down
أَنْزَلَ	يُنْزِلُ	إِنْزَالٌ	to send down
تَنَزَّلَ	يَتَنَزَّلُ	تَنَزُّلٌ	to descend
[اِمْرَأَةٌ]		نِسَاءٌ / نِسْوَةٌ	woman
نَسِيَ	يَنْسَى	نَسْيٌ	to forget
أَنْسَى	يُنْسِي	إِنْسَاءٌ	to cause to forget

أَنْشَأَ	يُنْشِئُ	إِنْشَاءٌ	to raise, create
نَصَرَ	يَنْصُرُ	نَصْرٌ	to help
نَصْرَانِيٌّ		نَصَارَى	Christian
نَاصِرٌ / نَصِيرٌ		s.p. / أَنْصَارٌ	helper
نِصْفٌ			half
نَاصِيَةٌ		نَوَاصٍ	forelock
نَظَرَ	يَنْظُرُ	نَظَرٌ	to look at (*ilā*), into (*fī*)
أَنْعَمَ	يُنْعِمُ	إِنْعَامٌ	to bless, be gracious to
نِعْمَةٌ			blessing, bounty
نَعَمٌ		أَنْعَامٌ	animal, livestock
نَفَخَ	يَنْفُخُ	نَفْخٌ	to blow
نَفِدَ	يَنْفَدُ	نَفَادٌ	to be exhausted
نَفَرَ	يَنْفِرُ	نَفْرٌ	to go forth
f. نَفْسٌ		أَنْفُسٌ	soul, self
نَفَعَ	يَنْفَعُ	نَفْعٌ	to benefit
مَنْفَعَةٌ		مَنَافِعُ	benefit
أَنْفَقَ	يُنْفِقُ	إِنْفَاقٌ	to spend
مُنَافِقٌ		s.p.	hypocrite
نَقِيبٌ		نُقَبَاءُ	chief
أَنْقَذَ	يُنْقِذُ	إِنْقَاذٌ	to save, rescue
اِسْتَنْقَذَ	يَسْتَنْقِذُ	اِسْتِنْقَاذٌ	to save, rescue
نَقَضَ	يَنْقُضُ	نَقْضٌ	to break one's oath
اِنْتَقَمَ	يَنْتَقِمُ	اِنْتِقَامٌ	to take revenge on (+ *min*)

أَنْكَرَ	يُنْكِرُ	إِنْكَارٌ	to deny, disapprove; not to know
نَمْلٌ			ants
نَهْرٌ		أَنْهَارٌ	river
نَهَارٌ			day, daytime
نَهَى	يَنْهَى	نَهْيٌ	to forbid
اِنْتَهَى	يَنْتَهِي	اِنْتِهَاءٌ	to cease, desist
أَنَابَ	يُنِيبُ	إِنَابَةٌ	to come back to; repent
نُورٌ		أَنْوَارٌ	light
نَارٌ		نِيرَانٌ	fire
نَاقَةٌ		[إِبِلٌ]	she-camel

ه

هَجَرَ	يَهْجُرُ	هِجْرٌ	to forsake, leave
هَدٌّ			crash, destruction
هَدَى	يَهْدِي	هُدًى	to guide
هَدْيٌ			offering
هُدًى			guidance
هَزَّ	يَهُزُّ	هَزٌّ	to shake
اِسْتَهْزَأَ	يَسْتَهْزِءُ	اِسْتِهْزَاءٌ	to mock (+ *bi-*)
هَشِيمٌ			dry twigs
هَلَكَ	يَهْلِكُ	هَلَاكٌ	to perish
أَهْلَكَ	يُهْلِكُ	إِهْلَاكٌ	to destroy
مُهِينٌ			humiliating, contemptible

و

وَبَالٌ			mischief
اَلْوُثْقَى		[وَثِيقٌ]	firmest
مِيثَاقٌ			covenant, pledge
وَجَدَ	يَجِدُ	وَجْدٌ	to find
وَجِلَ	يُوجَلُ	وَجَلٌ	to be in awe of
أَوْحَى	يُوحِي	إِيحَاءٌ	to inspire, reveal
وَحْيٌ			inspiration
وَدَّعَ	يُوَدِّعُ	تَوْدِيعٌ	to bid farewell to
	يَذَرُ		to let, allow
وَرِثَ	يَرِثُ	إِرْثٌ	to inherit
وَرَقَةٌ		وَرَقٌ	leaf
وَزَرَ	يَزِرُ	وِزْرٌ	to carry a burden
وَازِرَةٌ			soul bearing a burden
وَزْنٌ			weight
مِيزَانٌ		مَوَازِينُ	balance
وَسَطٌ			middle
وَسِعَ	يَسَعُ	وُسْعٌ	to be wide; encompass
وَاسِعٌ			wide, ample
سَعَةٌ			wealth
وَصَفَ	يَصِفُ	وَصْفٌ	to describe
وَصَلَ	يَصِلُ	وُصُولٌ	to arrive
وَضَعَ	يَضَعُ	وَضْعٌ	to put down; give birth to
وَعَظَ	يَعِظُ	وَعْظٌ / عِظَةٌ	to exhort, admonish
وَعَدَ	يَعِدُ	وَعْدٌ	to promise

وَاعَدَ	يُواعِدُ	مُوَاعَدَةٌ	to make an agreement with
وَفَّى	يُوَفِّي	تَوْفِيَةٌ	to pay, repay
أَوْفَى	يُوفِي	إِيفَاءٌ	to fulfil, give in full
تَوَفَّى	يَتَوَفَّى	تَوَفِّي	to take
وُقُودٌ			fuel
وَقَعَ	يَقَعُ	وُقُوعٌ	to fall, come to pass
اِتَّقَى	يَتَّقِي	اِتِّقَاءٌ	to protect oneself; to be god-fearing
أَتْقَى		[تَقِيٌّ]	more pious
تَوَكَّلَ	يَتَوَكَّلُ	تَوَكُّلٌ	to put one's trust in (*ʿalā*)
وُلِدَ	يُولَدُ	[passive]	to be born
وَلَدٌ		أَوْلَادٌ	child
وَالِدٌ			father; (dual) parents
وَلَّى	يُوَلِّي	تَوْلِيَةٌ	to turn
تَوَلَّى	يَتَوَلَّى	تَوَلٍّ	to turn away; to take on oneself
وَلِيٌّ		أَوْلِيَاءُ	friend, protector
أَوْلَى			nearer
وَهَبَ	يَهِبُ	هِبَةٌ	to give
وَهَّابٌ			forgiving
أَوْهَنُ			frailest

ي

يَئِسَ	يَيْئَسُ	يَأْسٌ	to despair
f. يَدٌ		أَيْدٍ	hand
يُسْرٌ			ease
يَسِيرٌ			easy
أَيْقَنَ	يُوقِنُ	إِيقَانٌ	to be certain
يَمِينٌ		أَيْمَانٌ	right, right hand; oath
يَهُودِيٌّ		يَهُودٌ	Jew
يَوْمٌ		أَيَّامٌ	day
يَوْمَئِذٍ			on that day